Aleksandar M. Ognjević, Branislav J. Mirkov

# Ikarus IK-2

KAGERO

# MORE FROM KAGERO

Ikarus IK-2 • Aleksandar M. Ognjević, Branislav J. Mirkov • First edition • LUBLIN 2019

 • ISBN 978-83-66148-62-8

Editing: **Aleksandar M. Ognjević** • Translation: **Maja Katanić, Milica Protić, Djordje Nikolić** • Proofreading: **Djordje Nikolić** • 3D illustrations and scale drawings: **Branislav Mirkov** • Photos: **AK NS, via Čedomir Janić, WPHP, AMB, via Nenad Miklušev, Author, GJV 1939, Petar Bosnić, GJV 1935, Kazimierz Puławski, Passingham – Klepacki via Nenad Miklušev, Miloš Milosavljević, Alex Imrie via Nenad Miklušev, Milan Micevski, Dalibor Jovanović, Šime Oštrić via Ognjan Petrović, Djordje Nikolić, Dejan Milojević, Dragan Kolundžić, Tomislav Aralica via Robert Čopec, AVII via Dejan Djerić, Josip Novak, Dragan Šaler, Ognjan Petrović, Tomislav Aralica, Jan van den Heuvel, Aleksandar Smiljanić, Vladimir Bosner Jr., NMU, Csaba B. Stenge, Mario Jelušić, Berndhard Tötchinger, Emil Smutni** • Design: **KAGERO STUDIO**

KAGERO Publishing
**Akacjowa 100, Turka, os. Borek, 20-258 Lublin 62, Poland, phone/fax: (+48) 81 501 21 05**
www.kagero.pl • e-mail: kagero@kagero.pl, marketing@kagero.pl
w w w . k a g e r o . p l
Distribution: **KAGERO Publishing**

First Ikarus factory at Novi Sad at No.12 Šumadijska street, photographed at the beggining of 1920's. After Ikarus moved to Zemun near Belgrade, the remaining real estate at Novi Sad was sold. [AK NS]

## Introduction

At the end of 1920s, at the initiative of the Army Air Force of the Kingdom of Yugoslavia and Royal Air Club, a few young ambitious aviation engineers were sent to France for professional development. The idea was for them to return to their homeland after the training where they would be offered specialist positions in the military aviation or the aviation industry. However, when they returned to the country, engineers Ljubomir Ilić and Kosta Sivčev were appointed to administrative positions, even though they completed the required training. In 1931, dissatisfied with their status, they decided to design substitution for Avia BH-33E fighter which was in use at the time. They worked secretly on their new design outside their working hours in a basement in Belgrade and at Ilić's apartment at Novi Sad. Their initial concept included low-wing airplane with retractible landing gear, but they modified this initial design to a fighter with fixed landing gear and gull wing, armed with engine mounted cannon and synchronized machineguns.

Ikarus IK-2 was a single seat fighter from the 1930s, the first one made as private endeavor according to the Yugoslav design, with intent to make the Aviation Command interested enough to buy the project. Only 12 series airplane were produced along with two prototypes, as it was already obso-

Dimitrije P. Konjović (31 Dec 1888 – 5 Jan 1982), former Austro-Hungarian naval pilot and founder of Ikarus airplane factory in 1923. [via Čedomir Janić]

Ikarus early advertising poster, late 1920's. [AMB]

**Ikarus advertisment with ŠM-1, representing the first Yugoslav construction hydroplane. [via Nenad Miklušev]**

lete at the time of its introduction in 1935. In April 1941, when Germany invaded Yugoslavia, eight operational airplanes were in use. Germans sold the four remaining airplanes to a newly formed aviation of the puppet Independent State of Croatia.

It is very important to add that there are almost no saved records for this rare airplane. Several decades of research have resulted in the discovery of a relatively modest amount of data, documents and photos. To date, no factory documents or factory plans were discovered. Recent publications are largely based on information found in the 1972 vintage IK Fighters (Airplane Profiles) booklet. Certain information from this publication has been overcome over time, while serious inaccuracies in technical drawings "survived" to this day, neatly repeating in several articles. The exterior and the interior of this exceptional airplane is for the first time elaborated to the finest of details in close cooperation with 3D illustrator Mr. Branislav Mirkov and the author.

**Josip Mikl (Josef Mickl, 1885 – 25 Aug 1965), an aviation and mechanical engineer, pilot, hydroplane designer at ÖFFAG and in the Kingdom of Yugoslavia, as well as Ikarus Technical director. [WPHP]**

## About Ikarus A.D.

Ikarus airplane factory emerged from a small plant "Industrija motora Protić i drugovi" (Motor industry Protić and Comrades), from Novi Sad, which in the fall of 1923 went bankrupt. At that time, it dawned on the Serbian corvette captain Dimitrije Konjović, who was a retired air force hydroplane pilot, that the aviation industry was the future. Konjović was joined by an engineer Josip Mikl, who used to construct hydroplanes for the Austro-Hungarian Navy before the Great War.

On 13 October 1923, an enterprise "Ikarus - Prva srpska industrija aeroplana, automobila i strojeva - Kovačević i drugovi" (Ikarus- The first Serbian industry of airplane, cars and machines - Kovačević and Company) was founded. On 28 July 1924, it became a joint-stock company. Its main office was at Novi Sad, which was convenient for many reasons. The Air Force Command was there, and the airfield was near the Danube, which was ideal for airplanes and hydroplanes. An arsenal of aviation items and workshops for airplane repair were in the vicinity at Petrovaradin. Also, craftsmanship and industry with qualified work force, good communication with other centers, both in the country and abroad (railway Belgrade – Budapest – Vienna) were developed.

In 1923, the Ministry of Air Force and Navy of Kingdom of Serbs, Croats and Slovenes, advertised a call for national enterprises, to which it would entrust the airplane construction with adequate technical, material and organizational state support. The number of state-owned and private companies which answered the advertisement was unexpectedly high. In a tight competition, the contract was signed with two small private companies – Ikarus from Novi Sad and Rogožarski from Belgrade. With only a general consent from the Aviation Department to commence the construction of four training airplanes ŠB-1 Mali Brandenburg (Small Brandenburg), which the state would buy in case they fit the needs and standards for aviation material, Ikarus management entered the adventure called "airplane production". Coincidently, a contract was signed at the same time with the Navy Command for production of six training hydroplanes

**Post card of Ikarus production plant at Novi Sad shows interior of the factory with unsuccessful sole prototype of IM hydroplane. [Author]**

ŠM constructed by Josip Mikl. ŠM was also the first national-made airplane.

By the end of 1924, Ikarus produced four airplanes and six hydroplanes, a construction bureau was built and the first credit was taken for the expansion of the factory. In 1925, 32 airplanes were produced. The greatest challenge in those days was to secure sufficient resources, so the company increased share capital on 1 March 1925, from two to five million dinars. All the airplane produced by Ikarus at that time, whether for the Air Force or Naval Aviation, were intended for pilot training. Owing to the quality of those airplanes, Ikarus, who became a reliable manufacturer, gained trust of the Air Force Command. Hence, the Command decided to entrust them with the production of a combat airplane. The Air Force Command purchased a license for production of 200 Potez XXV airplanes and assigned it to Ikarus on the condition that it moved its factory for strategic reasons further inland. The factory management conceded choosing Zemun as the new location as it was the most similar in terms of conditions to Novi Sad, while Kraljevo was considered as an alternative.

Zemun was convenient as the new location, since it was close to the capital Belgrade, the rail-

**Ikarus hydroplane launching post at Danube in Novi Sad during late 1920's. Photo shows domestic hydroplane ŠM-1 No.137 just before launching. [Author]**

Ikarus factory early type logo.

Ikarus management building, together with Ikarus factory plant buildings, photographed from the factory airfield. [Author]

Main entrance into the Ikarus assembly plant at Zemun at the end of 1920's. Note the huge cyrillic inscription "ИКАРУС" above the entrance. [AMB]

way Belgrade - Zagreb - Ljubljana was near and the construction of Zemun airport was ongoing (the construction commenced in 1923, and the airport was put in use on 25 March 1927). The Danube was only 200 meters away from the factory, while the pier was no more than 800 meters away. Also, the factory for the production of airplane engines was planned to be constructed at Rakovica near Belgrade, while Zemun had a complete infrastructure for building of an airplane factory (electricity, water, sewage, telephone, access roads and an industrial railway). An adequate parcel of 15 acres was bought on which the factory with an airfield was built. Construction was completed on 1 January 1928, and the total of 7,000 m$^2$ was covered with buildings, while the total volume of buildings was 61,660 m$^3$. Installation of equipment and machines was completed by March that year when the trial production started. The first Potez XXV was delivered in October 1928 and the last one in 1932.

Until 2 November 1932, the factory at Novi Sad produced hydroplanes, while the factory at Zemun produced military airplanes. Subsequently, the production at Novi Sad ceased and the entire facilities and the factory management moved to Zemun, while the remaining real estate at Novi Sad was sold. Organizing airplane production at Ikarus served to the Air Force Command to impose such model of production on other manufacturers. During that period, apart from regular production, a modification of 37 Dewoitine D.1 fighters was completed in accordance with the blueprints made by engineer Dušan Stankov.

Similar to the other factories, Ikarus was also struck by the world economic crisis which was most detrimental between 1932-1935. New orders were not placed and state failed to pay for already delivered airplanes. During the crisis, the factory managed to survive by producing airscrews, bomb carriers and aluminum reservoirs for the State Airplane Factory (DFA) in Kraljevo, and by reparing and overhauling airplanes and engines. Expenses were severely reduced, the number of employees was decreased but the factory survived. Period from 1935 until 1941 was marked as the period of progress. The average number of employees in that period was around

Aerial photo of Ikarus factory at the beggining of 1930's. Industrial railway track at the Dunav bank are visible on the right side of the factory. [AMB]

This Royal Yugoslav Army Air Force Potez XXV (No.169) powered by Gnôme et Rhône Jupiter (420HP) engine, represents one of 200 airplanes assembled by Ikarus under license in the first half of 1930's. [Author]

2,000, while the maximum was 3,140, and they worked in two and even three shifts.

The first model of combat airplane of domestic production – a prototype of a single-seat fighter IK-1L, designed by engineers Ljubomir Ilić and Kosta Sivčev, was produced in April 1935. This line included the total of 12 IK-2 fighters. Annual value of the delivered products was almost 100 million dinars. From 1923 and by the beginning of the Second World War in 1941, Ikarus produced a total of 477 aiplanes. Nine domesctically developed and assembled airplane prototypes produced, while eight airplane types were produced according to purchases licenses, which included amongst others Hawker Fury and Bristol Blenheim.

On 17 April 1941, following the capitulation of the Kingdom of Yugoslavia, Germans proclaimed Ikarus company as spoils of war, impounded factory buildings, equipment and machines, tools and production supplies, all the material, parts and airplane production which had already started, as well as the airplanes intended for repairs and overhaul. The confiscated factory continued its work for the needs of German occupational forces as Wiener Neustadter Flugzeugwerke (WNF) branch. During the occupation, various parts for Messerschmitt Me-109 structures were produced at Ikarus, together with overhauls and repairs of various airplanes which Germans impounded during the war. According to unreliable data, over 20 types of several hundred airplanes were repaired. Just before the liberation of Belgrade and Zemun, WNF Company transferred the most valuable equipment, tools and material from Ikarus to Germany and Austria.

**Ikarus A.D. factory advertisement was often seen in local and specialized magazines at the end of 1930's. [GJV 1939]**

**An end of an era. German military vehicles in front of the Ikarus factory during April/May 1941. Luftwaffe bomber crews were strictly instructed not to bomb aviation factories/ infrastructure in Serbia. It speaks about the quality of aviation industry in Serbia prior to the outbreak of WWII. [Author]**

**Royal Yugoslav Army Air force ppuk Ljubomir D. Ilić (14 Feb 1902 – 28 Sep 1974), Chief of Constructors Group and one of the most famous Serbian aviation engineers and constructors. He was also great opponent of the communist regime after WWII. Ppuk Ilić defected to the west in 1947. [Petar Bosnić]**

**Royal Yugoslav Army Air Force ppuk Kosta I. Sivčev (9 Feb 1903 – 1 Dec 1982), versatile aviation engineer and pilot. He was the Commanding Officer of the Military Technical Institute in Belgrade. [via Čedomir Janić]**

**Royal Yugoslav Army Air Force ppuk aviation engineer Srbobran M. Stanojević (19 Aug 1895 – 7 Aug 1939), acting Chief of Staff of the Technical Department of the Royal Yugoslav Army Air Force. His unreserved support was crucial in the creation of IK-L1. [GJV 1935]**

## Ikarus IK-2

The Ikarus IK-2 was the first fighter airplane of Yugoslav design and manufacture, as well as the first Yugoslav monoplane fighter with metal structure, the first cannon-armed fighter in the Royal Yugoslav Army Air Force (VVKJ) and the first Yugoslav airplane which reached the top speed of 435 km/h. It was designed as a private project by two Serbian engineers, Ljubomir D. Ilić and Kosta I. Sivčev.

The project was completed in 1933, in time when the conception of the gull-wing monoplane fighter with powerful engine and heavy armament represented a modern solution. Zemun-based Ikarus A.D. factory produced a total of 14 airplanes, IK-L1 Prototype I (1935), IK-02 Prototype II (1936) and 12 IK-2 series airplanes (1938-1939). Unfortunately, the IK-2 fighters were introduced in the 6. LP VVKJ in 1939, at a time when they were already outdated in comparison to the modern low-wing fighters. During the period between 1940 and 1941, the IK-2s were part of Zagreb-based 4. LP, and they also successfully participated in the so-called

In 1928 Puławski designed a modern all-metal gull-wing fighter with an inline engine, PZL P.1. The P.1 was flown in 1929, and among few others, it was a basic role model for Serbian engineers. [AMB]

Zygmunt Rafał Puławski (24 October 1901 – 21 March 1931), was one of the most famous among European and Polish pilots, Engineers and visionary ahead of his time. [Kazimierz Puławski]

April War against the modern Luftwaffe's Messerschmitt Bf-109's.

The early appearance of the IK-2 was not properly taken advantage of. The period of several years, when the gull-wing fighter was still modern and acceptable for equipping the front line units, passed as a consequence of unnecessary delays. The VV was affected the most, as they were forced to use biplanes in the meantime. Instead of ordering a series of IK-2s, Fury biplanes were purchased and their license production was ordered, at time when low-wing fighters already made their appearance. Besides the conservative attitudes, fluctuations in official circles and the financial situation, such decision by the VV was prompted, on the one hand, by desire for a good, useful and dependable supercharged engine, and the doubts whether the Yugoslav Aviation Industry was capable at that time to quickly start and complete a series of the metal gull-wing fighters.

Obsolete Avia BH-33 biplane fighter was the main among many other reasons why Serbian engineers Ilić and Sivčev decided to construct a new and modern fighter airplane project, to meet the needs of VVKJ. [AMB]

**Photo of IK wooden model airplane which was tested in famous French Eiffel wind tunnel. [AMB]**

**Ikarus airplane factory logo that was painted on the rudder of newly produced airplanes since mid 1930's.**

Viewed from a later perspective, the Air Force Command also had a certain amount of luck. If there had been a production of greater number of the IK-2s, large amount of resources would have been spent, and the Air Force would have found themselves in a situation to start the war with the already outdated fighters. Similar situation happened in other Balkan countries which entered the war with a significant number of gull-wing fighters and a small number of low-wing fighters. The Yugoslav Aviation Industry still had the greatest benefit from the IK-2s, as it provided it with an opportunity to gain experience in the production of modern metal construction fighters.

## The first prototype IK-L1

The choice and a decision to purchase a fighter airplane for the VV was not achieved during the first half of the thirties, which among other things, resulted in an idea to produce an indigenous fighter concept. Even before the appearance of the outstanding Rogožarski-built PVT fighter-trainer, which successfully beat the French competition and enabled the Yugoslav Aviation Industry to take over the production of almost all trainer types, a group of young and ambitious aeronautical engineers took a stand that the production of an indigenous-designed fighter airplane could also be organized, as opposed to the views of the conservative circles in the Air Force. Such attitude enabled the domestic Aviation Industry to become one of the important sources of supply for the war airplanes in the coming period.

Two young Serbian engineers, Ljubomir Ilić and Kosta Sivčev, were the first who came up

**Ikarus IK-L1 first prototype, final stage of work, with completed fuselage in front of the Ikarus Factory plant. [GJV 1935]**

Static test of the first prototype wing at Ikarus Factory in 1934. Test results were beyond the expected values. [GJV 1935]

First prototype without engine cover plates and without tail section during final adjustments and assembly at the Ikarus factory. [GJV 1935]

IK-L1 at Ikarus factory airfield during the initial trials in April of 1935. The wheel spats were removed for so far unknown reasons. [AMB]

Moments before the IK-L1 test flight in the spring of 1935. Beside mechanics and technical staff, it appears that the two gentleman with hats in front of the airplane are engeneers Ljubomir Ilić and Kosta Sivčev. [AMB]

First advertisement of Ikarus factory related to the new airplane, published in 1936 Aviation Year Book. [GJV 1936]

with the idea. They were both educated in France, and they returned to Serbia in 1931. Ilić finished his studies very successfully at the prestigeous French College of Aeronautics (École supérieure d'aéronautique et de constructions mécaniques – ESACM). Sivčev specialized at the design offices and in production of French Breguet and Hispano-Suiza factories, and during his stay in France, he also was acquainted with the work of 11 more airplane, engines and aeronautical equipment factories. As the first foreigner, he spent three months at the Department for Airplane Testing of the Technical Service of French Air Force (Service Technique de l'Aéronautique – STAé), as well as at the famous Centre for Testing Aeronautical Materials (Commission des d'Érudes Pratiques Aéronautiques – CEPA), both located at Villacoublay. They were both familiar with the modern airplane construction developments in France and all over the world. Following the return to the Kingdom of Yugoslavia, they were employed in the administrative jobs at the Technical Department of the Air Force Command.

Realizing the needs and estimating the capacities of the Yugoslav Aviation Industry, Ilić and Sivčev soon made the decision to design a fighter airplane, and as soon as the following year, 1932, they independently began working on a design of a single seat fighter. They carried out their work in an absolute secrecy at Ilić's appartment, after work hours at the Air Force Command, very often during the night hours. Although their initial intent was to create a low-wing fighter with retractable landing gear, due to certain prejudices and some contemporary trends, they decided to design a gull-wing monoplane fighter with strut-supported wings and fixed landing gear, with engine-mounted 20 mm cannon and with two synchronized machine guns. Therefore, they selected the most contemporary and extremely powerful French engine at that time, Hispano Suiza 12Ycrs, the so-called "*moteur cannon*", in which the cannon fired through the propeller hub. The powerful and heavy engine and heavy central armament required metal fuselage structure.

The parasol conception (wings above the fuselage), known since the period of World War One, was applied again during the second half of

**Serbian engineers Ljubomir Ilić and Kosta Sivčev proudly stand in front of their first jointly designed airplane, IK-L1, in the spring of 1935. [AMB]**

**Excellent three-quarter shot of the first prototype, Ikarus IK-L1 BR.01, during extensive testing with Aviation Test Group in Belgrade during spring of 1935. The photo was taken at early stage of testing, without armament and with streamlined wheel spats. [Passingham – Klepacki via Nenad Miklušev]**

the twenties and in the early thirties in France and Poland. French companies produced series of several types (Wibault 72, LGL-22, Morane Saulnier MS.225, Dewoitine D.27 and D.37) and Polish one type (PWS-10). As a logical development of the parasols, high-wing aiplanes appeared with the so-called "gull wing" which remained known as "Polish" or "Puławski wing", named after the famous Polish engineer Zygmunt Rafał Puławski, who designed the P-1 type, the first such fighter from 1929.

The relatively new conception of the high-wing fighter with the "gull wing" was applied successfully, especially in the Republic of Poland. The typical representatives were the P-family fighters produced by the Polish PZL factory, which produced metal fighters P.7 (1930), P.11 (1931) and P.24 (1933). Besides them, the same conception fighters were produced by other countries. The French factory ANF Les Mureaux was the first one to accept the "Pulawski" wing for their Mureaux 170 and 180, and the similar wings were produced in Czechoslovakia (Aero A-102), France (Arsenal - Delanne 10 prototype with thin wing, Dewoitine 560 and 570, Gourdou-Leseurre GL-482, Loire Type 43, 45 and 46), Germany (Henschel Hs-121), the USSR (Laville DI-4) and the Kingdom of Yugoslavia (Ikarus IK-L1 and IK-2).

**First International Aviation Exhibition at the Belgrade Fair, May – June 1938. First in line is Rogožarski R-100 trainer, than Ikarus IK-2 BR.01 (former second prototype IK No.02) and finaly Hawker Fury Mk.II produced at Ikarus factory under licence. [Miloš Milosavljević]**

The decision made by Ilić and Sivčev to adopt the conception of a gull-wing fighter with fixed landing gear was obviously in accordance with contemporary trends in fighter airplane design. The preliminary design, as well as aerodynamic and other calculations, were finished as soon as the beginning of 1933, and Ljubomir Ilić brought precisely made wooden model for testing to the Eiffel wind tunnel. After "blowing" the model, the designers made further necessary aerodynamic changes and started work on blueprints. The entire work, evenly divided between

**Ikarus IK-2 BR.01 during the exhibition with quite important spectators on its starboard side, General Ljubomir Marić - Army and Navy minister and Engineer Emilo Matić, Director of Engine Industry concern. [AMB]**

**Excellent photo of excellently prepared airplane for an exhibition. All metal parts were polished up to high gloss, together with the Ratier propeller. [Alex Imrie via Nenad Miklušev]**

Nice close up of unusual and quite complicated Messier fixed landing gear of IK-2 BR.01. French company Messier also provided hydraulic brake system. [Alex Imrie via Nenad Miklušev]

Starboard view of IK shows streamlined fuselage together with a huge Yugoslav cocade on the lower side of the wing. [Alex Imrie via Nenad Miklušev]

the two engineers, was completed without any help from other people and it was done on own expense. Somewhat later, Ilić and Sivčev showed the documentation to the Acting Chief of Staff of the Technical Department of the Air Force, ppuk engineer Srbobran M. Stanojević, who was also an advocate of indigenous design production and one of the most deserving people for the accelerated development of the Yugoslav Aviation Industry and the adoption of the indigenous conception airplanes in the years which followed. He provided the necessary official support and soon, on 22 September 1933, the Air Force Command issued the necessary requirements (specification) for the prototype production. However, the conception of the new fighter had many opponents among senior Air Force officers who thought that the light biplane was the greatest achievement for fighter airplanes. The metal gull-wing fighter with engine-mounted hub-firing cannon was certainly not the conception which they would support. Nevertheless, the support of younger and more visionary pilots, and especially the determined attitude of the Technical Department and its chief resulted in the ordering of the prototype with the Ikarus factory in 1934.

The engine for the prototype, HS 12Ycrs, arrived from France in August 1934 to the address of the AF Command in Novi Sad, and they informed the Ministry of Trade and Industry by notice dated 25 August. The notice specified that

**Still marked as the second prototype, IK stands in its full glory at the Zemun "Beograd" airport. Royal Air Club hangars could be seen in the background. The first flight was performed on 24 August 1936 with Aviation Test Group pilot por Janko Dobnikar at the controls. [Miloš Milosavljević]**

**Ikarus IK-2 BR.01 with its Hispano – Suza V12 engine, running at the "Beograd" airport. Spinner and engine panels were removed. Note large national cocades on both wing undersurfaces. [Milan Micevski]**

the Hispano-Suiza engine No.495.011 with the related tools, weighing 490 kg arrived and that its cost was 299,950 francs or 849,910.26 dinars. The first prototype was designated according to the French manner as IK-L1 Br.01 (i.e. No.01), where, according to the French designation practice used at the Army Air Force, number 01 presented the designation for the first prototype. In September 1934, about a year after winning the job, the prototype airframe was completed at Ikarus Prototype Workshop. However, the first prototype flight was delayed due to the certain modifications and equipment installation, and the wing structure was subjected to rigorous static testing because of certain doubts about its construction strength and the requirement that the safety coefficient must be higher than the British, German and French standards.

Kap Ik Leonid I. Bajdak, the Acting Chief of the First Department of the "Vazduhoplovna opitna grupa" (Aviation Test Group), the special unit for airplane and other aeronautical material testing formed on 14 December 1933, was selected as the test pilot in September 1934. Captain Leonid Bajdak was one of the first four Aviation Test Group pilots, a highly experienced test pilot but also one of the greatest biplane advocates and a great opponent of the conception of the airplane he was about to test. Unofficially, there was a rumour that he received a large sum of money from a Hawker representative in Yugoslavia, in order to favour the airplane from the British company. This was never proven, but his attitudes led to such a conclusion. He refused to accept the proposed testing programme, and he had already decided to act according to his own choices and system. According to the order issued by the designers and for the purpose of testing, the weight of the prototype was limited to 1,650 kg. The prototype was tested without

the armament and with 150-200 liters of fuel. The first flight was performed on 22 April 1935 at the Zemun-based "Beograd" airport and the next day, during the second flight, Bajdak performed unplanned acrobatics, taking the airplane into a series of sharp manoeuvres. After landing, there was a slight damage to the fabric skin on the leading edge of the starboard wing, but Ikarus experts explained that the skin would stiffen as soon as the varnish was completely dry. Unfortunately, during the third test flight on 24 April, Bajdak performed sharp extraction from a dive at an altitude of 1000 m, wherein the loosened fabric skin separated from the starboard wing leading edge. The airplane fell into a tailspin, Bajdak saved himself with a parachute, and the IK-1 crashed into the ground. In his accident report, Bajdak wrote that the airplane was well made, greatly trimmed, with the precise response to commands and manageable, but he had objections to the poor visibility from the pilot cabin and long take-off distance. Since this totalled 300 m, which was a normal take-off distnace for the monoplanes from that period (at a speed of about 400 km/h), Bajdak's objection spoke more about Bajdak himself then the airplane he was testing.

## The second prototype IK-02

The unpleasant situation following the loss of the first prototype was overcome by a wise decision by Ikarus and its general director Dimitrije Konjović to offer production of a new sample in order to prove their own high production standards and to justify the two designers' attitudes and conception. The offer was accepted and the Air Force Headquarters ordered the production of the second prototype from Ikarus.

However, the second prototype, marked as IK and labelled as No.02, arrived somewhat later. A new test pilot from Aviation Test Group formation, agile Por Janko A. Dobnikar, was determined to test it. The date when he sat in the new airplane was briefly written in Ikarus log book:

*"IK-2, test flight, taxiing, 24 July 1936, pilot Dobnikar".*

The airplane was completed in only ten months – the technical staff and production workers at Ikarus proved that they were up to the task. Cooperation between the two engineers was again based on the 50:50% principle. The engine of the same type as used in first prototype arrived in May 1936 to the address of the Air Force Headquarters, this time at Zemun. And again, the sender was Hispano-Suiza Company (S-te Française Hispano Suiza, Bois Colombes, Seine). The Headquarters sent a notice to inform Military Technical Instityte on 28 May, that they received a crate with the Hispano-Suiza 860HP 12Ycrs airplane engine number 495.172 with corresponding spare parts and accessories. The cost of the engine was 235,450 francs or 678,096 dinars.

Second prototype significantly differed from the first one in the metal sheet wing plating. Practically, the entire airplane, except the covering of the rear part of the fuselage and the horizontal stabilizer, was made of metal. At the request by the Air Force, one additional half-wing was made for the static tests which had satisfactory results. Some other changes were made – better aerodynamically profiled fuselage, reduced size and improved shape of the cooling radiator, modi-

**Main oponent of IK-2 was Hawker Fury biplane. Fury's major supporter was Captain Leonid Bajdak. There were "rumors" in Belgrade that Bajdak received a large sum of money for such support from British aviation industry. [Dalibor Jovanović]**

Kap Ik Leonid I. Bajdak, Aviation Test Group test pilot who was responsible for the loss of IK-L1. [AMB]

fied and improved air intakes and several minor changes. The first flight was performed by por Janko Dobnikar on 24 August 1936. A very intensive testing followed within the Aviation Test Group of the second prototype, IK No.02, which was the first Yugoslav indigenous-designed airplane to be submitted to such a detailed examination. They measured the speed, climb rate, load and other characteristics. The load of 6-7 g was achieved. Por Dobnikar also performed a series of acrobatics with negative g, such as the front loop and the reversed Immelmann while presenting the airplane to different review boards. During the visit by a Turkish President Mustafa İsmet İnönü to Belgrade in the autumn of 1936, he performed a complete acrobatic programme. In mid-October 1936, Dobnikar reached the maximum speed of 435 km/h, instead of the planned 415 km/h, which was an unofficial European record for the airplane with fixed landing gear and the absolute Yugoslav speed record. During the test flights it was found that the engine develops 15HP higher power than specified by the manufacturer at the altitudes from 4,000 to 5,000 meters. That meant that the IK-L1's engine was depressed, i.e. that, in calculation, the lower power was taken into account than the one which was later attained. Therefore, the higher speed was achieved. The full engine power was allowed later. In September 1936, IK No.02 was accepted by the Air Force board, and the testing continued until 8 November.

In mid-July 1937, 16 simulated dog fights between IK-02 and Hawker Fury II were performed, where the new fighter showed superiority in speed, climbing and combat manoeuvres. However, not even these results managed to convince "stubborn" Bajdak in the quality of the Ikarus airplane, and once he stated his views, por Dobnikar challenged him to an aerial duel.

The set conditions were:

1) Taking off and climbing to 4,000 m above the Zemun airport (with a barograph for control)

2) Race along the route Belgrade - Novi Sad - Belgrade along 140 km

3) "Dogfight" above the airport

Of course, Bajdak chose Hawker Fury II, the best biplane in Army Air Force (and the best of all versions of the Fury). Dobnikar easily won the first round with the IK by reaching the given altitude, as well as the other, as he returned first from Novi Sad, being considerably ahead. The final round was a spectacular dogfight. Both pilots invested maximum effort and all their pilot skills trying to go "behind each other's tails". In spite of greater experience, Bajdak could in no way position his Fury behind the gull-wing fighter, while Dobnikar managed to get "behind the tail" of his opponent and hold him at gunpoint until the end of the "fight". The duel was stopped and Bajdak was finally forced to admit his defeat, which was also the defeat of his attitudes.

The airplane was re-marked and re-labelled as IK-2 Br. 01 (No.01), and it was exhibited at the First International Aviation Exhibition in 1938, held in the period between 28 May and 13 June at the Belgrade Fair, constructed during the previous year. The airplane, engines and other aeronautical equipment were displayed in the newly built pavilions and in the open space in this first

Front view of the second prototype shows rather cumbersome Messier fixed undercarriage. [Šime Oštrić via Ognjan Petrović]

Second prototype, Ikarus IK No.02, Aviation Test Group, October 1936. Hub-firing cannon appears for the first time. Photo was personally signed by the test pilot por Janko Dobnikar. [Šime Oštrić via Ognjan Petrović]

great aeronautical exhibition in the Kingdom of Yugoslavia. According to the number of the displayed exhibits, the greatest exhibitors were the Kingdom of Yugoslavia, Germany and Italy (who had separate pavilions). Other foreign countries (Czechoslovakia, France, Great Britain and Poland) exhibited in the international pavilion. Besides the IK-2 Br. 01, Yugoslav indigenous-designed and licensed airplanes and prototype models were also exhibited there.

The IK-2 Br. 01 as the only example of that type, was used for demonstration and training of the capital's 6. LP pilots based at the "Beograd" airport. When that regiment received series IK-2s, Br. 1 was also included. Unfortunately, Br. 1 was destroyed at the end of June 1940, when the famous acrobatic and test pilot kap Ik Milan V. Bjelanović flew into a thundercloud and was forced to jump out of the airplane at the altitude of nearly 5,000 m as the airplane was struck by lightning. The pilot caught fire and was badly injured, spending a couple of months in hospital because of serious burns. According to Captain Bjelanović interview with "Politika" journalist dated on 12 June 1940:

*"With the airplane I was testing, I had to climb to an altitude of 5,000 meters. The weather was not favorable, because the sky was mostly covered with dark and rainy clouds, but at the altitude of 2,000 meters the airplane was above the clouds and covered with crystalline sun rays. The instruments show an altitude of 4,500 meters. The remaining 500 meters altitude I will reach very soon. The engine works impeccably. Underneath me the clouds look like snow mountain peaks ...*

*Suddenly - the plane shook strongly! At the first moment, I thought I collided with another airplane! But my airplane is still flying normally. As I feverishly thought about what had happened,*

Air Force por Janko Dobnikar, Aviation Test Group, pilot which tested the second prototype. [AMB]

*I felt a sudden warmth at my feet. Everything was clear to me at the moment. The engine is in flames, as I was convinced as soon as I opened the cabin lid in order to bail out. I did not feel the fire on my face and hands as I unbuckled the seat belts, after which I invested all my strength to get out of the cabin, because the air pressure pushed me backward. To make the situation worse, my right leg clung to something in the cabin, so I barely pulled it out ... As I pulled out of the cockpit, I do not even know now how or how long it lasted, but it seemed to me as eternity until I felt I was in the air. I was not safe even at that time, because*

Series IK-2 BR. 2109, 6. LP at Belgrade airport in February of 1939. The machine was in overall silver dope scheme. Note the hub-firing cannon. [Djordje Nikolić]

Ikarus IK-2 BR.2110 from 6. Fighter Regiment during the mid 1939. Airplane sports large black number 2 on both fuselage sides. [AMB]

*the burning airplane began to circle in my vicinity. There was danger that the airplane would hit and kill me. That is why I did not want to pull the parachute cord right away, expecting the airplane to move towards the ground.*

*For some reason, I had unlimited confidence in the parachute. When I jumped out of the airplane, I began to track time on my wristwatch. I guess I was in a free fall about 300-400 meters, until the danger passed. I opened the parachute at the altitude of 4,300 meters.*

*As I descended with parachute, I watched the airplane underneath as it left black smoke behind in small turns. Then I thought that it did not take much, that I could still be in it now ... The airplane soon disappeared into the clouds. Only then did it come to my mind, what awaits me under the clouds? To make matters worse, when I came through the clouds, a "sea" appeared beneath me! And I do not know how to swim!"*

The pilot was fortunate enough to descend on the terrain which was flooded by Sava river. Fortunately for him, the "sea" was only deep down to his knees. Injured and exhausted, he waited for a short time while an ambulance arrived.

Kap Ik Vasilije J. Stojanović, Aviation Test Group and Ikarus Factory test pilot. He tested and officially received all series built IK-2 fighters. [Dejan Milojević]

## The IK-2 series production

As the testing of the second prototype confirmed the anticipated characteristics, the Royal Yugoslav Army Air Force Headquarters finally gave their approval on 20 November 1937 and during December series production of 12 IK-2 was ordered at Ikarus. More precisely, it was a pre-series, the so-called "zero" series, which was usually used for additional testing and characteristics confirmation, with eventual finishing works

Extraordinary photo of IK-2 BR.2110 from the capital's elite 6. LP. Note the absence of engine mounted cannon. "Beograd" airport at Zemun, September 1939. [Milan Micevski]

before ordering a larger series (which never happened in case of the IK-2). Since August 1936, when the second prototype had its flight, more than 15 months have passed until the order for the IK-2 series production. In addition to a long and thorough examination, which was the consequence of destruction of the first prototype and suspicion of certain people from aeronautical circles, it was obvious that the Command hesitated with the order. The probable reason for hesitation might also be found in the fact that the Fury II fighter deliveries began from the UK in 1936, and during the following year there the licensed Yugoslav-built Furies also came. These deliveries met the most urgent needs for fighters in the Air Force, although, at that moment, it was perfectly clear to most of the aeronautical experts that the Fury biplanes arrived too late. In the meantime, the Air Force showed their interest in low-wing fighters, and that also to some extent, contributed to the Command's extension of the deadline for making a decision about the IK-2 production.

IK-2 BR.2110 "black 2" from 4. LP with collapsed starboard undercarriage leg, probably due to hard landing. Note large black "Z" (stands for Zagreb airport) on under wing surfaces which was standard Army Air Force manner during the thirties. [Djordje Nikolić]

Ground crew in front of the camouflaged IK-2 No.2107 "white 31" in a hangar at Zagreb-Borongaj airport during 1940. Note a small "white 2107" on propeller blades canvas cover together with the lack of engine mounted cannon. In the background is No.2110 "white 34". Both machines served within 107. E of 4. LP. [Dragan Kolundžić]

Ikarus IK-2 No.2105 "white 29" from 4. LP presented at Technical Exhibition in the French Pavilion at Zagreb Fair in 1940. [Tomislav Aralica via Robert Čopec]

The Ikarus factory management immediately took all the necessary measures to produce tools and procure materials and they urgently began to manufacture parts and assemblies. In the meantime, the factory completed the delivery of 24 licensed Fury II biplanes, which released part of their production capacities. By the end of the summer of 1938, about ten months after the production order, Ikarus was slowly bringing the series production of the IK-2 to an end. In this regard, it was necessary to engage a new civil test pilot for factory test flights. The management hired highly experienced military and acrobatic pilot and famous flight instructor kap Ik Vasilije J. Stojanović, who previously obtained a diploma and license for work in the civil air traffic. He got the license at the end of September, and he started his duty as a factory test pilot at Ikarus on 16 September 1938 with the salary of 5,000 dinars. Stojanović performed the first test flight of the first series IK-2 sample on 11 October 1938, and he finished all the testing, trimming and acceptance flights for all 12 machines until November 1939.

Six series airplanes first flew from mid-October to early December 1938, and the others were completed by the end of February 1939. First one on 11 October, another three on 21, 25 and 30 November and another on 2 December 1939. Another four were delivered in January 1939, and the last IK-2 flew over to the "Beograd" airport on 25 February. There ara no records for two airplanes. At the end of 1939 twelve IK-2s were delivered, which meant deliveres were completed.

In contrast to the prototypes which had the original engines built by French Hispanc-Suiza company, the series airplanes were equipped with licensed Czechoslovakian engines Avia HS 12Ycrs, imported from Czechoslovak Republic. Ikarus, in the order form No.3391-Z dated 31 December 1937, ordered engines from Avia company (Avia akc. společnost pro průmisl letecký, Čakovice) and that company delivered five engines on 1 March and six engines on 19 March 1938, and invoiced them somewhat later to Ikarus. In the first invoice No.248/4-1091 dated 1 April, the following was listed (in French): "5 moteur d'avions complets, type AVIA HS 12Ycrs, Nos de fabrication 21262, 21264, 21265, 21266, 21267" at the price of 435,260 CSK (Czechoslovak korunas) per piece i.e. a total of 2,176,200 CSK. In the second invoice No.353/4-1091 dated 20 April, six engines were listed as "Nos de fabrication 21268, 21269, 21270, 21271, 21272, 21273" at the total price of 2,611,560 CSK.

There are two facts that indicate that the Air Force Headquarters had no intention and did not plan to introduce a larger number of the IK-2 airplanes into its inventory. Firstly, a small series of 12 airplanes only was ordered, and, secondly, that order arrived too late, in time when everyone was absolutely clear that the future of the fighter aviation is exclusively related to the low-wing fighters. It can, therefore, be reasonably concluded that the Headquarters ordered the

**Fighter pilot nar Bogosav M. Stamatović (3 Oct 1913 – 1944) from 4. LP had an accident with IK-2 No.2103 while landinig at Belgrade airport on 10 November 1940. Damage was minor due to pilot's experience, while pilot remained unhurt. [AVII via Dejan Djerić]**

**Another view of IK-2 No.2105 at the Technical Exhibition at the Zagreb Fair French Pavilion in 1940. White escadrille numbers were overpainted during the April war. [Tomislav Aralica via Robert Čopec]**

Heavy landing accident of Ikarus IK-2 from 4. LP in the vicinity of Zagreb in 1940. Unknown pilot, date and airplane serial number. [Josip Novak]

IK-2 more as a test series to examine the possibilities, not only of the Aviation Industry but also of the IK-2 itself. This is also indirectly proven by the fact that there were newly-introduced serial numbers chosen (the so-called "Vebr" or military evidential numbers) at the beginning of 1940, when the IK-2s were assigned series from 2101 to 2150, which clearly showed that they did not take a greater number of this airplane type into account. Of course, only 13 airplanes were assigned numbers, from 2101 to 2113, out of 50 numbers given.

## Service before the 1941 war

Having completed factory and acceptance flights, 12 IK-2 fighters entered service within the elite capital's 6. LP based at Belgrade. The regiment was equipped with the Hawker Fury Mk.II biplanes until then, and since April 1939 they also had 12 newly arrived Hawker Hurricane Mk.Is (the so-called „first Hurricane batch"). Thus it happened that the 51. VG from the 6. LP received gull-wing IK-2s and the low-wing Hurricanes almost at the same time. The IK-2s became operational in mid-1939, but they did not stay long in the inventory of 6. LP.

Since the first fortyish new Messerschmitt Bf-109s, which were firstly introduced with the 51. VG, arrived from Germany by the end of 1939, the IK-2s and the Hurricanes were transferred from Belgrade to the Zagreb's 4. LP stationed at the Borongaj airfield. The IK-2s arrived at Zagreb as early as October 1939, and by the end of the next year all of them were concentrated at the 34. VG in the formation of the 4. LP. Introduction of the IK-2 to the mentioned VVKJ unit was a temporary transitional solution, until the final re-equipping of that regiment with the Hurricanes. During 1941, it was envisaged that all the IK-2s be transferred to the Niš-based 5. LP, whose basic equipment consisted of the Hawker Fury Mk.II biplane fighters. The Niš regiment received their Furies from the 4. LP, which was re-equipped with the Hurricanes and the IK-2s in the meantime.

The IK-2 No.2103 had a minor accident on 10 November 1940, with the damage of around 2%. In the Training Department HQ report, dated 15 January 1941, inter alia, it was stated:

*"On 10 November 1940, nar fighter-pilot Stamatović M. Bogosav from the 108. E/4. LP had an accident in the airplane type IK-2 No.2103 with the Hispano-Avia engine No.21262 at the "Beograd" aiport – under the following circumstances:*

*"The pilot was tasked to fly the airplane from Zagreb to Zemun for the armament supplement. The pilot was descending properly according to the windsock and the signals given by the duty officer at the airport. At the moment of landing, the wind was blowing at 5 m/s which made the pilot land at minimum speed. As the wind changed, it is probable that at one point he relented and the airplane went down from the altitude of 5-6 meters, and due to the airplane weight, the left landing gear collapsed. The airplane tilted to the left, struck the ground with the left wingtip and stopped. The pilot timely reduced the throttle thus saving the engine and the airplane from a larger fault and damage."*

One more IK-2 suffered an accident. A saved photograph shows a camouflage painted IK-2 which was heavily damaged, with the rear fuselage broken, probably due to a rollover. According to the available data, the accident happened on an unknown date in 1940 at the outskirts of Zagreb, and the pilot, also unknown, was not injured. The planned transfer of the IK-2 fighters to the Niš-based 5. LP did not happen out of the simple reason that there were not enough

Judging by the appearance of the airplane, it seems that the impact to the ground was extremely strong. There is no information about the fate of the pilot. [Josip Novak]

Hurricanes needed to complete the 4. LP to the full formation level. They waited for the delivery of the licensed Hurricanes from Zmaj A. D. factory, but they arrived too late, only at the end of March 1941, when those new airplanes were used to complete the newly formed 2. LP. That was why all the servicable IK-2s awaited the April War within the ranks of the 4. LP, more precisely, in the 107. E from the 34. VG from the same regiment. One of the pilots, nar Radivoje Stikić from the 107. E, described the activities of the 4. LP in the last peacetime year:

*„In the second half of the 1940, the rebasing of the regiment by groups started, from the regular Borongaj airport to the auxiliary airfields, like the village of Brežice near Vilen-Krški, Gorina Kurilovac and others. Every 15-20 days the groups interchanged. At that time, the order came that we should, since the dogfights would be led at high altitudes, in that half of the year, devote most of the tasks to high altitude flights, with barographs in the fuselage and the oxygen masks. In addition to that, we practised acrobatics with the Hawker Fury biplane, commanded by radio from the ground."*

The IK-2 airplanes were delivered from the factory without the armament and radio equipment, the installment of which was done, according to the established practice, in the Air Force avaition plants/workshops. The planned and officially adopted armament of IK-2 consisted of one 20 mm Hispano-Suiza type 9 cannon and two 7.7 mm M.30 Darn machine guns. According to the inspection on 14 July 1940, the IK-2s used

Accident of camouflaged Ikarus IK-2 No.2104 at Zagreb – Borongaj airport in 1940. It seems that the damage to the airplane is minimal. Note the presence of the engine mounted cannon. [Šime Oštrić via Ognjan Petrović]

Very interesting and very rare pre war post-card with a quite inexpertly drawing of the Ikarus IK-2 airplane on it. [Dejan Milojević]

the total of 24 7.7 mm machine guns and 13 20 mm cannons, with a notion that one of the cannons was used for training on the ground. That meant that the 12 series IK-2s were equipped by the form given, while the first airplane (No.1 ex second prototype) only had a cannon.

According to the approval, dated 31 August 1940, Ikarus installed the 7.92 mm F.N. machine gun instead of the 20 mm cannon. This work was completed at the end of September the same year

Famous pre war Aviation Test group pilot kap Ik Milan "Mak" Bjelanović. He was calm enough to bail out successfully from a burning second prototype. [via Čedomir Janić]

at the Aviation Test Group which provided the FN machine guns (AF designation M.38) and tested them in October. At the end of October, the same airplane was at the factory for the cannon installation, which meant that the airplane was returned to its original state. The parts for the FN machine gun installation were returned to the transit warehouse. On 22 November, the Air Force Headquarters issued an obligation to modify all 12 IK-2s, with the delivery deadline by 20 February 1941, and the reception of the finished modifications of eight IK-2s (No.2101, 2102, 2104, 2106, 2107, 2108, 2112 and 2113) was done in February 1941 (there is no data about the rest).

Unfortunately, no document have been be discovered (up to now) containing the description of these modifications of the above mentioned IK-2s. Judging by the example of the IK-2 No.11, which had M.38 installed instead of the cannon (at the price of 15,762.31 dinars), and then had the cannon returned to it, it is most probable that the IK-2s got two M.38 machine guns each (of course, at a lower price of only 4,013.93 dinars per airplane). Judging by the photographs, some of the IK-2s were equipped with a cannon in the April War, and some were not.

The installation of skis was planned for use in winter conditions, and the exemplary pair of skis was ordered at the beginning of 1940. According to the authors of the 1972 Airplane Profiles article "IK Fighters", there were also plans

Kindom of Yugoslavia 1941 map with the location of 4. LP at the beggining of April War. [Dragan Šaler]

to produce a two seater training/reconnaissance version (IK-4) out of the IK-2:

"*With, the IK-2 entering service and plans under active consideration for more of the type to be built to equip other fighter units, there vas an apparent need for a suitble advanced trainer. The straightforward solution, was to modify the IK-2 into a dual-control two-seat aircrart. Such a conversion of one or two series IK-2s was considered. Besides its training role, the new trainer, designated IK-4, was to be employed for high-speed reconnaissance, since it would be faster than types like the Henschel Hs 126 then in service.*

*All the characteristics of IK-4, were to be similar to those of the IK-2, differing only in fuselage and cockpil layout. The rear seat for the instructor or observer was to be located behind the pilot's cockpit and in a raised position so as to provide clear visibility.*

*However, the IK-4 project did not pass beyond the discussion stage and was abandoned when delivery of the series version or the IK-2 was delayed and the obsolescence of the high-wing monoplane fighter had been acknowledged.*"

## The 1941 April War

**2. Mixed brigade VVKJ**

Commander – puk Jakov Djordjević

Aide – kap IIk Luka Kandić

The brigade HQ was stationed at the village of Nova Topola, on the road between Banja Luka and Gradiška . The 704. E (liaison) was at the airfield in the vicinity of the village of Nova Topola near the HQ.

**4. LP**

Regiment Commander – ppuk Radoslav Djordjević

Aide – ppuk Artur Kirasić

Aide – kap Ik Vladimir Bosner

33. VG Commanding Officer – maj Nikola Nikolić, technical officer ppor Lazar Vukobratović, 105. E C/O kap Ik Aleksandar Radičević, 106. E C/O kap Ik Dragiša Milijević, 10. Airfield Company (AC) C/O kap Ik Miodrag Laušević.

34. VG C/O – maj Arsenije Boljević, aide kap Ik Vajo Grbić, 107. E C/O kap Ik Žarko Vukajlović, 108. E C/O kap Ik Mladen Milovčević, 11. AC C/O kap Ik Marjan Dvoršak.

According to the war plan R-41, the task of the 4. LP was to prevent the advance of the enemy air force from the direction of Austria and western Hungary over the territory of Slovenia, Croatia and Bosnia, as well as supporting the 8. BR actions. The protected zone was on the east to the line: Donji Miholjac - Đakovo - Bosanski Šamac – Tuzla - Vlasenica, and on the south to the line: Rogatica - Sarajevo – Bugojno – Drvar – Otočac - Senj. Combat engagement of the regi-

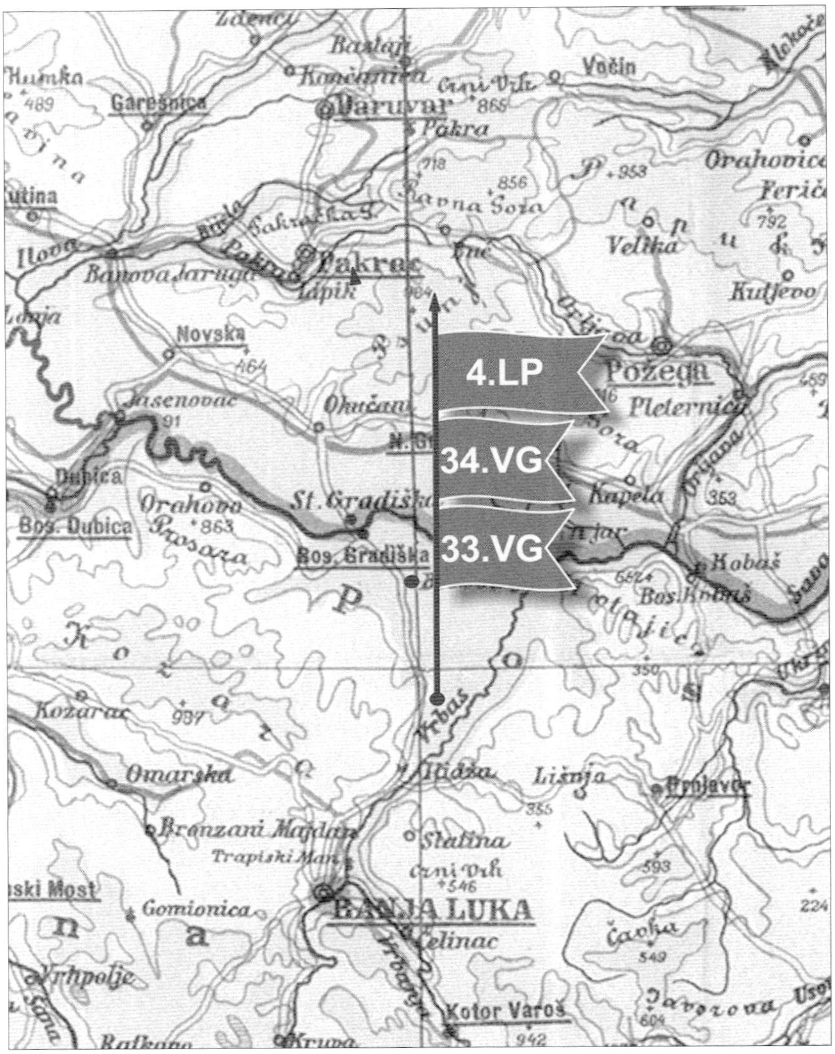


Close up extract from the map, with detailed position of the 4. LP with both fighter groups. [Dragan Šaler]

ment was determined by the strictly confidential Instruction No.1, issued by the Air Force Command in mid-March 1941.

In the peacetime, the regiment was situated at the Borongaj airport near Zagreb. They dislocated to the Bosanski Aleksandrovac war auxiliary airfield, north of Banja Luka, in mid-March 1941. The regiment equipment consisted of British-built Hurricanes (105., 106. and 108. E) and Yugoslav Ikarus IK-2s (107. E). The total number of Hurricanes was 16 plus eight IK-2's. There were 11 Hurricanes in the 106 and 108. E, while there were five airplanes in the 105. E. Each escadrille had one Bücker Bü-131D-2 trainer and one Rogožarski PVT fighter-trainer. There were nine pilots flying IK-2s in the 107. E: kap Ik Žarko Vukajlović, por Djordje Supić, ppor Radomir Milačić, ppor Lazar Vukobratović, nar Radivoje Stikić, por Spasen Zarević, nar Janko Lakić, pnar Branko Jovanović and the reserve kap IIk Milan Zemljić.

The Telefunken FuG VII (Funk Gerät VII) radio stations were installed in the IK-2, while the Standard R-10 radio stations, meant for the Hurricanes, were not installed by the beginning of the war, but they were in the technical armoury, according to por Stjepan Pažamenta's report. It is unknown what the reason was for not installing them, although it would facilitate flying in the conditions of war. Was it gross negligence, irresponsibility, sabotage or something else?

Djordjević J. Jakov, Commanding Officer of 2. MB. Although he was of high repute as a good troop officer in peacetime, he proved to be totally unfit and incompetent commanding officer during the April War. [AVII]

Due to the ustaša (anti-Yugoslav, anti Serbian, pro-Axis Croatian rebellion) sabotage of the communications centre, the brigade's headquarters did not receive two very important dispatches. The first one, dated 5 April, 1941, in the period between 08.00 and 09.00 o'clock, when the Air Force Command informed them that the German attack was expected the next day in the early morning hours and that they should be in the state of ground alert. The second one, dated 6 April, informed them that Germany attacked Kingdom of Yugoslavia and that they should act as instructed in the previously given Instruction No.1. Shortly before the beginning of the war, 105. E with five Hurricanes, under the command of kap Ik Aleksandar Radičević, was transferred as reinforcement to the formation of the 6. LP at the Mali Radinci auxiliary airfield in Srem.

4. LP airplanes deployed at the edge of the airfield, drawn into courtyards and around the farms in the village, camouflaged very well with stacks of hay, straw and reeds. The airfield terrain was in itself intersected by meadows and fields planted with different crops, so it stayed completely unobserved by Germans during the war, although they flew directly above it several times in the attempt to locate it. The airfield anti-aircraft (AA) defence was formed by two small anti-aircraft machine-gun platoons in the formation of the two aforementioned airfield companies with 24 obsolete Schwarzlose machine guns. According to the memory of ppor Lazar Vukobratović:

*"With regards to the anti - aircraft defence, it acted in the most primitive way. We had machine guns, but we didn't have sighting sets, so we were forced to make primitive sighting sets ourselves. The air defence personnel consisted of different service arms. There was a case of a former male nurse who came to be a gunner. It was out of the question to prepare soldiers by explaining them the current state in the world or informing them about the dangers that threatened us."*

There were no shelters for men and material, all of it caused by the passive behaviour of the brigade commander. The regiment was connected to the observation service by intelligence centres Bosanska Gradiška and Banja Luka. The 4. LP had been on strict ground alert since 22 March 1941. It was supplied from the 9. Air Force Base and transit station in Banja Luka. The state of the 9. VB was best described by statement of the technical armoury manager, por Franjo Vognar:

*"On the first day of the war we didn't get any orders, until late night hours when it was*

4. LP Commanding Officer during the April War, ppuk Radoslav M. Đorđević. [Ognjan Petrović]

Maj Arsenije T. Boljević (19 August 1904 - 1953) Commanding Officer of 34. VG/ 4. LP during the April War. [AVII]

*announced that every officer should act at their discretion. A German airplane appeared the next day, and that caused turbulence in the entire base although the attack was not dangerous at all. The German airplanes appeared more often during the next couple of days, but there were no attacks. They dropped four bombs in the afternoon of the fifth day of war. The turbulence overflowed the entire base and the first Croatian flag, which could be well discerned from afar, was observed at the railway station Predgrađe – Banja Luka. For the majority of personnel in the base that brought good mood as it presented the establishment of the Independent State of Croatia."*

On Sunday morning at about 07.00 hours the personnel found out about the attack on Belgrade by listening to the ordinary radio. They had never received radio dispatch sent by the Air Force Command. They did not receive any information from the home base Zagreb (Borongaj airport), although Germans performed the attacks on the airfields in the zone of operations of the 4. LP. The Luftwaffe fighter units, stationed in the South Reich territories, attacked the airports and airfields Borongaj, Lučko, Pleso and Gorica near Zagreb, Cerklje, Bregje, and after that Polje near Ljubljana, Težno near Maribor and Varaždin. Four Messers from the Stab II./JG 54 took off to "frei jagd" from Graz - Thalerhof airport at 06.21 hours. They were followed by three more, also from Stab JG 54, which took off at 06.25. On the basis of the information about the disposition of the Air Force Command and the locations of the airfields which the defected kap Ik Vladimir Kren gave to the Germans, the leader, Maj Hannes Trautloft and his wingmen's, Oblt Otto Kath and Oblt Werner Pichon-Kalau von Hofe, headed to Zagreb. According to the memory of Maj Trautloft:

*"Our mission was "frei-jagd" in the area around Zagreb and low-level attacks at the enemy airfields. Excited and with strained nerves, we stormed into the enemy territory. We must be extremely cautious, because, ironically, there are also German planes, Do 17 and Me 109, which were recently delivered to Yugoslavia, on the opposing side. The cowlings on our engines are painted bright yellow, but nevertheless, the highest degree of attention is required. There is no movement whatsoever. The ground looks quiet and sleepy on an early Sunday morning. A tower of a church looms out of the dense fog on our right. We are above Zagreb. Suddenly, I see a long freight train moving towards the southeast. We will not allow such a desirable target to escape. We lashed at the train and our machine guns hit the locomotive, which was forced to stop, covered with dense clouds of steam from all sides. The track was blocked for a while! A couple of minutes later, the outlines of the airport, revealed*

IK-2 and Hurricane fighter-pilots from 34. VG at an unknown auxiliary airfield, summer of 1940. [Tomislav Aralica]

4. LP ground crew with Hawker Hurricane Mk.I at Borongaj airport, summer of 1940. [Dragan Kolundžić]

*to us by the Croatian captain, appear out of the fog. I counted eight parked machines, seven of which were left in flames. Anti-aircraft defence is mediocre and nothing happens in the air yet. While leaving, I look around and I see the airport again, shrouded in thick black smoke from burning oil and gasoline. We must have done a good job. My other squadrons had similar experiences."*

There is a statement about the loss of the Messerschmitt Bf 109E (W.Nr.4115) from the Stab JG 54 "Grünherz" which confirms that the situation was not so "idyllic" on the German side. The pilot, Oblt Otto Kath, unit's aide and Maj Trautloft's wingmen said:

*"I was hit in the cooler on both sides. The engine started breaking down as we were climbing. Immediately after flying over the River Mura, I landed the airplane on its belly on the other bank of the river, but it was still the enemy territory. While I was making an emergency landing, I grazed the willows on the right, which turned me towards the embankment that I passed over and I fell straight into the water. It sank right away. I hit the gun sight with my head and lost consciousness, but I regained it in rising cold water and I pushed the cabin canopy with all my strength despite the murky water full of bubbles. I fell out over the yellow nose of the plane*

Another photo of 4. LP perssonel during the pre war period. Photo was taken at an unknown auxiliary airfield during the summer time and in quite casual mood. [Tomislav Aralica]

*and got away completely. When I only partially regained consciousness in the airplane, the dirty water filled my mouth and nose. I would have surely drowned if a brave boy from the nearby farm hadn't pulled me out of the machine to his boat, only a few seconds before it disappeared in the fast river current. He took me to a river mill. Luckily, the Chetniks quest came without dogs! The boy was sent as a messenger to our remote lines, but he never came back. After many hours of being haunted in the direction of north at the edge of the forest, I suddenly saw an ambulance car with the Red Cross flag fluttering on top at the embankment. They conducted me through the lines. Fritz, my saviour, came with me.“*

Most probably, the airplane was brought down by the fire from the members of the Drava Division. Germans suffered losses during the attack on ground targets by the Royal Yugoslav AA defence at about 08.00 also. Junkers Ju 87B (S2+BM, W.Nr.5286) from the II./StG 77 fell about 1.5 km away from the Hajdine village near Ptuj. The pilot, Ofw Heinz Ritter, and the gunner ‚Uffz Heinz Hertel, died. According to the German documents, it happened because of the alleged engine failure in the vicinity of Celje. They were shot at by the AA company under the command of por Miloš Čomagić from the 128th Infantry Regiment of Drava Division.

Certainly, the most interesting detail relates to the German ace and the future "Star of Africa", which was unknown at that moment, Oberfähnrich Hans-Joachim Walter Rudolf Siegfried Marseille from the 3./JG 27 "Africa", who was not shot down by the Yugoslav AA defence from the Ljubljana airfield only by chance. He managed to return to the departure airport at Graz-Thalerhof, landing normally with a large hole on the engine cowl, dangerously close to the engine compressor air intake. He was hit by the 602th AA battery of the Ljubljana Aerial Defence. Immediately upon learning that the war had started, the C/O of the 4. LP, ppuk Radoslav Djordjević, ordered the take-off of the first patrols and the ground alert, informing the Commander of the 2. MVB puk Jakov Djordjević by phone. The Hurricanes took off and patrolled towards Zagreb, Ljubljana, the border of Austria and Hungary, while the slower and

**Commanding Officer of 107. E (armed with IK-2s), 34. VG/4. LP, kap Ik Žarko M. Vukajlović. He bravely led his escadrille into the combat. [Aleksandar Smiljanić]**

**Pnar Branko Jovanović who entered the combat with an obsolete IK-2 fighter airplane against nine JG 54 Messerschmitts on 7 April 1941. He landed without taking a single hit on his airplane. [Author]**

**Luftwaffe Messerschmitts 109 from JG 54 at Hungarian airfield prior to campaign against the Kingdom of Yugoslavia. [Jan van den Heuvel]**

Commanding Officer of 107. E, fighter pilot kap Ik Žarko Vukajlović stands in front of the IK-2. Note the absence of engine mounted cannon. [Milan Micevski]

less armed IK-2s cruised over the territory of Bosnia, in the area between the Sava and Una rivers.

There were encounters with solitary Luftwaffe reconnaissance airplanes which avoided combat by hiding in the clouds. During the morning, immediately after landing at Thalerhof near Gratz, the fire broke out on Messerschmitt Bf 109E-7 (W.Nr.1586) from the I./JG 27, which resulted in 40% damage. It is possible that the fire was the consequence of the engagement of the Yugoslav AA guns.

The order arrived in the early morning hours that two of the Hurricanes from the 4. LP escort a pair of 8. BP Blenheim's, stationed at the Rovine airfield in the vicinity. The Blenheims were supposed to attack the railway installations at Graz, with the aim to disturb the concentration and transport of German units. It is known for sure that kap Ik Dobnikar flew in one of the Hurricanes, while there is no precise data about the other one. Although they flew together for a short period of time, because por Ivan Pandža, a Blenheim observer, decided to perform a sweeping flight instead of flight at the altitude of 2,500 meters as was ordered. Captain Dobnikar continued towards Austria by himself.

The Messerschmitt Bf-109E "White 1" from the 2./JG 27 "Africa" fell near Maribor at about

13.00. The pilot, Lt Wilhelm Kothmann, the ace with seven victories, disappeared, but he returned to his unit later. The first German report dated on 8 April, stated that there was a complete loss (100 %) of the airplane and that the pilot was reported as missing. The report dated on 11 April, stated that he was wounded, while the last report on 11 January 1942 claims that the plane returned to base and the pilot was not injured (?!). Most probably, Kotman was shot down by the fire from 128th AA battery of the Yugoslav Air Defence. There was also a possibility that his airplane was damaged during aerial combat with the Yugoslav Hurricanes, which had several engagements that day, but the Yugoslav pilots didn't claim any victories. According to the post-war report by Brigadier General Ferdinand Janež, artillery commander of the Drava Division, one airplane was hit and made emergency landing near the village of Pragersko, near Ptuj. The pilot was captured and taken to the HQ of the VII Army for questioning. Eleven days later, he was liberated by German troops, while his airplane was taken by German technical service which transported it to be repaired.

During the afternoon, the C/O of the 2. MVB ordered to determine a permanent patrol consisting of two IK-2s which will provide immediate protection, in order to protect the airfield with the Blenheims belonging to the 8. BP. The orderly pilots should rotate on daily basis. Two IK-2s from the 107. E flew over to Rovine auxiliary airfield immediately. The balance of the first day of the war for the 4. LP was about 50 take-offs with 50-60 hours of flight, without any losses.

During the 7 April 4. LP was supposed to continue air defence of the territory it protected and support the operations of the 8. BP. Accordingly they were supposed to provide escort for the bombers, which were tasked with attacking German air bases in Hungary near Szeged and Pécs at dawn, used by the Luftwaffe for the attacks on Belgrade. This mission was addressed to the C/O of the 2. MVB via the Operational radio network of the Air Force Command on 6 April, in the period between 21.00 and 22.00 hours, which was confirmed by the brigade's radio station, but the commander was only given the dispatch at 07.00 on 7 April. The deciphering of this radio dispatch lasted nearly two hours due to the lack of professional personnel for the new code, so that the brigade commander was familiar with the task at about 09.00 on 7 April, which was too late to carry out the task. The 8. BP was supposed to perform a sudden attack on the Luftwaffe airfields in Hungary at dawn. This delay was caused by the ustaša sabotage in the 2. Liaison Centre of the 2. M manager B. Puk Jakov Djordjević faced a very awkward situation. It was either to perform a daily attack on the targets heavily defended by AA weapons and fighters, protected by 12 Hurricanes from the 4. LP, without the necessary element of surprise, or to abandon a very risky mission. IK-2s should take cover of both airfields in the meantime. Finally, he chose the daily attack without consulting the Air Force Command. At about 10.00, he issued an order to the C/O of the 8. BP ppuk Stanko Diklić to perform bombing of the airfields in Szeged and Pécs at about 11.00, and to the C/O of the 4. LP to organize escort of the bombers, provided that the details about the cooperation will be agreed by the regiment commanders. Since the order to attack the targets in Hungary arrived too late, the Blenheims flew to attack the targets at the Austrian bor-

Rudder of an Me-109 ace, Hubert Mütherich, who claimed two Ikarus fighters during brief aerial combat over Rovine/Bosanski Aleksandrovac airfields. He lost his life on 9 September 1941 on the Eastern Front. [AMB]

Fighter pilot of 107. E, nar Radivoje Stikić in front of the IK-2. He will be the only pilot shot down in aerial combat in IK-2 during the April war. [Milan Micevski]

Bosner F. Vladimir, fighter pilot and a 4. LP C/O Aide. Beside he was one of the most expirienced pilots in 4. LP, he did not participate in aerial combat during the April War. On the other side, he joined Croatian Air Force without hesitation. [Vladimir Bosner Jr.]

Meserschmitt Bf-110C (L2 + HR, WNr.2318) from the 7 (F)/ LG 2 which force landed on the Hungarian territory after combat with 4. LP fighters. [Csaba B. Stenge]

6./KG 51 "Edelweiss" Junkers Ju-88 (9K + LP, WNr.8201) three crew grave, included its commander Captain Jürgen Berlin that crashed into Lijevče polje near Nova Gradiška. [NMU]

der area before the break of dawn. In addition to the fact that the unfavourable weather and low clouds prevented them from precise bombing, they were also deprived of fighter escort as they could not fly under such weather conditions. Nevertheless, Blenheims returned without any losses, except one airplane which was damaged and had to make an emergency landing on the Austrian territory.

After a lull between two attacks of the 8. BP, there was an incident with a German airplane near Novska. In fact, at about 09.15, Do 17Z (U5 + HR, W.Nr.1146) from the 7./KG 2 "Holzhammer" grazed a telegraph pole in a sweeping flight and crashed eight kilometres north-west of Novska near Lipovljani. The four men crew lost their lives: navigator Maj Friedrich Dreyer, commander of the III./KG 2, pilot Lt Franz Mayerhofer, Ofw Fritz Schmidt and radio-operator/ gunner, Uffz Richard Zachart.

Due to the in short range, the IK-2 patrols cruised along the line: Slavonski Brod - Bosanska Gradiška – Jasenovac - Bosanski Novi, and the Hurricane patrols were in front of that line all the way to the Hungarian and Austrian border. The Territorial Air Surveillance operated somewhat better and reported about the appearance of the enemy planes in the border zone and in Varaždin - Maribor region. However, these telephone reports arrived late, so that the fighter patrols took off too late and they couldn't intercept or approach the Germans, especially the fast twin-engine Messerschmitt Bf 110s which were most often flying above the regiment territory . It was agreed that, due to the improving weather conditions, Hurricanes should provide the escort to the Blenheims during the attack at 11.00 hours. The escort fell behind out of completely inexplicable reasons, because the Blenheims departed not waiting for the Hurricanes?! This resulted in horrible losses of seven Blenheims and twenty-two crew members. In this particular case, almost the entire 2. MVB command personnel consisted of Serbians. The chain of command failed completely, primarily due to the brigade's C/O, causing enormous victims and extensive material damage. The deputy of the C/O, ppuk Artur Kirasić, who was a Croat, was absolutely side-lined from any specific tasks. Ppuk Kirasić stated as follows:

*"On 7 April, I was invited by the brigade commander puk Djordjević Jakov, who was in the village of Nova Topola, which was about five kilometres away from us, and he ordered me to go to Banja Luka and to flatten the airfield. I have a feeling that I was deliberately removed from the regiment, because when I arrived to the airfield I saw that it was an impossible task to do, as there were ground works which were being carried out by the contractors, and he, together with his expert personnel, couldn't finish that job in six months!"*

The Air Force Command, as ppuk Pavlović Andrija remembers, ordered an investigation into these tragic events, in order to determine liability, but the quick end of the April War made it impossible. Shortly after the return of survived Blenheims from the tragic mission over Hungary, while the impressions were still being gathered, a large formation of enemy airplanes appeared in the sky. It was obvious that their arrival was related to the 8. BP's attack on targets in Hungary, because little time passed since Blenheims returned. The reason for the additional concern was the nearby village, inhabited almost exclusively by German population. Three groups from JG 54 "Grünherz", consisting of nine airplanes each, flew over both airfields, not noticing brilliantly camouflaged Yugoslav airplanes on the ground. The first two groups already dove towardss the road to Banja Luka, strafing Yugoslav troops. According to the memory of kap Ik Svetozar Lolić:

*"On 8 April (7 April - a.c.) 1941, at about 15.00 hours, pnar Jovanović (Branko - a.c.), landed with obsolete IK-2 at the auxiliary airfield Rovine near Bosanska Gradiška, where the 68. VG/8. BP was based. He approached me with his machine, and jumping out of it and leaving the en-*

Burnt and destroyed aircraft at Bosanski Aleksandrovac auxiliary airfield. Three IK-2 remains photographed by an unknown VVKJ officer observer from 1. BP., 13 April 1941. [Author]

Almost totally burned Ikarus IK-2, photographed with German soldier standing by, April/May 1941. Note a small Yugoslav cockade on port wing upper surface. [AMB]

*gine running, he asked me if this was the airfield of the 8. BP. At that moment, a group of 16 (18 - a.c.) Messerschmitt 109s appeared and flew over the airfield in a sweeping flight at an altitude of 100 meters. The commander of the German unit started climbing up to about 500 meters, and the other German pilots began to circle receiving instructions via radio to attack the ground targets. Noticing the Germans, pnar Jovanović jumped into his machine, and he just said: 'I am going to the combat!!'"*

The leader of the aforementioned patrol from the 107. E, ppor Supić Djordje, landed at Rovine with his IK-2 together with Jovanović, but he turned off the engine. Pnar Jovanović took off at full throttle, while ppor Supić tried several times without success to start his Hispano-Suiza. The mechanics from the 8. BP rushed to help, but they could not do anything either. As kap Ik Lolić remembers, he was on the verge of tears of fury because he could not start the engine and take off to join the combat. Immediately after taking off, pnar Jovanović flew his IK-2 into the formation of nine Luftwaffe Bf 109s which were much faster and better armed. There was an aerial combat in the ratio 9:1, in which pnar Jovanović, thanks to the excellent knowledge of the airplane he was flying, as well as skilled manoeuvres and agility of the IK-2, led successfully, going from one manoeuvre to another, closing extremely narrow combat turns which the Germans could not follow due to their higher speed and much larger turning radius, and also because of the turmoil caused by competing which of them would bring him down first!

In the meantime, the first two German groups, called back over the radio, came back from the direction of Banja Luka towards the airfield of the 8. BP. In order to stop the German attack against the airfield and to help pnar Jovanović, who fought heroically flying an obsolete machine in absolutely surreal conditions against nine Messerschmitts, the C/O of the 4. LP, ppuk Radoslav Djordjević, used the banners as the agreed signal to order all the regiment es-

German photo of captured Ikarus IK-2, ex 107. E machine, with unusual field camouflage. Note the nonstandard Kosovo Cross on both underwing surfaces. [Nenad Jovanović]

cadrilles to scramble. At this sign, within only a couple of minutes, having already been at the first degree alert, 13 fighters took off from the Bosanski Aleksandrovac airfield and then headed in the direction of Rovine, flying separately or in patrols formed after the take-off.

The 106. E was the fastest one, consisting of four Hurricanes divided into two patrols; the first with the commander of the 106. E kap Ik Dragiša Milijević, accompanied by nar Milan Mitić; the second, which was probably led by kap Ik Života Petrović with an unknown wingman. The 107. E followed with five IK-2s, consisting of kap Ik Žarko Vukajlović, ppor Lazar Vukobratović, nar Radivoj Stikić in one group, and ppor Radomir Milačić and, according to the unproven data, reserve kap IIk Milan Zemljić or nar Janko Lakić in the second group. And finally, the 108. E with four Hurricanes. So far, only the name of nar Živorad "Žika" Tomić from the 108. E is known. The first patrol to arrive at Rovine was the one of kap Ik Milijević and his wingmen nar Milan Mitić, and after that the others arrived. There were arguments about who would fly into the combat during the scramble, so that nar Tomić, although he was a non-commissioned officer, managed to "expel" 34. VG C/O aide, kap Ik Vajo Grbić, from the Hurricane cockpit despite the fact that he was already at the commands. Nothing could help, not even the threats by captain Grbić that he would be reported to the superiors and that he would be taken to the military court. Basically, nar Tomić was right because it was his turn to fly. According to the statement of the 34. VG commander, maj Arsenije Boljević, who did not participate in the combat:

*"All the serviceable airplanes took off in pairs, there were four Hurricanes and six IK-2s from my group. The take-offs of the first pairs were performed while the Messerschmitts were flying towards Banja Luka (the first two groups consisted of 18 planes - a.c.). Therefore, some of the pairs evaded the Germans, and three IK-2s and two Hurricanes from my group as well as two Hurricanes from the 33. VG participated in the combat over the Rovine. The German Messerschmitts formed combat circles. Our fighters attacked in pairs and separately (nar Jovanović and nar Stikić). Two of the Me 109s (one - a.c.) were shot down in the fierce combat with the enemy that was three times more superior in numbers, technique and tactical experience."*

Nar Stikić M. Radivoje, only 107.E pilot who was shot down by Germans but managed to survive despite being heavily wounded. [VA]

There was a fervent aerial combat between 14 fighters on the Yugoslav side and 27 fighters on the German side, but at two separate locations in the immediate vicinity. Being very skilful in combat, Germans formed three circular levels according to altitude, with the lowest one formed by the group intended for strafing the 8. BP's planes. They only managed to damage one Blenheim and one Jupiter-powered Breguet Br 19 biplane. The Yugoslav pilots, without any combat experience and tactic, attacked in patrols or individually, and surprisingly, they managed to involve the Germans, who were very disciplined as a rule, in such a disorganized way of fighting. Nar Stikić was in the first trio of IK-2s which entered the combat with the Germans at about 15.30 hours:

*"Our take off was straight south towards Banja Luka, then a left U-turn towards Topola. I made the turn before Vukobratović managed to do his, which meant that I cut him off, in order to catch up with our commander and join him. I found out later that my leader, Supić, didn't take off at all (Por Supić remained at the Rovine airfield – a.c.). However the c/o's aircraft engine had just come back from overhaul, so I never really caught up with him. There was an 8/8 overcast that day and the cloud base was at appx 1500 meters ; climbing immediately to 1000 meters a group of nine Messerschmitts flew by above me in a westerly direction coming as they did from Slavonski Brod and if I recall correctly in a single wedge formation. The swastikas on their tails were very visible as were their yellow wingtips, tails and propeller hubs, which was inducing respect. At first it seemed they wouldn't fight, but they made the U-turn and headed towards us. At that very moment, another squadron of Messerschmitts appeared, and there began an uneven combat. At the beginning of the combat I saw one or two IK-2s, and later I didn't see anybody although the entire regiment took part in the combat.*

*I was aiming with short bursts, and when I saw a Messerschmitt "parading" horizontally in front of me, I aimed with deflection and pulled the trigger, which was on my joystick. Although I immediately let go of the trigger and brought it back to its original position by closing the valves, where the gas throttle was, nothing helped and my left gun kept firing until all its ammunition was gone. There were moments when I was attacked by six aircraft simultaneously, two from the back and two on each side. I didn't care about those on the sides because I knew that there was a small probability that they would hit me. On the other hand I never flew straight and level for a single moment but constantly twisted and turned every second, so to speak. As long as I did so, they couldn't harm me, in spite the fact that "Meho" whizzed next to IK-2 as a hawk next to a chicken... Since I was slower than them, I could never get on their tails but had to satisfy myself with those who flew past in front of me, and since by now also my cannon and right machine gun had ceased to function, my only defense was to try and outmaneuver them.*

*It is very likely that they noticed that something was wrong with my armament, because I was attacked for a long time by a lot of them. I was trying to activate the starboard machine gun and the cannon, but the machine gun and cannon bullets kept falling out complete in the net for collecting the empty shells. It was probably because the trigger wire had been cut off. I was quite demoralized by this, because seconds are eternity in a combat, so I decided to get down lower, reckoning that they would not be able to attack me at low altitude. I pitched the plane' s nose downwards, and in one steep spiral- imitating a tailspin, I descended to the altitude of about 50-100 meters, straightened the plane and continued flying horizontally and in a straight line, thinking that the Germans had gone.*

*What a mistake! I wasn't flying for a long time when I noticed that the dust was raising on the floor and I felt something lukewarm leaking down my lower back. I moved my arms and my legs and everything felt alright. But I started to feel lightheaded. My IK was still working like a clock, but since I had begun to feel light headed, and certainly was to late to climb and try to parachute I had to get down, quickly. Not wanting to land back on our auxiliary airfield (I was scared to reveal it to the enemy) I looked for some place to land. There wasn't much time left for thinking and choosing, so I landed on a plowed field. I knew that there was nothing good awaiting for me in this case, because the IK-2 had a fixed undercarriage meaning I would most likely somersault on the soft ground. That was exactly what happened. At ten meters above the ground I noticed a big hole in the field, so, in order not to go straight into it, I gave full left rudder and caved in right side first and of course rolled over straight away, loosing consciousness. Blood was dripping down my back to the neck. The IK-2 had a steel plate behind the pilot, serving to protect him from being wounded in the back. But the Germans had special ammunition with heavier charge, so the bullet pierced the body armor plate, flying suit and uniform and it stayed in the flesh, not breaking through it all the way."*

Nar Stikić crashed very close to the airfield, so the personnel rushed to help him. Nevertheless, they had to wait, because the Germans were machine gunning the wreckage of his airplane with him still being inside! Luckily, there was no fire, and the mechanic Rade Vučković with two soldiers managed to pull out wounded and unconscious pilot. A couple of moments later, a fire broke out and the plane was completely burnt. Stikić was put into the ambulance, and before being transported to the hospital in Banja Luka, the ambulance door were opened and there appeared aide of the 4. LP C/O, kap Ik Vladimir Bosner, as Stikić remembered later, with the words:

*"You want to fight more, it serves you right!"*

And then he slammed the door. The aerial combat lasted only seven to eight minutes, and then the Germans abandoned the combat and thanks to the higher speed, they flew north in the direction of their airfields in Hungary. During this short combat, the commander of the 106. E, kap Ik Dragiša Milijević, was killed. According to the testimony of the civil mechanic Radojko Mašković, captain Milijević was either wounded or his plane was severely damaged, as he separated suddenly from the combat and, not taking the direction towards the airfield, he pulled out the landing gear on the Hurricane, trying to land on a higher plateau near the Vrbas River. The mechanic said that even four or five German fighters stormed on Milijević, who was absolutely helpless in his attempt to force land. After the

**Another view of the same airplane from 107. E with German soldier sitting in the cockpit. It seems that unservicable machines were not burned like servicable ones. [Mario Jelušić via Djordje Nikolić]**

Por Supić S. Djordje, 107.E pilot whose IK-2 engine failed to start and prevented him to join aerial combat with JG 54 fighters. [VA]

second or third attack, a large fire broke out on the Hurricane, which turned over its wing and crashed to the ground. His wingman, nar Milan Mitić, had more luck, so he managed to rescue himself by jumping out of the burning airplane with a parachute, but he had significant burns on his face and one hand. The eyewitnesses of his landing said that he was badly burnt, but that he firmly held a gun in his right hand. The gun had a crooked barrel, which was a consequence of its hitting the ground at landing. Namely, Mitić told them that one of the German pilots tried to shoot at him with while he was descending with his parachute, so he reached his gun and shot back at him.

Nar Radivoj Stikić from the 107. E was severely wounded, but he managed to perform the emergency landing. The German pilots claimed two IK-2s and one PZL-11 because of the similarity between two airplanes, and they were: Oblt Hans-Ekkehard Bob from the 9./JG 54 and Oblt Hubert Mütherich from the 5./JG 54 claimed the IK-2s, and Oblt Gerhard Koall from the 7./JG 54 shot the aforementioned "PZL". Claims related to three Hurricanes were submitted by: Lt Josef Pöhs from the 5./JG 54, Lt Erwin Leykauf from the 8./JG 54 and Lt Max Clerico from the 7./JG 54. One German fighter was shot down allegedly by kap Ik Milijević, and the other by nar Živorad Tomić from the 108. E /34. AG. There is no confirmation for the first claim, and as for the other it was Bf 109E (KV+LI, W.Nr.5570) from the 7./ JG 54, which, according to the German data, had an emergency landing in the area Marcali-Balaton in Hungary, which was incorrect, as he did so near Bosanski Aleksandrovac. The pilot was Gefr Günther Fabian who was declared missing, but he returned to his unit after a couple of days. There was a geographical map with six German airfields marked in the Pécs area in the downed airplane. The pilots suggested that the map should be used to perform immediate counter attack at the marked airfields but the brigade commander refused it for unknown reasons. That evening, the commander of the 34. VG, kap Ik Boljević, assembled the pilots and worked out the tactic for the upcoming aerial combats:

*"At the sign 'both escadrilles in the air' – the 107. E with IK-2's assembles and circles over our base, while the 108. E assembles and circles above the Rovine, 8. BP war base; the pairs must not be split up; aide (kap Ik Grbić) and I will be the reserve; the IK-2s should fly in a combat circle in groups of four, with the smallest possible diameter; open fire in every favourable situation of encounter; leave the circle only briefly, because of favourable targets and return right away; the Hurricanes can leave the circle in pairs for longer periods in pursuit of favourable targets."*

The 4. LP had about 40 take-offs with about 50 hours of flight. Two of the Hurricanes and one IK-2 were lost. One pilot died, two were wounded, one of whom severely. The Yugoslav AA defence shot at its own airplane in the area of Zagreb, Sisak, Slavonski Brod and other places, despite the given instructions about the recognitions and agreed signals...

8 April found the 4. LP with nine Hurricanes and seven IK-2s at the Bosanski Aleksandrovac airfield. They got an assignment to continue with the air defence of its territory and to support the 8. BP operations. The commander of the 2. MB, puk Jakov Djordjević, conveyed the received assignments to the regiment commanders, but he stayed inactive leaving the initiative to subordinate commanders, while he was obstructing every initiative of the regiment commanders in the previous two days, although they only blindly executed his decisions. Such attitude of the brigade commander was probably a consequence of the great losses of the 8. BP the day before, which he was most responsible for. Such passive attitude had a negative impact on the operation of both regiments which restricted their activity on this day.

Puk Djordjević neither submitted his daily report to Air Force Command on the brigade's

Like IK-2's, all servicable Hurricanes from 4. LP were burned as well. [Mario Jelušić]

actions that day, nor did he address the Air Force HQ to get the information about the situation and to receive assignments for the following day, which was his duty and obligation. In order to execute the task in question, the 4. LP units performed IK-2 patrol flights over the territory of Bosnia, while the Hurricane patrols flew over the territory of Croatia and Slovenia. The Observation and Reporting Service periodically informed about the appearance of German airplanes in the area of Varaždin, Maribor and other places, but with a delay of half an hour to half a day. The 4. LP's fighters were taking off too late, so interception and successful pursuit were not possible. German reconnaissance airplanes managed to avoid combat by flying one by one most of the time. That was why the Hurricane patrol consisting of maj Arsenije Boljević as a leader, and nar Živko Džal as a wingman, had two dogfights, without claims.

While cruising over the valley of the river Sava along the route Bosanski Novi - Bosanska Gradiška to Jasenovac, one of the two IK-2s from 107. E patrol had to perform emergency landing, during which the airplane rolled over its nose and was severely damaged, and the pilot remained uninjured. Por Spasen Zarević held the commands of the IK-2:

*"I was on patrol in the area Bosanska Gradiška - village of Davor, with the patrol leader, ppor Radomir Milačić. Our task was to close the direction from Vrbas towards Banja Luka. As the weather conditions started to get worse, we patrolled at lower altitude in the "front" combat ready formation. There weren't any interceptions, but I ran out of fuel due to uneconomical fuel consumption, so I had an emergency landing which passed without consequences for me as the airplane rolled over to its back."*

During the day, one IK-2, which was under repair at the Ikarus factory, was flown to the 105. E at the Radinci airfield. There are indications that either kap Ik Milan Bjelanović or the Ikarus' test pilot kap Ik Vasilije Stojanović were the ones who flew it. The regiment again had about 40 take-offs, with about 50 hours of flight.

The task for the 4. LP on 9 April was to continue the aerial defence of its territory. In order to execute this task, the regiment units went on patrol flights despite the bad weather conditions, and they chased some German reconnaissance airplanes which were flying over the 4. LP's zone. The Observation and Reporting service was very ineffectual on this day as well, which came as the result of withdrawing of units of the Yugoslav IV and the VII Army and the sabotage by the Croatian personnel. These made the work of the 4. LP more difficult, as they couldn't apply the interception tactic, but the take-off was performed only when they saw German planes in the air. However, that afternoon at about 16.30, one more German loss was recorded on the territory covered by the 4. LP. It is worth to mention the downing of the German Dornier in the vicinity of Banja Luka. It was Do 17Z (U5+BT, W.Nr.1190) of 9./KG 2 "Holzhammer". It performed emergency landing and it was damaged heavily near the railway station Predgradje in the vicinity of Banja Luka. The crew consisted of non-commissioned officers, pilot Uffz Ulrich Sonnemann, who was wounded, and navigator Uffz Hans Wimmer, as well as gunners Gefr Karl Weetmar and Gefr Heinz Waldraff, who was also wounded. Firstly, they were reported as missing in action, but they later returned to their unit. According to the Yugoslav data, the crew was killed. The aforementioned Dornier was shot at from several locations. First from the train travelling in the direction Otočac-Caprag, at about 1.5 kilometres outside Caprag, then the remaining soldiers from the Alpine Regiment under the temporary control of pilot por Pero Zdjelar, and, according to some information there was also AA defence of Banja Luka under the command of reserve por Skender Kulenović, later known as a famous writer and member of the Serbian Academy of Sciences. The number of 4. LP flights and flight hours for 9 April 1941 is still not known.

On 10 April, the task of the air defence of the territory covered by the 4. LP still remained unchanged. Informing the regiment about the flights of the enemy aviation also remained at the same poor level, so the take-offs under alarm were still dependant on the visual observation from the regiment airfield. In spite of the unfavourable weather conditions with low cloudiness and occasional rain, which was threatening to turn into snow, there were patrol flights with the expulsion of some of the lonely German airplanes flying over the regiment zone. IK-2s kept flying their patrols. Later, during the day, due to the bad weather, there were only individual take-offs. In one such occasion, captain Janko Dobnikar in a Hurricane successfully attacked one Messerschmitt Bf 110, which was hidden in the clouds, but, according to the unconfirmed information, it later crashed in the nearby village. Even the villagers after some time told captain Vukajlović, the commander of the 107. E, about the airplane which fell "somewhere near". According to the Hungarian sources, it was Bf 110C (L2+HR, W.Nr.2318) of 7(F)./LG 2, which had emergency landing at the Pécs airport without landing gear. The crew and the pilot Uffz Karl Rimmer remained uninjured. The news about the difficult position of the Yugoslav armies on the battlefield began to arrive, as well as about the proclamation of the Independent State of Croatia, pro-Axis puppet state.

During the evening of 10 April, the commander of the 2. MVB got the order to continue

**Nar Lakić G. Janko, 107.E pilot, he was most probably the participant of unequal combat with numerous Luftwafe pilots. [VA]**

**Por Zarević Z. Spasen, 107.E pilot. Due to own negligence during patrol flight on 8 April 1941 he performed force landing when his IK-2 ran out of fuel. [VA]**

the air defence of his territory together with the 4. LP, and to bomb German armoured columns which were advancing through Slavonija in the direction of Slatina - Našice - Đakovo - Vinkovci and Slatina - Donji Miholjac - Osijek - Vukovar. The brigade commander, puk Djordjević, conveyed the given tasks to the regiment commanders who performed all the necessary technical and tactical preparations in the night between 10 and 11 April. Most of the tasks weren't performed due to the unfavourable weather conditions such as fog, low clouds and poor visibility, which prevented flying in most cases. The constitution of the NDH had tremendous consequences on the 2. MVB units, as well as on the 4. LP which had a large percentage of the personnel of the Croatian nationality who began leaving the unit. According to the orders given by the competent military authorities, the brigade commander ordered on 11 April that all the officers and soldiers of the Croatian nationality could leave the units if they wished, but that they must hand over their weapons before doing so. Almost all of them left the unit, leaving it almost entirely to the Serbian personnel. There was also the order of the Air Force Command for the 2. MVB to retreat to the area of Sarajevo during 11 April. The ground crew of the 4. LP and the 8. BP was to start retreating towards Sarajevo in the afternoon, in the direction Banja Luka - Jajce - Travnik - Sarajevo, and the flight crew at the end of the day, after finishing the given tasks. The flight crew of the 4. LP and the 8. BP, with the exact number of crew personnel was to remain with the airplane and the most necessary number of mechanics until the weather got better, when they were to perform the flight to Sarajevo, except that the order for this flight would be issued later by the brigade commander who would remain in the village of Nova Topola. On 11 April, the action of the 4. LP was restricted to persecuting individual German airplane. There were only sixteen flights of IK-2s and Hurricanes because of the extremely bad weather conditions for flying. A lonely German twin-engine airplane appeared somewhere around the noon, most probably KG 51 "Edelweiss" Ju 88 and bombed the 4. LP Headquarters. It dropped two 250 kg bombs, one of which hit the house with the regiment Headquarters and killed one and badly wounded another radio-telephone operator, blowing his leg off. At the unknown time during the day, Ju 88A (9K+LP, W.Nr.8201) of the 6./KG 51 crashed into Lijevče polje near Nova Gradiška. The four-men crew was killed, pilot Oblt Helmut Westen, navigator Hptm Jürgen Berlin, radio-operator/gunner Fw Heinrich Langlotz and gunner Uffz Wilhelm Vossen. It was obvious that the villagers who were talking to captain Vukajlović thought of this airplane. According to the statement of IK-2 pilot, por Spasen Zarević, without stating the exact date of combat:

**Burnt Ikarus IK-2 at Mali Radinci auxuiliary airfield. This machine was flown after the major overhaull from Ikarus factory to 105. E on 8 April 1941. [Jan van den Heuvel]**

*„The second interception which was also unsuccessful in its outcome, i.e. unsuccessful in terms of using the firearms of the airplane, was the one of the commander of the group of that time, maj Arsenije Boljević, as the pair leader with captain Dobnikar, who managed to head off one of the enemy's twin-engined airplane at low altitude. Our men were in the Hurricanes, each armed with eight machine guns. Our fighters' machine guns were shooting heavily, but the German continued his flight in spite of that.“*

There is no data about the actions in the defence of Belgrade for the 105. E detached to the formation of the 6. LP. One of the rare details known is the report about the downing of one German Ju 88 by kap Ik Milan Bjelanović in the area of Ruma. There is no confirmation of this loss from the German side.

Having received the order to retreat, the commander of the 4. LP, ppuk Radoslav Djordjević, directed the ground crew, led by the commander of the 33. VG kap Ik Nikola Nikolić, loaded in the trucks and automobiles to Jajce via Banja Luka at about 15.00 hrs, where they arrived at the end of the day. The flight crew of the 4. LP, with nine Hurricanes and six IK-2s with their pilots, as well as the most necessary number of the mechanics with four to five trucks, stayed at the Bosanski Aleksandrovac airfield, waiting for better weather conditions and the commander's order to fly in the area of Sarajevo. Both the commander of the regiment and the commander of the 34. VG stayed with the flight crew. As the weather conditions didn't improve by dark, and the order of the brigade commander for this flight wasn't issued, the flight crew of the regiment spent the night at the Bosanski Aleksandrovac airfield.

In the night between 11 and 12 April, the commander of the 2. MVB received the order that the 4. LP, after the flight to Sarajevo, should become the part of the Sarajevo air defence, which was to be led by the commander of the 1. LB, puk Dragutin Rubčić. The flight crew of the 4. LP spent the night on their airfield, ready to perform all the aforementioned tasks at dawn of 12 April. The ground crew of the 4. LP continued their retreat to Sarajevo, in the direction Jajce - Travnik, where they were held by the Royal military authorities who demanded their urgent return to Banja Luka. Allegedly, the regiment's flight crew could not perform the flight to Sarajevo due to the unfavourable weather conditions. However, the Hurricanes were occasionally engaged to pursue separate German, mostly twin-engine airplanes which were flying over the direction Bosanska Gradiška - Banja Luka - Prijedor, i.e. south of the river Sava. According to this data, there certainly were conditions for the take-off to Sarajevo and to the Rajlovac and Butmir airfields. It remains unclear why they were not performed! Aide of the 34. VG C/O, kap Ik Vajo Grbić, flew one of the interceptions of the German twin-engine airplane. He managed to come close to and to attack it, which was observed from the airfield near Bosanski Aleksandrovac. The Hurricane was hit by the return fire, and the pilot was heavily wounded in his knee, which led to the landing accident. kap Ik Grbić was transferred to hospital in Banja Luka, where his leg was amputated.

That day, at about 14.00, the Luftwaffe lost one Bf 110D (W.Nr. unreadable) from I./ZG 26 "Horst Wessel" which crashed in immediate vicinity. According to the German data, the reason for this was unknown. The two officer crew, pilot Uffz Rudolf Flähmig and gunner Gefr Paul Weiler, was killed. The same day, also according to the German report, Ju 88A from 5./KG 51 "Edelweiss" was damaged by Yugoslav AA fire near Slavonski Brod. The crew members, Uffz Hugo Dönig and radio-telegrapher gunner Uffz Ernst Ruhland were wounded, while the navigator Gefr Helmut Hannig was killed. It is also stated that there was a similar damage of one more Ju 88 from the same unit at the same location, with a note about the wounding of Fw Willi Born.

The order that the 4. LP flight crew with the airplane crews and with the most necessary number of the mechanics should wait the order to fly at the airfield was still in effect. Although the meteorological conditions allowed flying, the commander of the 2. MVB, puk Jakov Djordjević, out of the absolutely inexplicable reasons, somewhere around 14.00 hours, ordered to burn all the airplanes and the flight crew to start retreating by trucks!!

In a period between 14.00 and 15.00, most of the undamaged airplanes of the 4. LP were burnt, as well as part of the liaison airplanes from the 704. E, which were, in any case, able to perform a flight with light airplanes like Fi 156C Storch and Bü 131D-2 Jungmann! According to the known data, the Germans seized one undamaged but defective Ikarus IK-2, the severely damaged and overturned captain Grbić's Hurricane and a pair of Jungmanns. This catastrophic development of events occurred because the commander of the 2. MVB, puk Djordjević, didn't keep in touch with the Air Force Command, which would instruct him when and where to perform this flight and prohibit burning the airplane without necessity. He also didn't ask the meteorological data from the 2. Air Force Base in Sarajevo, which would certainly inform him that it was possible to perform the flight in the area of Sarajevo. To make the matters worse, the commander of the 2. MVB didn't even organize the necessary reconnaissance of the directions where the German units were advancing. That way he would find out that the flight units of the 2. MVB were not endangered from the ground and that

**Ppor Vukobratović S. Lazar, 107.E pilot and 4.LP/33.VG Technical Officer. Also joined the combat on 7 April 1941 and survived. [VA]**

**Ppor Milačić R. Radomir, 107.E pilot. He landed after the battle without sustaining any damage. [VA]**

**Wehrmacht soldier poses in front of the surviving Ikarus IK-2 of unknown s/n from 107. E. Note the unusual camouflage with absence of light blue-grey color on the fuselage, undercarriage and wheels surfaces. [Djordje Nikolić]**

they could remain at their airfields even until 14 April, as the German panzers didn't arrive in Banja Luka until the evening hours of 13 April 1941. Although he was of high repute as a good troop officer in peacetime, puk Jakov Djordjević proved to be totally unfit and incompetent commanding officer in wartime. The 4. LP and the 8. BP paid the price of that, having huge human and material losses.

The flight crew and the mechanics got on the trucks and started retreating in the direction of Banja Luka - Jajce - Travnik, where they arrived the following morning and found the ground crew, which were detained there by the military authorities. The move towards Sarajevo was necessary now, as there was imminent danger of being captured by the German tank units.

At this time, identical drama was happening at the Srem auxiliary airfield Radinci, where the members of the 105. E couldn't fly over in the direction of Bosnia due to the bad weather conditions and soggy ground. During the day, the personnel of the 105. E burnt all five Hurricanes and a sole IK-2, as was done with the remaining airplanes of the 6. LP. The personnel started retreating towards Sarajevo on 12 April 1941, while the 4. LP ceased to exist as a combat unit.

The 2. MVB, i.e. what was left of it, retreated towards the city of Sarajevo on 13 April. The Brigade Headquarters, retreating by cars and trucks, from Jajce, via Travnik and Kiseljak, arrived at the area of Sarajevo around noon, and stayed at the village of Blažuj. The rest of the personnel of the 4. LP were going with them, expecting orders for further movement. They spent the night in the village of Blažuj near Sarajevo, the lights of which they saw. Without any logistic support, hungry, abandoned and left to themselves and the goodwill of the people from the Serbian villages in the vicinity, who helped them as much as they could.

The 4. LP remained at the outskirts of Sarajevo on 14 April. Together with the Serbian personnel from the 8. BP, they formed two Aviation Detachments, which closed the directions leading to Sarajevo from Konjic and Kiseljak, and all that by the orders of the Air Force Command. More morally than materially ready for battle with the German panzers, they awaited the enemy at the entrance to Sarajevo. The First Aviation Detachment, commanded by maj Arsenije Boljević, who took up the position near Kiseljak, closed the route to Sarajevo. During that time, the 4. LP Headquarters with the rest of the personnel stayed in the area of the village of Blažuj, where they remained until the further orders by the Air Force Command. During the day they entered combat with German advanced guard. Although poorly armed, only with infantry weapons and without antitank weapons, the Aviation Detachment accepted the combat and managed to detain the weak German motorized patrols during the day. With the arrival of the German tanks, the situation completely turned in favour of the Germans and the Detachment left the region of Kiseljak under heavy combat, and retreated quickly towards Kalinovik. In the ground combat led with the Germans, pnar Branko Jovanović, the hero of 7 April 1941, pilot of the IK-2 who fought alone against nine Messerschmitt fighters, lost his life.

A part of the fliers from the 4. LP, mainly from the 34. VG, in the formation of the Aviation Detachment, under the command of maj Arsenije Boljević, retreating via Kalinovik, arrived to a small town of Ulog in Herzegovina on 15 April 1941.

The fliers from the 34. VG, 4. LP commanded by maj Boljević, retreating from Ulog, arrived in Nikšić at the end of the 16 April, i.e. at the Kapino Polje auxiliary airfield, only to be captured by the Italian army during the following day.

## In Croatian service

The newly formed Croatian quisling state NDH used a total of four IK-2 fighters in their Zrakoplovstvo NDH (ZNDH i.e. Air Force of the NDH) until the beginning of 1943, and only two of them until the beginning of 1944. Almost all of the former Yugoslav military airplanes from Wehrmacht booty were sold by the Germans in the period between 1941 and 1942 to their new allies, the Croats. Among these airplanes there were IK-2s from Ikarus as well as

Photo of Ikarus hangars during the autumn of 1941. Just behind modified a Blenheim B.1 sold to Romanian Air Force (AAR), is an IK-2. Brand new VVKJ camouflage, with Axis yellow bands on the fuselage is visible too. Airlane is prepared for delivery to the ŻNDH. [Berndhard Tötchinger]

Ikarus IK-2 pressed into Croatian (ZNDH) service. It is almost certainly 2903, since it was the only airplane registered at Rajlovac base flight book to have made four flights, before all IK-2s were moved to Banja Luka. Ground crew stand in the front; second from the left is mechanic Mate Smutni. Rajlovac airfield in the summer of 1942. [Emil Smutni via Tomislav Aralica]

one inoperative airplane, seized at Nova Topola auxiliary airfield in the vicinity of Bosanski Aleksandrovac. Different parts of the IK-2, including complete wings and fuselages, were seized at the same airfield in the various state of damage. From the above, the ZNDH completed two more IK-2s at the Ikarus factory. According to the unconfirmed information, IK-2 2106, which was attempted to be repaired in Rajlovac, was also seized there, but it didn't get Croatian serial number. All of the Croatian IK-2s were stationed at the ZNDH 2. Air Force Base Rajlovac near Sarajevo in the formation of the 6. Group, in the 17. E ZNDH. According to some sources, at the end of 1942, they were transferred to the 5. E at Banja Luka. Croatian pilots refused to fly them due to the poor visibility from the cockpit, obsolescence and lack of spare parts, so the IK-2s were relatively rarely used. During the six months period from 27 April up to 14 October 1942, only four test flights were registered in Rajlovac base flight book, on 8 May, 5 September, 6 and 14 October 1942, all of them on 2903. First three flights lasted only ten minutes each (pilots Marjanović, Pavlović and Cvikić), listed as "training circles" above the base, while the last one lasted 55 minutes listed as "checking of an airplane" in base vicinity with nar Šerif Mehanović at controls. There are no records for three other machines as they were probably checked on the ground (starting of engines, regular maintenance, etc.). There is also no trace of their transfer flight

**Another photo of ZNDH IK-2, this time 2901 in one of Rajlovac hangars. Note the Croatian green/grey camouflage. [via Nenad Jovanović]**

to Banja Luka at the end of 1942 that is quite strange. Only logical conclusion is that they were transported by ground/train transport, or that they were transferred there after 24 June 1943 (last entries in Rajlovac flight book).

The Croatian IK-2s flew without cannons, although their planned standard armament consisted of "2 cm cannon and two machine guns".

They were painted according to the new painting scheme and they got Croatian serial numbers 2901-2904. They were (supposedly) former 2104, 2103, 2111 and 2113. However, there are certain doubts recently about the accuracy of (some of) the aforementioned No. marks. Primarilly because of the data discrepancies. According to the report dated 28 March 1941, there were two IK-2s at the overhaul in Ikarus, 2103 and 2113. In a German list dated 20 May 1941, there were two IK-2s seized in the same factory. Although the Germans didn't specify the Air Force serial numbers, it was considered up to now that the seized airplanes were the same ones mentioned in the report from 28 March, i.e. 2103 and 2113. However, we know now that one of the IK-2s from Ikarus flew to auxiliary airfield Radinci on 8 April 1941, and that it was, somewhat later, burnt at the same airfield as the only IK-2. The logical question would be: Which airplane was that? Was it one of the two known Nos, or was it the third IK-2? There is no data about that so far. In this respect, the origin of at least one of the Croatian airplane is unclear. Unfortunately, none of the remaining IK-2s survived the Second World War.

## Conclusion

Athough a small number of them was produced, the IK-2 fighters had certain significance for the development of Yugoslav Aeronautic Industry, as well as for the Air Force. There is no doubt that the early development (1932-1933) of that type contributed much to engineers Ilić and Sivčev as it helped them to improve on time and to gain necessary experience and, more importantly, confidence to go over to making a design for the modern low-wing fighter of the IK-3 type, immediately after finishing the designing of the gull-wing fighter. On the other hand, the production of the IK-2 brought precious experiences and improved the technology of the production of metal airplane constructions to Ikarus factory and its technical and production staff. In that sense, IK-2 was an important airplane.

IK-2 fighter had excellent flying characteristics. All fighter pilots which piloted this fighter had words of praise. The airplane had extraordinary maneuverability and was very agile and easy to manage. Relatively high maximum speed of this high-wing monoplane fighter was appropriate to the conception and the time when it was designed. Powerful engine and a well-positioned powerfull weapons have also contributed to IK-2 is what he was – a true representative of its conception and right fighter type for the 1933-1936 period.

## Camouflage, markings and inscriptions

Designation IK-L1 was given to the first prototype and was the first of new-kind designations which was assigned to Air Force airplanes. The first part of designation (IK) stands for initials of the designers, the second (L1) means Lovac 1 i.e. single-seat fighter. The second prototype had designation IK-02, for same reasons as the first prototype. Series airplanes were officially designated as IK-2. In the foreign literature, the type was known (in French) as Ilitch-Sivchev IK-2. Official designation was applied on the rudder, superimposed over the state flag in the case of peacetime camouflage, or over camouflage areas in the case of wartime camouflage.

Military series numbers (s/n) were assigned due to standardised Air Force manner which was, again, very similarly to French one. Prototypes (and pre-series airplane) were assigned 01, 02, etc. First prototype had Serbian abbreviation Br. i.e. No. (Br. 01), while the second prototype had simply No. (No.02). The second prototype later became No.1, as the first machine of the se-

Group of Royal Yugoslav engineers (Air Force and civil ones) in Italian No.32 POW camp near Lago di Garda. Kosta I. Sivčev stands in the middle, while engeneer ppuk Dušan D. Lučić stands first from the left. After capitulation of Italy, Sivčev managed to escape to Switzerland. [Djordje Nikolić]

ries. After new system for air force military series numbers was introduced, the second prototype became BR. 2101 i.e. No.2101. Series airplanes were originally marked as No.2 to No.13 (as extension behind the front No.1) and, in 1940, they received new serials 2102 to 2113. Series numbers were always applied across the rudder flag in the form BR.2101 etc. (BR in Cyrillic – БР.), and over camouflaged area in form No.2101.

Construction numbers (c/n) of first prototype was 01. Contrary to that, second prototype got c/n 1 instead of expected 02. Series machines carried c/nos 2 to 13.

During the peacetime IK-2's had standard national markings known as "Kosovo cross" of 125 cm diameter placed on the four positions on the wings. National flag was placed over the entire rudder on both prototypes.

At first, IK-2's wore national markings (100 cm) in four positions on wings and small (30 cm heigh) national flag on the rudder. The so-called asymmetric system of national markings was introduced later, in which the "Kosovo crosses" were placed in only two positions. Smaller one (75 cm) was painted on the upper surface of the port wing, while the bigger one (100 cm) was retained on the lower surface of the starboard wing. However, as with other types of VVKJ airplanes, both large markings under the wings were usually retained in combination with the small upper one.

According to Federal Standard, colors used for Royal Yugoslav national markings were: Light Blue (FS 25450); Insignia White (FS 27875); Insignia Red (FS 21136) and Insignia Dark Blue (FS 25053).

Croatian IK-2's wore national markings in the form of Croatian red/white chessboards in five positions on wings and on both sides of the rudder.

According to some studies, black numbers 1 to 5 painted on fuselage (50 cm heigh) were used in 1939, while IK-2's were on strength within 6. LP at Belgrade.

Camouflaged IK-2's carried white escadrille numbers during 1940, while they were in the 4. LP at Zagreb. Photographs showing numbers 29, 31 and 34, and according to some assumptions, IK-2's had white numbers from 25 to 36.

Regarding the small inscriptions, on all silver IK-2's on the white field of national flag was painted (in Latin) HS 12Ycrs (engine type) and above it was the black logo of the factory Ikarus. Also, on the rear of the fuselage, above the lifting port, it was written (in Cyrillic) – "ДИЖИ ОВДЕ" (lift here).

VVKJ usual manner from the 1930s was painting of large initial letter of the city or airport below the lower wing on the outer side of the "Kosovo cross". The IK-2 was not an exception and during peacetime there was a large Latin letter "Z" for Zagreb. Camouflage airplanes had small all black Ikarus factory logo painted above the national flag on the rudder.

During the VVKJ service, IK-2's sport two color schemes. At first, the entire airplane was silver. More precisely, the metal parts were polished, while the fabric was painted in silver, which is known as the Aluminum dope (FS 17178). Propellers were silver on the front and matt black on the back side on both prototypes. According to Air Force regulations, IK-2's were painted on the upper side with camouflage spots in three colors. These colors were ochre yellow (FS 30219) , dark green (FS 34108) and dark brown (FS30108). The lower surfaces were painted in a light gray-blue color (FS 35352).

The propellers were painted in light gray, similar to light gray-blue (FS 35352).

The Croatian IK-2's were painted in dark green (FS 34096) upper and lateral surfaces, as well as parts of the lower surface of the fuselage (from the beginning of the radiator to the frame behind the cabin), and the lower surface in gray (FS 35526). The propeller was dark gray.

## IK-2 technical information

IK-2 was a gull wing monoplane of mixed construction with metals making 75% and wood the remaining 25%. It had an inline engine, fully enclosed cockpit, fixed landing gear, cantilever type tail assembly and armament comprising of both cannon and machine guns.

### Cockpit

The cockpit area was constructed from steel and duraluminium pipes joined together with stainless steel couplings. On the exterior, it was lined with 1 mm thick duraluminium plates, which were riveted together. Cockpit area was used as a junction between the fuselage and the wing spars as well as the fuselage and the engine frame. Across the base of the cockpit, stainless steel rods supported the cockpit floor, control cables, oil and centrally mounted fuel tanks, pilot seat and the machine gun mounts. An all metal pilot's seat was vertically adjustable to accommodate for pilot's height.

Windshield was made from Plexiglas and the canopy was hinged to one side. Some airlanes flew without the canopy as well, that is with open cockpit.

### Engine

The IK-2 was powered by a Hispano-Suiza HS 12YCrs, inline V 12-cylinder, liquid cooled carbureted engine. The engine was supercharged and connected via the reduction gear drive to a variable pitch all metal Ratier-Figeac propeller. The propeller had a left hand tractor prop. Propeller pitch was adjustable by controlling the lever on the right hand side of the pilot's seat.

Each cylinder block was a single casting bolted to the crankcase. Open ended cylinder barrels were nitrated inside and their upper ends were screwed into the cylinder blocks. A special steel sealing ring was installed at the upper and two rubber sealing rings at the lower end. Portions of walls were directly in contact with the coolant and were cadmium plated. Coolant was fed into tops of blocks by longitudinal tube pierced to distribute liquid to the hottest points.

The pistons were manufactured from high strength aluminium alloy forgings with low coefficient of friction. One fire ring, two conical compression rings and one scraper ring were included, all four above gudgeon pin. Latter was fully floating and restrained from sideways motion by aluminium pads.

The connection rods consisted of one forked and one plain rod per crank pin, each tubular and manufactured from nickel-chrome steel. Both were split with cap of plain rod tongued and grooved to fit grooves and tongues on the rod and were fastened by conical pins. Main bearing was steel lined with lead bronze.

The crankshaft was single piece nickel chrome forting with six throws at 120°, running in eight white metal bearings in the crankcase. Torsional vibrations were prevented by dynamic absorbers at extreme back end of crankshaft.

Crankcase was manufactured from special alloy and was practically incorrodible. The main bearings were cooled by cast in air passages.

Valve gear consisted of one inlet and one exhaust valve per cylinder, and was manufactured from hollow chrome-sillicum steel forgings filled with sodium for cooling. Valves were operated directly by overhead camshafts working on mushroom ends of valves. Double valve springs were used of which one alone was strong enough for emergency operation if the other broke.

Hispano-Suiza carburetors, one for every two cylinders, were supplied with air from centrifugal supercharger placed at the rear of the engine. An automatic air pressure regulator was placed in the intake of the supercharger. It consisted of an aneroid capsule in a chamber under the same pressure as the exit of the supercharger. The deformations of the capsule controlled a hydraulic relay working off the lubrication system of the engine. This opened or shut a vane in the supercharger entry. This arrangement had advantages that if supercharge stopped, the carburetors would continue to work unchanged.

Supercharger was centrifugal type of light alloy construction. It was installed at the back of the engine, was running at ten times the engine speed and was driven through centrifugal clutch and train of gears.

Propeller drive consisted of straight toothed crown wheel on propeller shaft which ran in journal bearings and bore against double ball trust race and was driven by piston solid with crankshaft. Provisions were made for hydraulically controlled variable pitch propeller. Raised propeller shaft clearance made it possible to have sufficient ground clearance for the propeller. Hollow shaft made it possible to install a 20 mm cannon.

Lubrication was provided by three vane type pumps. The single pressure pump worked at 6 kg/cm$^2$ and two pumps removed a maximum of 30 l/min of oil. To reduce time for take off, supplementary oil could be put in action by the pilot by diverting oil from central bearing to six jets which were positioned on crank pins with oil sprayed on the connecting rods and cylinder walls.

For cooling a special allow centrifugal pump was placed below the oil pump. It delivered 500 l/min of coolant at 2,400 RPM.

The engine was mounted on a riveted stainless steel tubular frame with bracing cables used to additionally stiffen the assembly. The fuselage truss was connected inseparably to the engine mount frame and shock absorbers were used to minimize transfer of vibration during engine operation. At the very bottom of the engine frame provisions were made to enable complete engine lifting with ease for servicing.

Several components were driven by the engine such as the fuel pump, oil pump, coolant pump, compressor and an electrical generator.

Each Hispano Suiza engine was scheduled for a mandatory inspection every 100 hours and a major overhaul every 300 hours.

| Hispano Suiza 12YCrs technical specifications | |
|---|---|
| Horse power at altitude | 860 |
| Horse power at ground level | 760 |
| Horse power on takeoff | 835 |
| Nominal vacuum pressure | 880 mm Hg |
| Vacuum pressure on take off | 960 mm Hg |
| Nominal RPM | 2,400 |
| Maximum RPM | 2,520 |
| Gear box ratio | 2:3 |
| Nominal propeller revolutions | 1,600 |
| Number of cylinders | 12 |
| Cylinder arrangement | V |
| Cylinder bore diameter | 150 mm |
| Cylinder stroke | 170 mm |
| Cylinder volume | 36,05 liters |
| Compression ratio | 5.8:1 |
| Supercharger drive | 10:1 |
| Fuel consumption at nominal RPM | 206 gr. |
| Fuel consumption at altitude | 218 gr. |
| Oil consumption | 6,25 gr. |
| Nominal oil inlet temperature | 50 °C |
| Minimal oil inlet temperature | 30 °C |
| Maximum oil outlet temperature | 105 °C |
| Nominal oil outlet temperature | 80 °C |
| Maximum coolant outlet temperature | 100 °C |
| Nominal coolant outlet temperature | 80 °C |
| Engine weight | 470 kg |
| Engine length | 1,722 mm |
| Engine height | 935 mm |
| Engine width | 764 mm |
| Crankshaft rotation | clockwise |

With each delivered engine, a set of equipment and tools was delivered. This set included the following:

| Part | Make | Quantity |
|---|---|---|
| Carburetor | Hispano-Solex 56 S2 | 6 |
| Magnetos | Voltex ROD-12 / Scintila GM 120 | 2 |
| Spark plugs | Avia B 10 | 24 |
| Ignition cables | - | 24 |
| Fuel pump | A.M. Rotativ N° 2 | 2 |
| Compressor | Viet C. 8 | 1 |
| Vacuum limiter | Vénus | 1 |
| Gun synchronizer | - | 1 |
| Generator | Labinal 1200W / Labinal 600W | 1 |
| Tool kit | - | 1 |
| Propeller axle | S. AE -50 Type Spleine | 1 |
| Exhaust pipes | - | 12 |
| Hydraulic pump | Laceba P13D | 1 |
| Hand crank | Viet 1525 | 1 |

## Fuel System

The fuel system consisted of one fuselage and two wing mounted fuel tanks. The fuselage fuel tank together with two wing fuel tanks had a capacity of 240 liters of 85 octane fuel. The material of construction was duraluminium and the interior of each tank had several bulkheads. Fuel tanks were interconnected via piping and fuel was supplied to the engine through the two engine mounted pumps.

## Ignition System

The engine was equipped with two magnetos. The ignition switch was on the right-hand side of the instrument panel. The engine start was initiated by actuating the hand crank on the right-hand side of the instrument panel.

## Lubrication System

The lubrication system consisted of the oil tank, filters, a pump, hoses and the oil radiator. Oil tank had a volume of 30 liters and was constructed out of copper plates stiffened with steel ribs. It was mounted ahead of the pilot and incorporated two passageways for the nose mounted machine guns. An oil radiator was placed in a small tunnel beneath the airplane's nose. Depending on the time of the year, different oil was used. During the warmer months INTAVIA Green Band 120M was used and during the cooler months INTAVIA Red Band 100M. The highest permitted oil temperature was 100 °C.

## Coolant system

The coolant system consisted of the coolant tank, pump, mesh reinforced rubber hoses and

Hispano – Suiza 12 Ycrs, 860HP, V12, liquid cooled engine. [Author]

the radiator. The coolant tank had a total volume of cca 70 liters. Ethylene - Glycol radiator system was placed in an aerodynamically shaped housing below the fuselage between the landing gear. The pilot had the ability to control the degree of cooling by adjusting the air flow by positioning the movable gills on the radiator intake but in practice this was done automatically with help of a thermostat. The coolant pump was mounted directly on the engine, which provided power for it. The highest permitted Ehylene - Glycol temperature was 105 °C.

## Hydraulics system

A hydraulics system was used to operate flaps. It was constructed out of high pressure piping. The hydraulic system was charged to 115 atm. pressure.

## Compressed air system

Apart for starting the engine, the compressed air system was used for cocking the machine guns. The compressed air bottle was located below the pilots' seat in a horizontal position. An engine mounted pump type Viet was used to maintain the pressure at a constant 30 atm.

Black Storch; Hispano – Suiza Factory Logo.

## Fuselage

The main structural component of the fuselage was a riveted and welded stainless steel and duraluminium tube truss with varying cross section. The fuselage was divided into four main sections: cockpit, mid section, aft section and the engine area. The cockpit area was constructed out of stainless steel and duraluminium tubes connected together with stainless steel bands. The cockpit area of the fuselage housed the bolted junctions for the engine mount. The stainless steel tube floor frame ensured that the weight of the entire cockpit, oil and central fuel tank as well as machine gun mounts was securely supported. The fuselage surface was covered with different materials based on the location. For example, the engine area was covered with 1 mm thick duraluminium riveted sheets, and aft fuselage was covered with fabric infused with Bakelite and covered with nitrocellulose varnish. While servicing an airplane, a single pipe was provided spanning from the left to the right side of the fuselage and its location was marked accordingly with inscription "ДИЖИ ОВДЕ" (lift here).

## Wings

The gull wings were constructed entirely out of metal with several steel tubes used for reinforcement.

### Ailerons

The ailerons were located at the trailing edge of each wing. The aileron frame consisted of a round front and flat rear stainless steel tube spars, which were welded to stainless steel tubular ribs. The leading edge was covered with 1 mm thick duraluminium, except on the first prototype where leading edge was covered with canvas.

### Flaps

The IK-2 used two flaps, below both wings. The wing trailing edge split flaps were made of duraluminium 1 mm thick. Flaps were hydraulically operated simultaneously and were controlled via pulleys and rigid linkages.

### Horizontal stabilizer

The horizontal stabilizer was constructed from metal and its surface was covered with wooden profiles. It was connected to the fuselage with two bolts at fuselage frames. It featured two spars, at the front and at the back, which were joined by inspar ribs. A horizontal stabilizer was covered both with 3 mm thick wooden profiles and fabric. All internal components were infused with clear varnish to preserve the wood structure.

### Vertical stabilizer

Constructed entirely from metal, the vertical stabilizer was bolted to the fuselage at four junctions. It had two spars with five ribs in between them of which only the top one was reinforced. Within the vertical stabilizer passageways, the trim tab controls were pulled through. The vertical stabilizer surface was covered with the identical materials as the horizontal stabilizer.

### Rudder

Both of the rudder spars and ribs formed the rudder frame and were made from stainless steel welded tubing. A rudder trim tab was located at the rudder trailing edge. Two ball bearing hinges connected the rudder to the vertical stabilizer.

### Landing gear

Fixed type produced by French Company Messier. Oleo-pneumatic wide track elastic legs, without central axle, and with a tail wheel. Messier wheel drum brakes with oleo-pneumatic control. Brake swich was located on the control column.

Landing gear wheels were manufactured by Dunlop and had dimensions of 750 x 150 mm for the main gear and 260 x 180 mm for the tail wheel.

### Oxygen system

For high altitude flights, the pilot used an oxygen system, which consisted of an oxygen bottle, regulator, manometer, flow control valve and an automatic mask type Minerelle M.34. An oxygen bottle was located behind the pilot's seat and was charged with a total of 5 kg of oxygen at 150 atm. pressure.

**Advetrisment of Hispano – Suiza, Representative Office in Zemun/Belgrade. [GJV 1939]**

### Electrical system

Electrical system consisted of the engine mounted 1200W or 600W generator, one 24 V battery in the wings and various electrical wiring.

### Lighting system

IK-2 was equipped with position lights on each wing tip (red on port and green on starboard) and the tail (clear). Light bulbs were protected from the elements by glass covers. For flying at night, two dimmable lamps lit up the control panel and two were mounted on both sides of the cockpit and could be positioned by the pilot as required.

### Flight monitoring instruments

Instrumentation was standard for single seat fighters produced in mid 1930s. Prototype was equipped exclusively with the French made instruments while the first series production airplanes used a mix of French and locally produced Teleoptik, Mikron and Nestor instruments. All instruments were labeled in accordance with the kilogram, meter and second unit system. Each instrument was labeled with "Svojina vojnog vazduhoplovstva" (Property of the Air Force). The instrument panel as attached to shock absorbers intended to minimize engine vibrations.

## Radio

Telefunken FuG VIIa radio station was installed in the first series IK-2 airplanes. This radio station had a range of 60 - 80 km between airplane and ground station and 40 -60 km between airplanes. It was located behind the pilots' seat and was protected from damage by a steel shroud.

## Weapons

The IK-2 featured centrally mounted armament. The IK-2 prototypes were without armament. The first series IK-2 armament consisted of one 20 mm Hispano Suiza HS9 cannon firing through the propeller hub with 60 tracer or incendiary rounds total.

Two Saint Etiene Darne M.30 7.7 mm (it's not sure if they were replaced with FN Browing M.38, 7.92 mm prior to the outbrake of the war) machine guns with 500 armor piercing or incendiary rounds per gun were placed above the engine. The machine gun and cannon trigger, along with arming and securement was installed at the control column and was pneumatically operated. The cannon with magazine weighed 68.7 kg and machine guns installation weighed 21/18 kg, a total of 86.7 kg. without ammunition.

The cannon was mounted on top half of the crankcase in the Vee of the cylinders with muzzle passing through the upper spur reduction gear pinion and the propeller boss. The distributor of the compressed air starter was mounted at the back end of the valve gear casing so as to leave the Vee space between the cylinders for the cannon. The right handed auxiliary drive shaft was provided with a gun synchronizing drive, so that the additional machine guns firing through the propeller could be installed.

The gun sight was a simple French Collimateur Chrétien E.T.Aé Modèle 1933 brand ring and bead type installed forward of the windshield.

Avia Factory Logo.

Moderan avion snabdeva se uređajima:

MESSIER

IK2. IK3. ORKAN. R313

Messier Company advertisment with a list of Yugoslav airplane types which used their equipment. [GJV 1939]

French Company Ratier Factorie Logo.

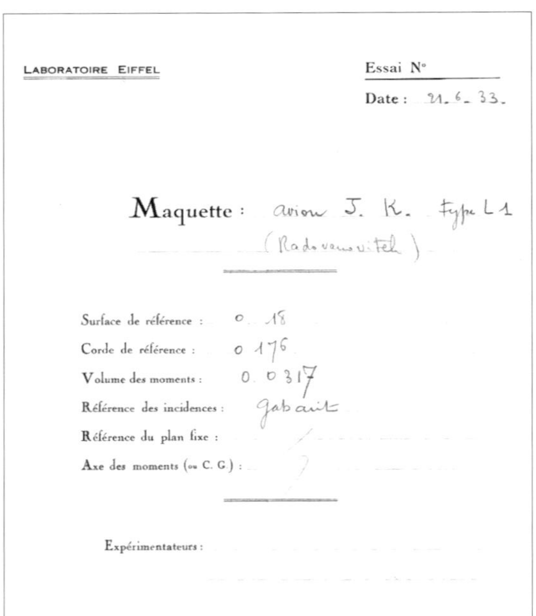

LABORATOIRE EIFFEL

Essai N°

Date : 21.6.33.

Maquette : avion J. K. type L 1 (Radovanovitch)

Surface de référence : 0.18

Corde de référence : 0 176

Volume des moments : 0.0317

Référence des incidences : gabarit

Référence du plan fixe :

Axe des moments (ou C. G.) :

Expérimentateurs :

Original Laboratoire Eiffel document regarding wind tunnel testing of IK-L1 wooden model, published here for the first time! 21 June 1933, Paris. [Laboratoire Eifell]

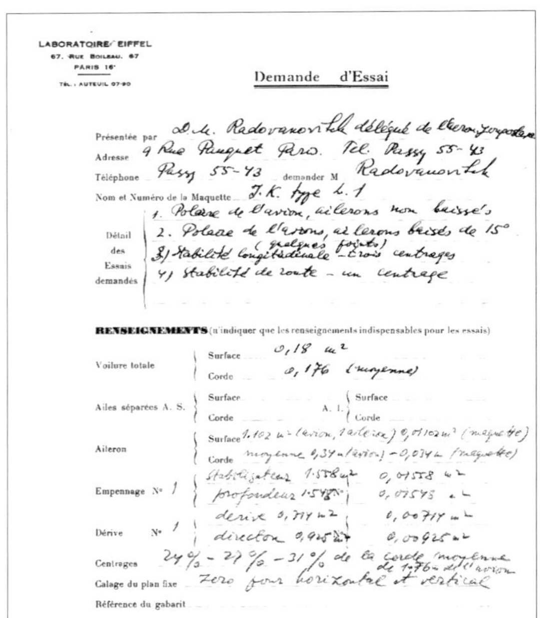

LABORATOIRE EIFFEL
67, Rue Boileau, 67
PARIS 16e
Tél. : AUTEUIL 07-90

Demande d'Essai

Présentée par: D. M. Radovanovitch
Adresse: 9 Rue Pauquet Paris. Tel. Passy 55-43
Téléphone: Passy 55-43 demander M Radovanovitch
Nom et Numéro de la Maquette: J. K. type L. 1
Détail des Essais demandés:
1. Polaire de l'avion, ailerons non baissés
2. Polaire de l'avion, ailerons baissés de 15°
3) Stabilité longitudinale – trois centrages
4) Stabilité de route – un centrage

RENSEIGNEMENTS (n'indiquer que les renseignements indispensables pour les essais)

Voilure totale — Surface: 0,18 m² — Corde: 0,176 (moyenne)
Ailes séparées A. S. — Surface — Corde; A. I. — Surface — Corde
Aileron — Surface: 1,102 m² (avion, 1 aileron) 0,01102 m² (maquette) — Corde: moyenne 0,34 m (avion) – 0,034 m (maquette)
Empennage N° 1 — stabilisateur 1,558 m² 0,01558 m²; profondeur 1,543 m² 0,01543 m²
Dérive N° 1 — dérive 0,714 m² 0,00714 m²; direction 0,925 m² 0,00925 m²
Centrages: 24 % – 27 % – 31 % de la corde moyenne de 1,76 m de l'avion
Calage du plan fixe: zero pour horizontal et vertical
Référence du gabarit

Second page of so far unknown IK-L1 document, showing aerodynamic characteristics of precisely manufactured wooden model. [Laboratoire Eiffel]

# Appendix

## Appendix 1 Weapons Technical Data

| Hispano - Suiza HS 9 | |
|---|---|
| Caliber | 20 mm |
| Weight with drum magazine | 68.7 kg |
| Length with muzzle brake | 2.52 m |
| Barrel length | 0.8 m |
| Rate of fire | 700/min |
| Rounds | 60 |
| Muzzle velocity | 840-880 m/s |
| Max. range | 6,500 m |

| Saint-Étienne Darne M.30 | |
|---|---|
| Caliber | 7.7 mm |
| Mass | 10,5 kg |
| Barrel length | 0,696 m |
| Rounds | 250 |
| Muzzle velocity | 700 m/s |
| Rate of fire | 1,200/min |

| FN Browning M.38 | |
|---|---|
| Caliber | 7.92 mm |
| Mass | 9 kg |
| Barrel length | 0.606 m |
| Rounds | 250 |
| Muzzle velocity | 800 m/s |
| Rate of fire | 1,300/min |

## Appendix 2 Abbreviations

| | | |
|---|---|---|
| Vazduhoplovstvo vojske Kraljevine Jugoslavije | VVKJ | Kingdom of Yugoslavia Air Force |
| Komanda vazduhoplovstva | KV | Air Force Command |
| Lovačka Brigada | LB | Fighter Brigade |
| Lovački puk | LP | Fighter Regiment |
| Vazduhoplovna Grupa | VG | Aviation Group |
| Eskadrila | E | Escadrille |
| Ministarstvo Vojske | MV | Air Ministry |
| Akcionarsko Društvo | AD | Joint Stock Company |
| Broj | Br. | Number |
| Vojno evidencijski broj | Vebr. | Army Evidence Number |
| Sturzkampfgeschwader | StG | Dive Bomber Wing |
| Kampfgeschwader | KG | Bomber Wing |
| Jagdgeschwader | JG | Fighter Wing |
| Zerstörergeschwader | ZG | Destroyer Wing |

## Appendix 3 Air Force rank comparison

| Royal Yugoslav Air Force | | Luftwaffe | | Royal Air Force | |
|---|---|---|---|---|---|
| Armijski đeneral | Arm đen | General Oberst | GenOb. | Air Chief Marshall | ACM |
| Divizijski đeneral | Div đen | General Leutnant | GenLt. | Air Marshall | AM |
| Vazduhoplovni brigadni đeneral | vazd brig đen | General Major | GenMaj. | Air Vice Marshall | AVM |
| Pukovnik | puk | Oberst | Oberst | Group Captain | G/Cpt |
| Potpukovnik | ppuk | Oberstleutnant | OberstLt. | Wing Commander | W/Cdr |
| Major | maj | Major | Maj. | Squadron Leader | S/Ldr |
| Kapetan I klase | kap Ik | Hauptmann | Hptm. | Flight Lieutenant 1st class | F/Lt |
| Kapetan II klase | kap IIk | - | - | - | - |
| Poručnik | por | Oberleutnant | Oblt. | Flying-Officer | F/O |
| Potporučnik | ppor | Leutnant | Lt. | Pilot-Officer | P/O |
| Narednik-vodnik I klase | nv Ik | Stabsfeldwebel | Stfw. | Flight Sergeant | F/sgt |
| Narednik-vodnik II klase | nv IIk | Oberfähnrich | Obfhr. | - | - |
| Narednik-vodnik III klase | nv IIIk | Oberfeldwebel | Obfw. | - | - |
| Narednik I klase | nar Ik | Feldwebel | Fw. | Sergeant | Sgt |
| Narednik II klase | nar IIk | Unterfeldwebel | Ufw. | - | - |
| Podnarednik I klase | pnar Ik | Unteroffizier | Uffz. | Corporal | Cpl |
| Podnarednik II klase | pnar IIk | Stabsgefreiten | Stgefr. | Senior Airplaneman | SAC |
| Kaplar | kpl | Gefreiter | Gefr. | Airman 1st Class | A1C |
| Redov | red | Flieger | Flg. | Airman 2nd Class | A2C |

## Appendix 4 VVKJ unit structure

| | |
|---|---|
| Brigada | Comprised of 2 Bomber or Fighter Regiments, or mixed Fighter/Bomber |
| Puk | Composed of two to three fighter groups or two Bomber Groups |
| Grupa | Tactical unit consisting of two to three Escadrilles |
| Eskadrila | Unit consisting of nine to twelve airplanes |

## Appendix 5 34. VG structure on 6 April 1941

| 34. Vazduhoplovna grupa (VG) | |
|---|---|
| maj Arsenije T. Boljević | |
| kap Ik Vajo N. Grbić | |
| 107. E, IK-2 | 108. E, Hurricane Mk.I |
| C/O kap Ik Žarko M. Vukajlović | C/O kap Ik Mladen B. Milovčević |
| rez kap IIk Milan M. Zemljić | kap Ik Janko A. Dobnikar |
| por Djordje S. Supić | nar Živko I. Džal |
| por Spasen Z. Zarević | nar Mehanović B. Šerif |
| ppor Radomir R. Milačić | nar Bogosav M. Stamatović |
| ppor Lazar S. Vukobratović | nar Živorad Tomić |
| nar Radivoj M. Stikić | |
| nar Janko G. Lakić | |
| pnar Branko A. Jovanović | |

## Appendix 6 Ikarus IK-2 individual airplane history as known so far

| No./IK Type | VeBr. | Delivery | Black/White N° on fuselage | Fate |
|---|---|---|---|---|
| 1. IK-L1 | - | 22 April 1935 | - | 1st prototype crashed on 24 April 1935, pilot bailed out |
| 2. IK-02 | 2101 | 11 October 1938 | - / 25 | 2nd prototype crashed during June 1940, pilot bailed out |
| 3. IK-2 | 2102 | 25 November 1938 | - / 26 | * |
| 4. IK-2 | 2103 | November 1938 | - / 27 | Captured and sold to Croat AF (ZNDH), became 2901 |
| 5. IK-2 | 2104 | 21 November 1938 | - / 28 | Captured and sold to Croat AF (ZNDH), became 2902 |
| 6. IK-2 | 2105 | 30 November 1938 | - / 29 | * |
| 7. IK-2 | 2106 | 2 December 1938 | - / 30 | * |
| 8. IK-2 | 2107 | January 1939 | - / 31 | * |
| 9. IK-2 | 2108 | January 1939 | - / 32 | * |
| 10. IK-2 | 2109 | January 1939 | 1 / 33 | * |
| 11. IK-2 | 2110 | January 1939 | 2 / 34 | * |
| 12. IK-2 | 2111 | February 1939 | 3 / 35 | Captured and sold to Croat AF (ZNDH), became 2903 |
| 13. IK-2 | 2112 | February 1939 | 4 / 36 | * |
| 14. IK-2 | 2113 | 25 February 1939 | 5 / 37 | Captured and sold to Croat AF (ZNDH), became 2904 |

* Note:
Only one Ikarus IK-2 was lost in combat with Germans on 7 April 1941, and another one in an emergency landing accident on 8 April, both with so far unknown VeBr's, so it is not possible to determine precisely which VeBr's were destroyed by own crews.

## Appendix 7 Ikarus IK-2 technical data

| | First prototype | Second prototype | First series production |
|---|---|---|---|
| Wing span | 11.4 m | 11.4 m | 11.4 m |
| Overall length | 7.9 m | 7.9 m | 7.9 m |
| Overall height | 3.8 m | 3.8 m | 3.8 m |
| Wing surface area | 18.0 m$^2$ | 18.0 m$^2$ | 18.0 m$^2$ |
| Wing loading | 103 kg/m$^2$ | 103 kg/m$^2$ | 103 kg/m$^2$ |
| Weight empty/loaded | 1,575 / 1,930 kg | 1,502 / 1,857 kg | 1,502 / 1,857 kg |
| Fuel | 250 kg / 332 l | 250 kg / 332 l | 250 kg / 332 l |
| Oil | 26 kg/ 30 l | 26 kg/ 30 l | 26 kg/ 30 l |
| Climbing time to 5,000 m | 5 min. 30 sec. | 5 min. 25 sec. | 5 min. 25 sec. |
| Max. speed (3,000 m) | 415 km/h | 435 km/h | 435 km/h |
| Max. speed (sea level) | 340 km/h | 340 km/h | 340 km/h |
| Cruising speed | 250 km/h | 250 km/h | 250 km/h |
| Landing speed | 104 km/h | 130 km/h | 130 km/h |
| Maximum altitude | 12,000 m | 12,000 m | 12,000 m |
| Maximum range | 700 km | 700 km | 700 km |
| Take off distance | 300 m | 300 m | 300 m |
| Landing distance | 350 m | 350 m | 350 m |

### Appendix 8 Technical data comparison of the Ikarus IK-2 against two most modern Royal Yugoslav Army Air Force fighters

| Specification | Ikarus IK-2 | Bf 109E-3 | Hurricane Mk. I |
|---|---|---|---|
| Wing span | 11.4 m | 9.9 m | 12.2 m |
| Overall length | 7.9m | 8.8 m | 9.7 m |
| Overall height | 3.8 m | 2.5 m | 3.9 m |
| Wing surface area | 18.0 m$^2$ | 16.4 m$^2$ | 29.9 m$^2$ |
| Weight empty/loaded | 1,502 / 1,857 kg | 2,005 / 2,505 kg | 2,259 / 2,937 kg |
| Climbing time to 5,000 m | 5 min. 25 sec. | 5 min. | 5 min 42 sec. |
| Max. speed at 5,000 m | 435 km/h | 560 km/h | 510 km/h |
| Maximum altitude | 12,000 m | 10,972 m | 10,900 m |
| Maximum range | 700 km | 663 km | 804 km |

### Appendix 9 Geographical locations with coordinates

**Banja Luka** (Bosnia and Herzegovina, Republika Srpska) **44.7722° N, 17.1910° E**
**Beograd** (Serbia, Capital, Belgrade Municipality) **44.7866° N, 20.4489° E**
**Bijeljina** (Northeastern Bosnia and Herzegovina, Republika Srpska) **44.7570° N, 19.2150° E**
**Bosanski Aleksandrovac** (Bosnia and Herzegovina, Republika Srpska) **44.5655° N, 17.2058° E**
**Bosanski Novi (today Novi Grad)**(Bosnia and Herzegovina, Republika Srpska) **45.0487° N, 16.3746° E**
**Bosanski Šamac** (Bosnia and Herzegovina, Republika Srpska) **45.0611° N, 18.4690° E**
**Bugojno** (Central Bosnia and Herzegovina, Central Bosnia Canton) **44.0562° N, 17.4498° E**
**Butmir** (Bosnia and Herzegovina, Sarajevo Canton) **43.4909° N, 18.1934° E**
**Caprag** (Croatia, Sisak-Moslavina Region) **45.2800° N, 16.2300° E**
**Doboj** (Republika Srpska) **44.8004° N, 18.0603° E**
**Donji Miholjac** (Croatia, Osijek-Baranja County) **45.7621° N, 18.1651° E**
**Drvar** (Western Bosnia and Herzegovina, Canton 10) **44.3711° N, 16.3813° E**
**Đakovo** (Croatia, Osijek-Baranja County) **45.3100° N, 18.4098° E**
**Gorica** (Zagreb County, Croatia) **45.7142° N, 16.0752° E**
**Grab** (Bosnia and Herzegovina, Trebinje Municipality, Republika Srpska) **43.2203° N, 17.1057° E**
**Gradiška** (Northwestern Bosnia and Herzegovina, Republika Srpska) **45.1466° N, 17.2544° E**
**Han Pijesak** (Republika Srpska) **44.0672° N, 18.9433° E**
**Ilidža** (Bosnia and Herzegovina, Sarajevo Canton) **43.8314° N, 18.3002° E**
**Jasenovac** (Croatia, Slavonia, Jasenovac Municipality) **45.2707° N, 16.9114° E**
**Kalinovik** (Bosnia and Herzegovina, Republika Srpska) **43.5007° N, 18.4494° E**
**Lipovljani** (Croatia, Slavonia, Sisak-Moslavina County) **45.3982° N, 16.8946° E**
**Maribor** (Slovenia, Maribor Municipality) **46.5547° N, 15.6459° E**
**Nikšić** (Montenegro, Nikšić Municipality) **42.7805° N, 18.9562° E**
**Nova Topola** (Northwestern Bosnia and Herzegovina, Republika Srpska) **45.0520° N, 17.3081° E**
**Novska** (Croatia, Slavonia, Sisak-Moslavina County) **45.3400° N, 16.9786° E**
**Otočac** (Croatia, Northwestern Lika) **44.8689° N, 15.2375° E**
**Pragersko** (Northeastern Slovenia, Slovenska Bistrica Municipality) **46.3951° N, 15.6592° E**
**Ptuj** (Northeastern Slovenia, Ptuj Municipality) **46.4200° N, 15.8697° E**
**Reljevo** (Bosnia and Herzegovina) **43.5315° N, 18.1844° E**
**Rogatica** (Eastern Bosnia and Herzegovina, Republika Srpska) **43.7988° N, 19.0021° E**
**Rovine** (Bosnia and Herzegovina, Republika Srpska) **45.0801° N, 17.2997° E**
**Sarajevo** (Bosnia and Herzegovina, Sarajevo Canton) **43.8563° N, 18.4131° E**
**Senj** (Croatia, Lika-Senj County) **44.9894° N, 14.9036° E**
**Slavonski Brod** (Eastern Croatia, Slavonia, Brod-Posavina County) **45.1631° N, 18.0116° E**
**Sokolac** (Bosnia and Herzegovina, Sokolac Municipality) **43.9341° N, 18.8019° E**
**Trebinje** (Bosnia and Herzegovina, Republika Srpska) **42.7082° N, 18.3503° E**
**Tuzla** (Bosnia and Herzegovina, Tuzla Canton) **44.5375° N, 18.6735° E**
**Ulog** (Bosnia and Herzegovina, Kalinovik Municipality) **43.3949° N, 18.3149° E**
**Varaždin** (Northern Croatia, Varaždin County) **46.3057° N, 16.3366° E**
**Veliki Radinci** (Serbia, Province of Vojvodina, Syrmia District) **45.0361° N, 19.6705° E**
**Vlasenica** (Bosnia and Herzegovina, Republika Srpska) **44.1800° N, 18.9418° E**
**Zagreb** (Croatia, Capital) **45.8150° N, 15.9819° E**
**Zemun** (Serbia, Belgrade Municipality) **44.8532° N, 20.3556° E**

# Bibliography


**Aleksandar M. Ognjević**: Bristol Blenheim - The Yugoslav Story, Operational Record 1937-1958 (LeadenskyBooks, Beograd; 2014)

**Aleksandar M. Ognjević**: Ratni Dnevnik - Knjiga 1 (LeadenskyBooks, Beograd; 2016)

**Andrija Pavlović**: Jugoslovensko vazduhoplovstvo u aprilskom ratu 1941 (Glasnik RV i PVO broj 5; Beograd, 1972)

**Andrija Pavlović**: Jugoslovensko vazduhoplovstvo u aprilskom ratu 1941 (neobjavljena studija; Beograd)

**Andrija Pavlović**: Za istoriju, Jugoslovensko vazduhoplovstvo u aprilskom ratu 1941. godine (Vazduhoplovni glasnik br. 348 god. XL, London; avgust 1988)

Aprilski rat 1941 - Kapetan I klase Vukajlović Žarko, 107. Eskadrila 4.vazduhoplovnog puka. Memorijalni skup vazduhoplovstvo u Aprilskom ratu 1991;

**Arsenije Boljević**: Jugoslovensko vazduhoplovstvo u ratu aprila 1941. (Vojno delo br.1; Beograd, 1952)

**Arsenije Boljević**: Jugoslovensko vazduhoplovstvo u ratu aprila 1941 ( Vojno delo, br.1; Beograd, 1952)

**Werner Held, Hannes Trautloft, Ekkehard Bob**: Die Grünherz-Jäger, Bildchronik des Jagdgeschwaders 54 (Podzun-Pallas-Verlag, Friedberg; 1985)

**Biserka Isaković**: Svedočanstva iz Aprilskog rata 1941 (AERO magazin-specijalno izdanje, br. 2-3, Portorož; mart-jun 1991)

**Bojan Dimitrijević, Milan Micevski, Predrag Miladinović**: Kraljevsko Vazduhoplovstvo 1918-1944 (Beograd; 2012)

**Boris Ciglić with Dragan Savić, Milan Micevski & Predrag Miladinović**: Messerschmitt Bf 109 The Yugoslav Story Vol. I (Jeroplan, Beograd; 2016)

**Branko Obradović**: Protiv-avionska odbrana bivše Jugoslavije (Artiljeriski glasnik br. 3; Beograd, maj-jun 1952)

**Branko Petranović**: Srbija u Drugom svetskom ratu 1939-1945 (Vojnoizdavački i novinski centar, Beograd; 1992)

**Čedomir Janić**: Sedamdeset godina vazduhoplovne industrije Jugoslavije 1923-1993 (Beograd, 1993)

**Christopher Shores and Brian Cull with Nicola Malizia**: Air War for Yugoslavia, Greece and Crete (Grub Street; London, 1987)

**Csanady, Nagyvarady & Winkler**: A Magyar repules tortenete (Muszaki konyvkiadó, Budapest; 1977)

**Danijel Frka, Josip Novak, Siniša Pogačić**: Zrakoplovstvo NDH (P.C. grafičke usluge; Zagreb, 1998)

**Dr. Nikola Žutić**: Avioindustrija i vazduhoplovstvo u Kraljevini Jugoslaviji 1918-1945 (Beograd, 2004)

**Dr. Pagáts Pál**: Légitámadás Pécs és Siklós ellen (Aero Historia; Budapest, Augustusz 1991)

**Dušan Ćirović**: Jugoslovensko vazduhoplovstvo u aprilskom ratu 1941 (neobjavljena studija; Zemun, 1956)

**Dušan Ćirović**: Vazduhoplovne žrtve 1913–1945 (privatno izdanje; Zemun, 1970)

**Eric Mombeek, Jean-Louis Roba & Martin Pegg**: Jagdwaffe-Strike in the Balkans April-May 1941(Classic Publications; 2002)

Fighters of the Royal Yugoslav Air Force - Naša krila, specijalno izdanje (Beograd; april 2001)

**Greiner/Schramm**: Srbi u ratnom dnevniku Vermahta (Službeni list SCG; Beograd, 2003)

Hrvatska krila (više brojeva; Zagreb, 1941-1945)

**Jerry Scutts**: Bf 109 Aces of North Africa and the Mediterranean (Osprey; London, 1994)

**Jerry Scutts**: JG 54 Jagdgeschwader 54 Grünherz, Aces of the Eastern Front (Airlife; Shrewsbury, 1994)

**Jochen Prien, Gerhard Stemmer, Peter Rodeike & Winfried Bock**: Die Jagdfliegerverbände der Deutschen Luftwaffe 1934 bis 1945, Teil 5 ...Einsatz im Mittelmeeraum, Oktober 1940 bis November 1941... (Struve druck; Eutin, 2003)

**Karl Ries**: The Luftwaffe a Photographic Record 1919-1945 (B.T. Batsford Ltd, London; 1987)

Kriegstagebuch des oberkommandos der Wehmacht, zusammengestellt und erlautert von Hans-Adolf Jacobsen

Kriegstagebuch III./KG 51, Kopija izvoda iz ratnog dnevnika (Muzej vazduhoplovstva; Beograd)

**Milorad Janković**: Aprilski rat (Dnevne novine „Politika" od 1.aprila do 15.avgusta; Beograd, 1973)

**Milorad Janković**: Peta kolona (Dnevne novine „Politika" od 10.novembra do 26.novembra; Beograd, 1972)

**Miloš Aćin**: Spomenica palih Srba vazduhoplovaca 1941–1945 (Srpska krila; Vašington, 1975)

**Miloš Čomagić**: Feljton: Svedoci aprilskog rata pričaju (Politika; Beograd, 2. VIII 1973)

**Nenad Miklušev**: Lovački avioni, IK Fighters (Model Art & YASIG Special, Zrenjanin; 1998)

**Njegoslav Puharić**: Kako smo oborili nemački bombarder (Front br. 1184; Beograd, april 1981)

**O. Petrović i N. Đokić**: Protivavionska odbrana u ratu aprila 1941 (AERO magazin-specijalno izdanje, br. 2-3, Portorož; mart-jun 1991)

**Paul H. Wilkinson**: Airplane Engines of the World 1946 (London, 1946)

**Petar Bosnić**: Naše nebo–April 1941 (privatno izdanje; Beograd, 1997)

**Petar Vukčević**: Operacije Jugoslovenskog vazduhoplovstva u ratu 1941 ( Glasnik srpskog istorijsko-kulturnog društva "Njegoš", sveska decembar; Kanada, 1967)

**Šime Ostrić & Čedomir Janić**: Airplane Profile 242: IK Fighters (Yugoslavia: 1930-1940s), London, UK 1972

**T. K. Milićević**: Kraljevsko jugoslovensko vazduhoplovstvo pred rat i za vreme rata 1941. godine (Glasnik Srpskog istorisko-kulturnog društva "Njegoš"; juni 1965)

**Ulf Balke**: Der Luftkrieg in Europa 1939 - 1941 (Bechtermünz Verlag; Deutchland, 1997)

Vazduhoplovni glasnik (više brojeva; London)

**Velimir Terzić**: Jugoslavija u aprilskom ratu 1941; (Pobjeda; Titograd, 1963)

**Velimir Terzić**: Slom Kraljevine Jugoslavije 1941 (Širo Srbija; Beograd, 1983)

**Vojislav V. Mikić**: Zrakoplovstvo NDH 1941-1945 (VII Vojske Jugoslavije i Target; Beograd, 2000)

Vojna enciklopedija (Vojnoizdavački zavod; Beograd, 1978)

Vojno-istorijski institut: Drugi svetski rat - pregled ratnih operacija;( Knjiga 1; Beograd, 1957)

**Wolfgang Dierich**: Kampfgeschwader "Edelweiss" - The History of the unit 1939-1945 (Ian Allan, London; 1975)

**Wolfgang Dierich**: Kampfgeschwader 51 "Edelweiss", Eine Chronik aus Dokumenten und Berichten 1937-1945 (4. überarbeitete und ergänzte Auflage, Motorbuch Verlag; Stuttgart, 1975)

Zbornik radova memorijalnog skupa – Učešće vazduhoplovstva vojske u Aprilskom ratu 1941 (Beograd, 1995)

**Zlatko Rendulić**: General avnojske Jugoslavije, sjećanja (Golden marketing, Tehnička knjiga; Zagreb, 2004)

**Royal Yugoslav Army Air Force - personal statements**:

- **Arsenije Boljević** - puk, k-dant 34.VG, pismena izjava, AVII, K.37 reg.br. 6/1;
- **Artur Kirasić** - ppuk, pom. k-danta puka, pismena izjava, AVII, K.66, reg.br.23/1;
- **Božo Lazarević** - pilot 218.E, izjava Andriji Pavloviću.
- **Ferdinand Janež** - izjava brigadnog generala, komandanta artilerije Dravske divizije, date 8. IV 1953. u Ljubljani.
- **Janko Dobnikar** - izjava vazduhoplovnog kapetana u Bariju, 1. avgusta 1944, vazduhoplovnom oficiru za vezu VŠ NOVJ sa BAF
- **Janko Dobnikar** – Opis života, izjave date vazd. oficiru za vezu sa BAF-om (najverovatnije majoru Svetlinu), 8.jula, 1.avg i 10.avg 1944. godine. Bari, Italija.
- **Janko Dobnikar** - zapisnik saslušanja satnika, od 30. studenog 1941. po prijavi radnika puškara Mate Baturine od 4. rujna iste godine.
- **Janko Drobnikar** - k1k, usmena izjava A.Pavloviću.
- **Krunoslav Dogan** – izjava satnika, 15. XII 1941. u Sarajevu
- **Luka Kandić** - ađutant IV.brigade, pismena izjava posle rata u RV
- **Luka Pezelj** - izjava satnika data 10. XII 1941 u Sarajevu.
- **Matija Petrović** - komandir i pilot 217.E, AVII, K.37, reg.br.6/1;
- **Matija Petrović** - komandir i pilot 217.E, AVII, K.68, reg.br.1795/1;
- **Mihailo Petrović** - izviđač 215.E, izjava Č. Janiću.
- **Miloš Glišić** - ađutant 8.BP, AVII, K.37, reg.br.6/1;
- **Nestor Gabrovšek** - izviđač 216.E, AVII, K.37, reg.br.6/1
- **Nikola Nikolić** - major, k-dant grupe, pismena izjava posle rata, Wagrain, Austrija
- **Pavao Sić** - pomoćnik komandanta 8.BP puka, AVII, K.68, reg.br.1781/12
- **Radojko Mašković** - civilni mehaničar 34.VG, usmena izjava Aleksandru Ognjeviću. Zlatibor, 1990
- **Radomir Anđelković** - izviđač 218.E, izjava Andriji Pavloviću.
- **Radoslav Djordjević** - potpukovnik, komandant puka, usmena izjava A.Pavloviću.
- **Spasen Zarevski (Zarević)** - ppuk, pilot 107.E, izjava, AVII, K.37 reg.br.6/1;
- **Stjepan Pažameta** – poručnik, pilot 108.E, pismena izjava, AVII, K.66, reg.br.34/1;
- **Svetozar Lolić** - komandir 12.AČ i pilot 216.E, AVII, K.8, reg.br.38/1;
- **Svetozar Lolić** - pilot, komandir 12.AČ, 8.BP (lični ratni dnevnik, neobjavljen);
- **Vićentije Milanović** - izjava posle rata u ratnom vazduhoplovstvu.
- **Vićentije Milanović** – Sećanje na rad 8.BP u Aprilskom ratu 1941, pisana izjava (sine anno).
- **Vladimir Bosner** - k2k, ađutant 4.LP, pismena izjava, AVII, kutija 66, reg. br.21/1;
- **Žarko Vukajlović** - k1k, k-dir 108.E, usmena izjava A.Pavloviću;

**Selected archival funds:**

- Arhiv vojno-istorijskog instituta (AVII), Srbija, Beograd:
- Documents on German Foreign Policy, 1918-1945, Series D, 1937-1945, Washington 1957, U.S. Department of State.
- National Archive Washington (NAW), NT 501-251-551.
- Notice technique des moteurs Hispano Suiza Type 12 Y, Notice No. 110, 1.1940, Ministère de l'air
- State Department Documents No.9183/Bern, Swiss (now in U.S. State Archive No.860N/9-844/)

Arhiv BJV:K.8, K.8A, K.37, K.68 Arhiv NDH: K.12-K.30, K.71-K.80, K.89, K.92, K.93, K.125–K.133B-XII

- Bundesarchiv Militärarchiv, Немачка, Фрајбург (Freiburg im Breisgau):

Luftflotte IV, Balkan Feldzug: Film C. 2036/II Anerk: Nr.11/12/13/14/15/16

Film RL 2/III. 753/118/4; 753/176/2; 753/178/9; 753/178/10; 753/182/14;

753/180/15; 753/181/16, 756/255/s; 753/178/8; 753/178/11; 753/218/28;

753/218/29; 753/184/3; 753/194/8; 753/194/9; 753/194/10; 753/194/11;

753/185/17; 753/241/34; 753/190/15; 753/194/3; 753/190/14; 753/195/17;

753/194/4; 753/216/16; 753/241/29; 753/261/19; 753/253/11; 753/272/44;

753/314/27;

**Selected internet sources:**

- luftwaffe-research-group.org/
- forum.12oclockhigh.net/
- www.avijacijabezgranica.com/forum
- www.paluba.info/smf
- www.aeromagazin.rs

**Institutions:**

- Muzej vazduhoplovstva Beograd, Beograd, Serbia
- Vojni arhiv Srbije, Beograd, Serbia
- Biblioteka grada Beograda, Beograd, Serbia
- Arhiv grada Beograda, Beograd, Serbia
- Bundesarchiv Militärarchiv, Freiburg, Germany
- Centar za vojno-naučnu dokumentaciju i informacije, Beograd, Serbia
- Hrvatski povijesni muzej, Zagreb, Croatia
- Hrvatski državni arhiv, Zagreb, Croatia
- Magyar Országos Levéltár, Budapest, Hungary
- Muzej istorije naroda Jugoslavije, Serbia
- Muzej vazduhoplovstva, Beograd, Serbia
- Narodna biblioteka, Beograd, Serbia
- National Archive, London, United Kingdom
- National Archive Washington, USA
- Stato Maggiore dell' Aeronautica Militare Italiana, Roma, Italy
- Vojni muzej, Beograd, Serbia
- Vojno-istorijski institut, Beograd Serbia
- Vojno-geografski institut, Beograd, Serbia

**Personal collections:**

- **Netherlands:** Jan Van den Heuvel (†)
- **Austria:** Berndhard Tötchinger (†)
- **Romania:** Dénes Bernad
- **Serbia:** Aleksandar Ognjević, Dejan Milojević, Milan Micevski, Miloš Milosavljević, Nenad Miklušev, Ognjan M. Petrović, Čedomir Janjić (†), Šime Oštrić, Dragan Kolundžić, Nenad Jovanović (†)
- **Croatia:** Tomislav Aralica, Emil Smutni, Mario Jelušić, Josip Novak, Robert Čopec
- **Slovenia:** Dalibor Jovanović
- **USA:** Djordje Nikolić
- **UK:** Alex Imrie (†)

**Special thanks to Djordje Nikolić, Dragan Šaler, Robert Čopec and Tomislav Aralica**

## Acknowledgments

This book would not be possible without the generous help from my numerous friends and fellow aviation enthusiasts around the world. I would like to use this opportunity to most sincerely thank: Djordje Nikolić, Dragan Šaler, Jan Van den Heuvel, Berndhard Tötchinger, Dénes Bernád, Csaba B. Stenge, Dejan Milojević, Milan Micevski, Miloš Milosavljević, Nenad Miklušev, Ognjan Petrović, Čedomir Janjić, Šime Oštrić, Dragan, Kolundžić, Nenad Jovanović, Tomislav Aralica, Emil Smutni, Mario Jelušić, Josip Novak, Robert Čopec, Dalibor Jovanović and Alex Imrie.

I am forever grateful for persistent support I received from my wife Biljana and my children Sara Milena and Vukašin, for their everlasting encouragement. I love you with all my heart!

Sheet 1

# IKARUS IK-2

## PRODUCTION SERIES

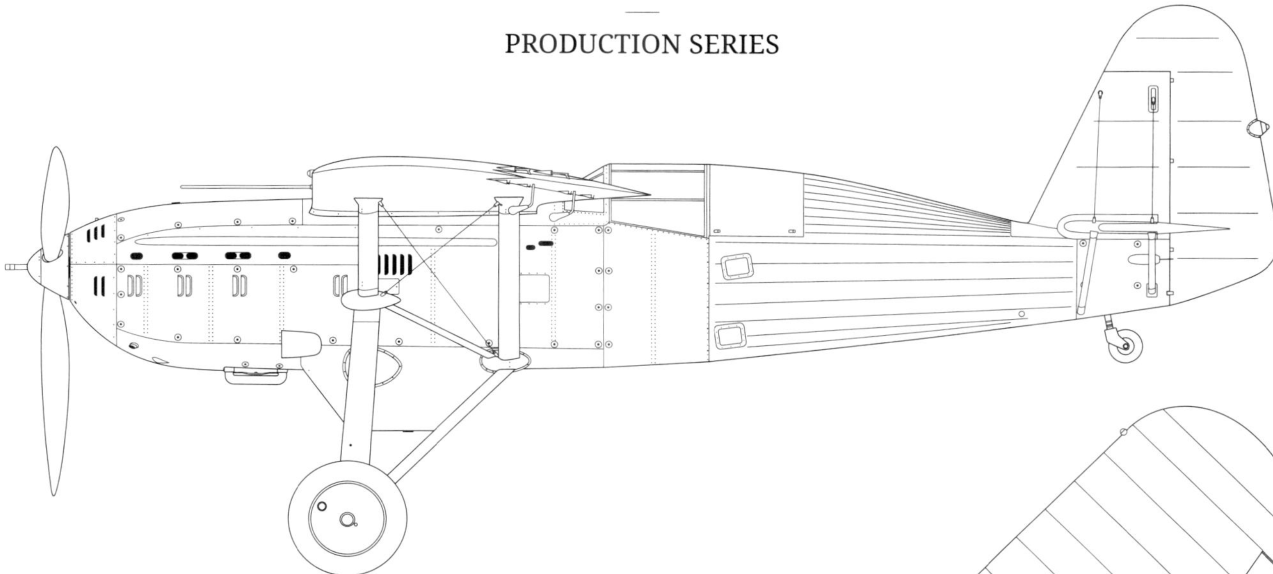

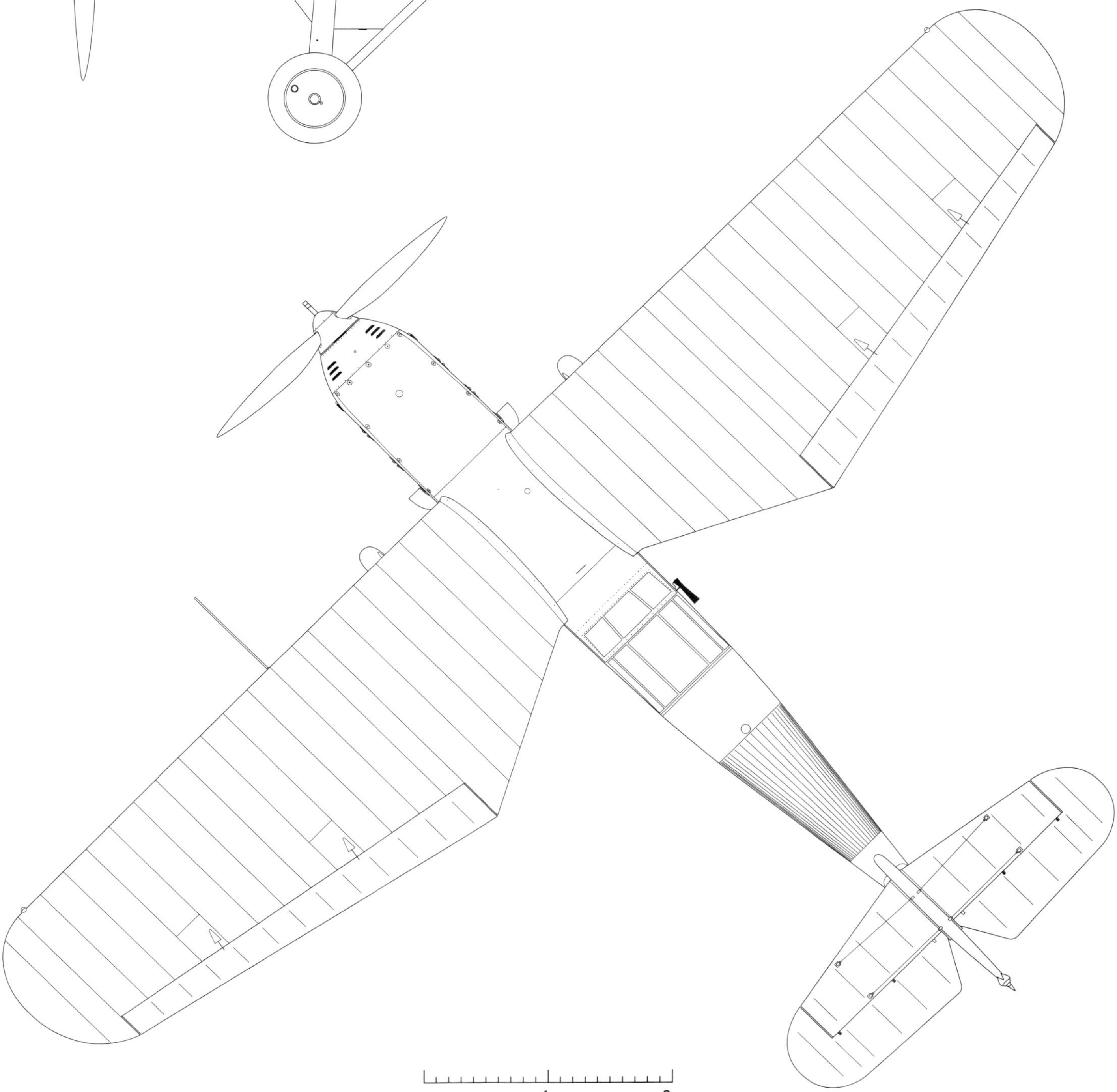

1m 2m

SCALE 1:48

Drawings: Branislav Mirkov, 2019

MONOGRAFIE MONOGRAPHS SPECIAL EDITION

**Sheet 2**

# IKARUS IK-2

## PRODUCTION SERIES

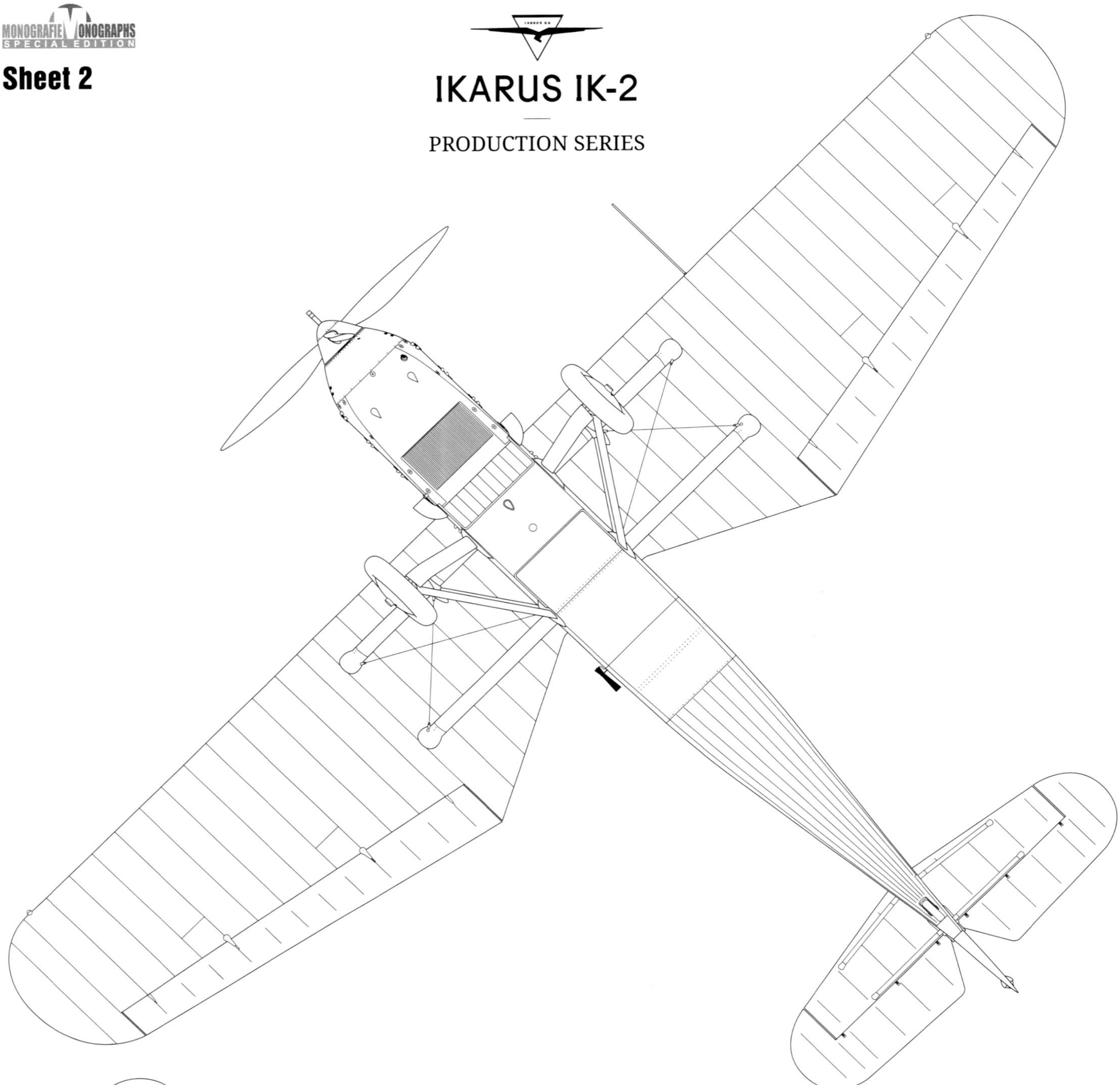

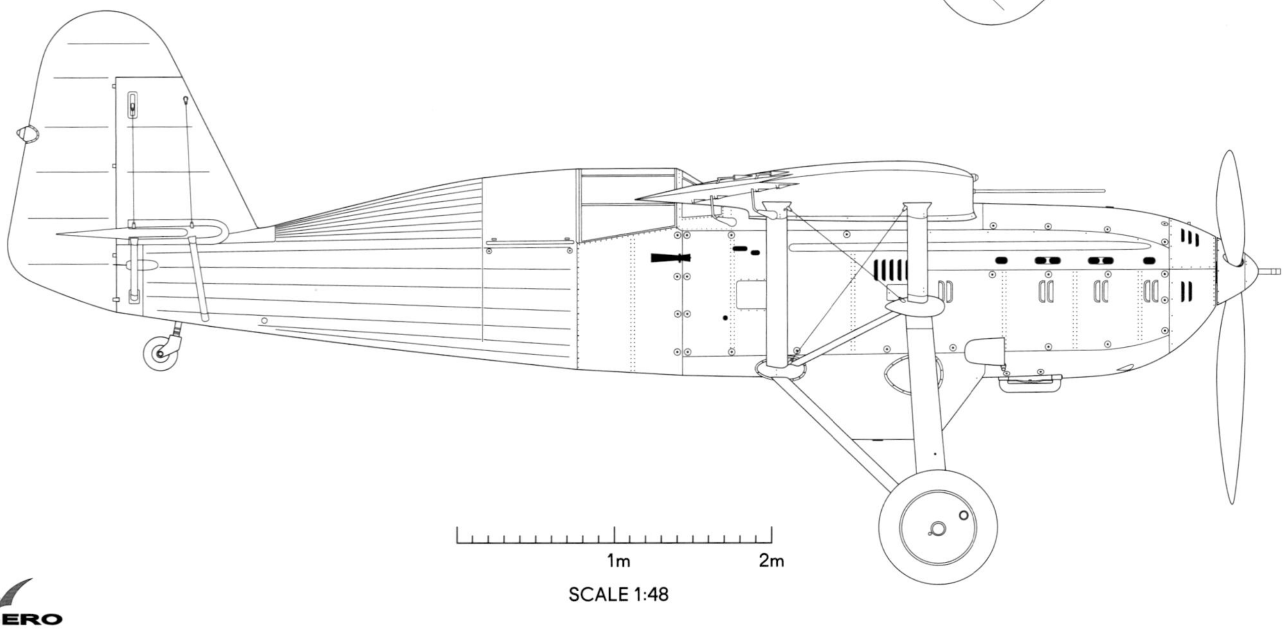

1m 2m

SCALE 1:48

KAGERO

Drawings: Branislav Mirkov, 2019

# IKARUS IK-2

PRODUCTION SERIES

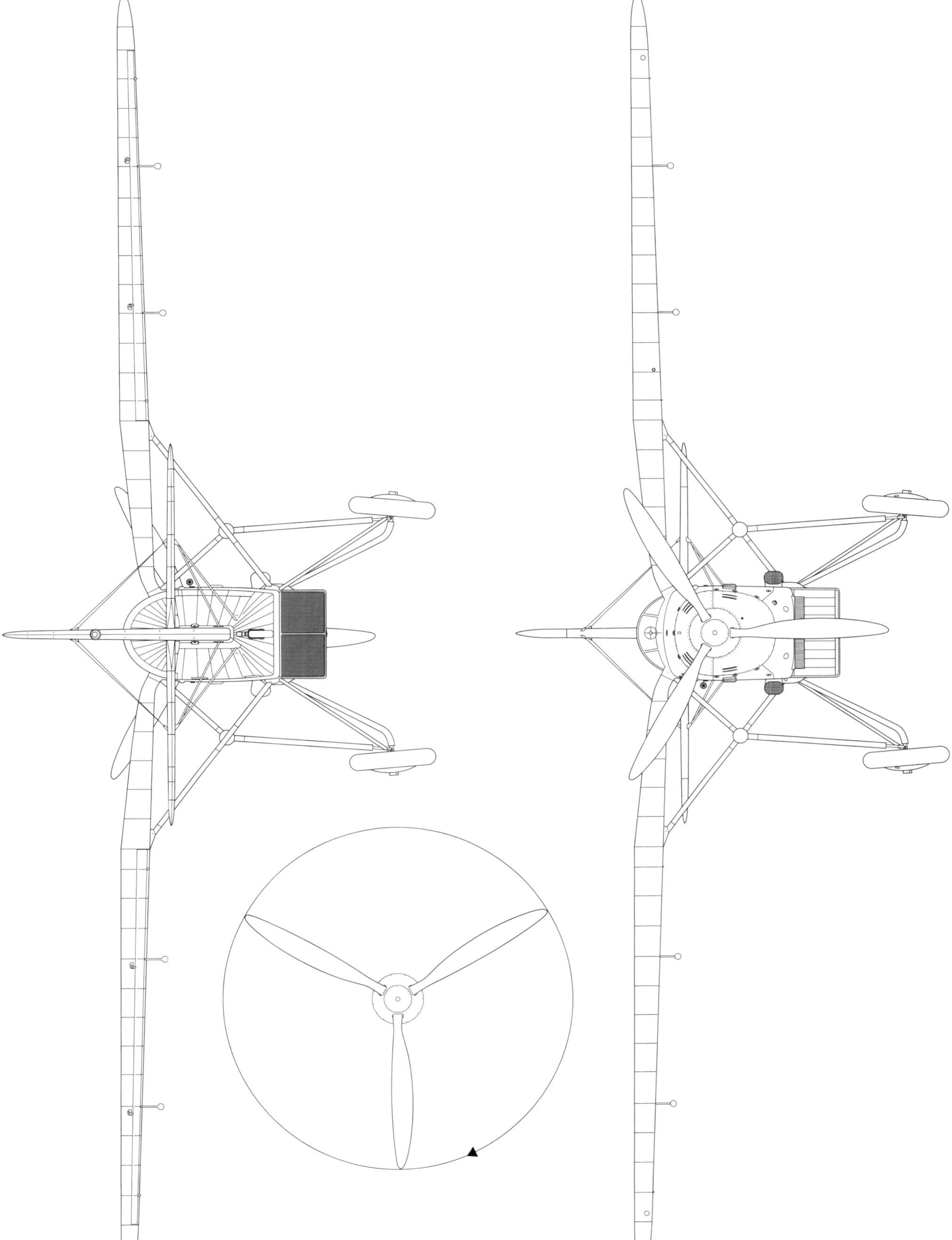

1m 2m

SCALE 1:48



Drawings: Branislav Mirkov, 2019

# IKARUS IK-2

## PRODUCTION SERIES

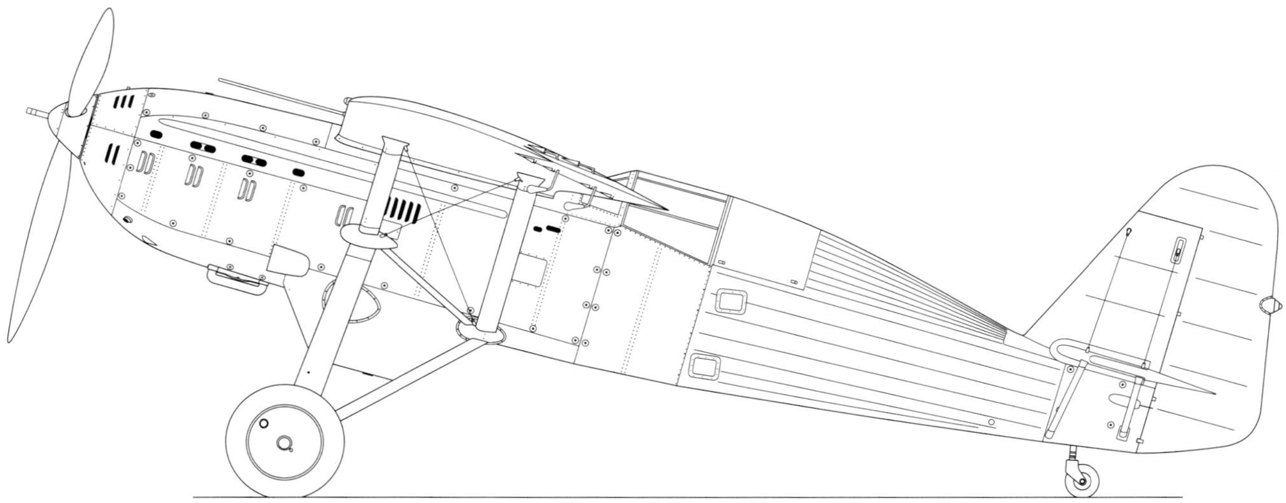

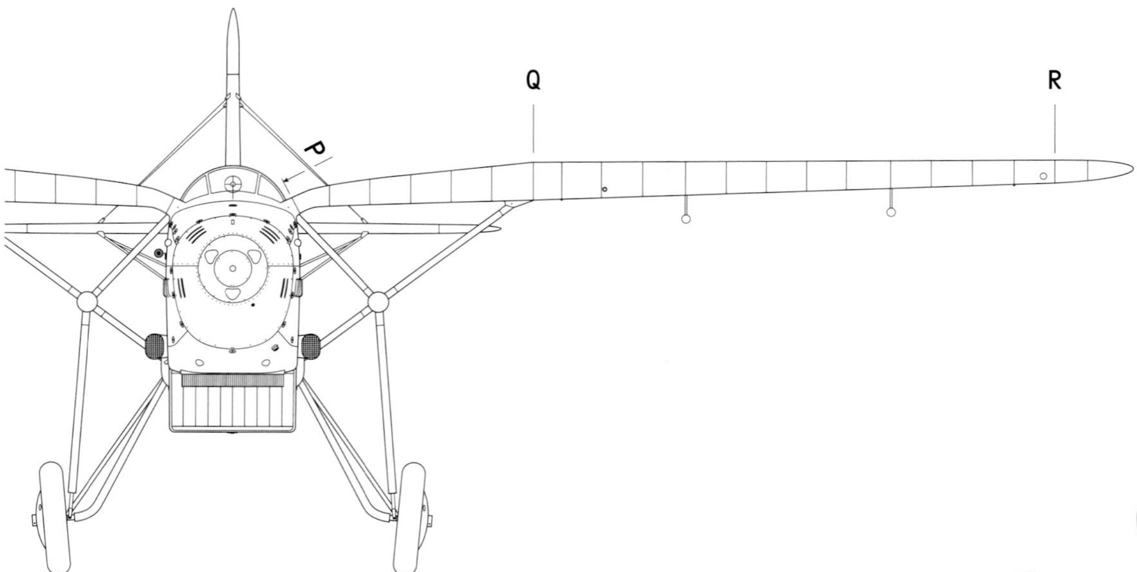


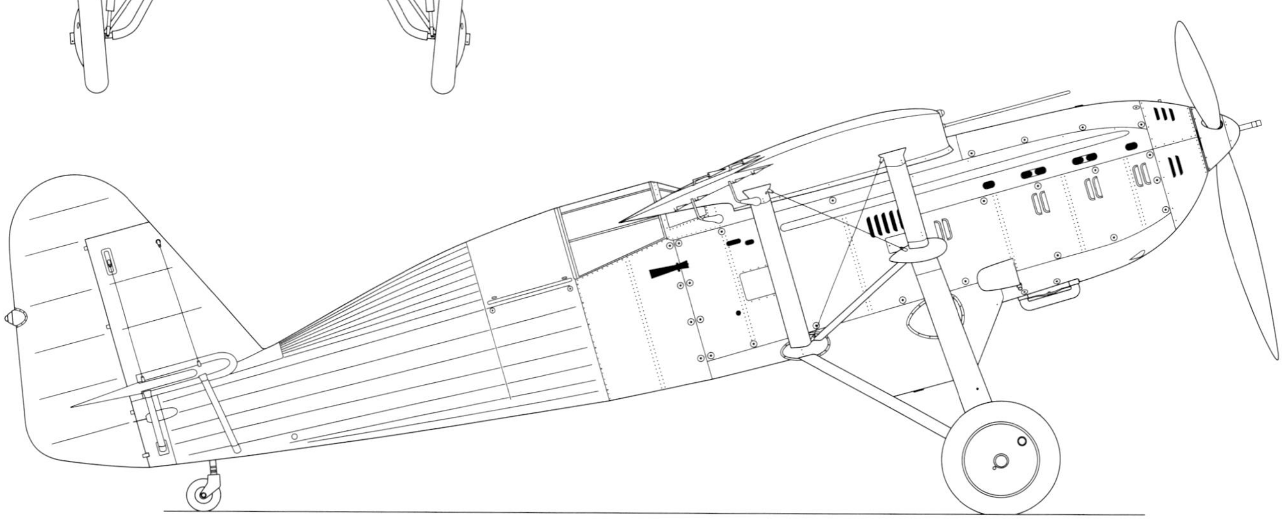

1m 2m

SCALE 1:48

Drawings: Branislav Mirkov, 2019

# IKARUS IK-2

## PRODUCTION SERIES

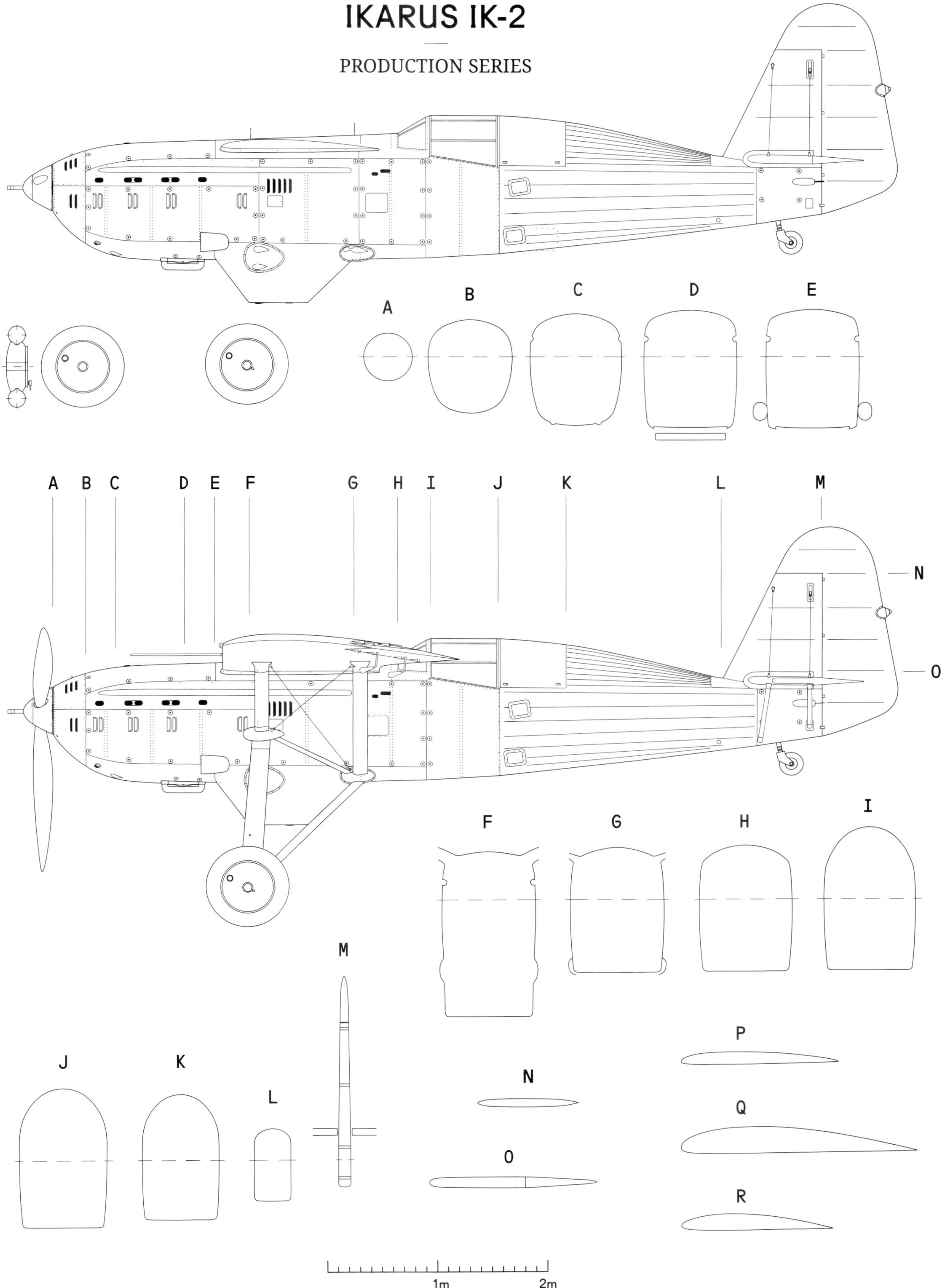


SCALE 1:48

Drawings: Branislav Mirkov, 2019

Sheet 6

# IKARUS IK-2

1st PROTOTYPE

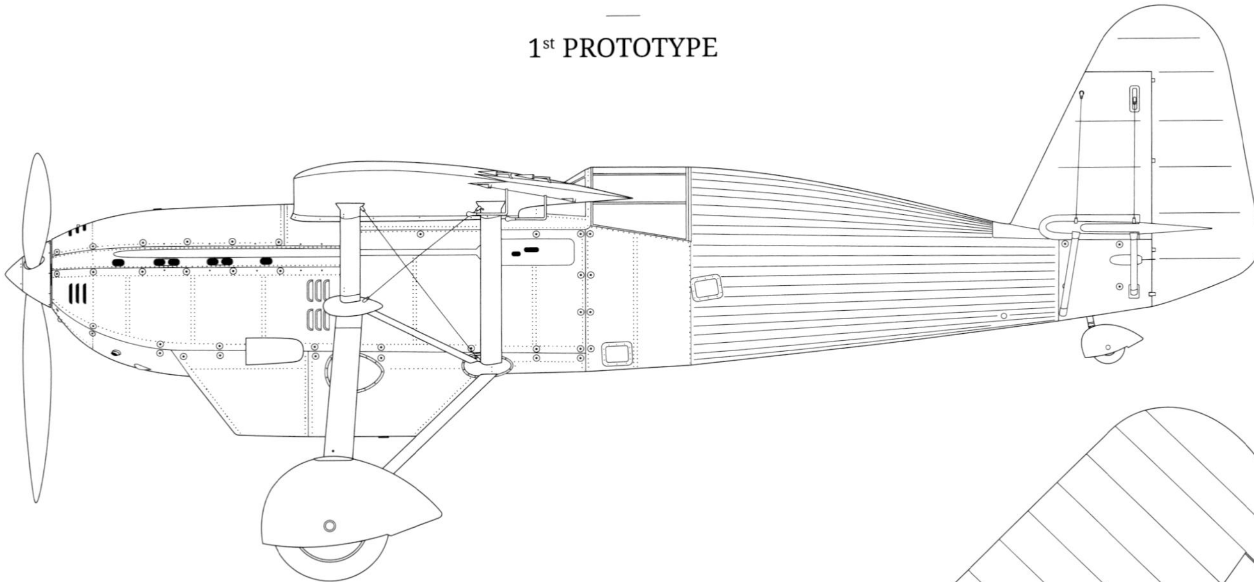

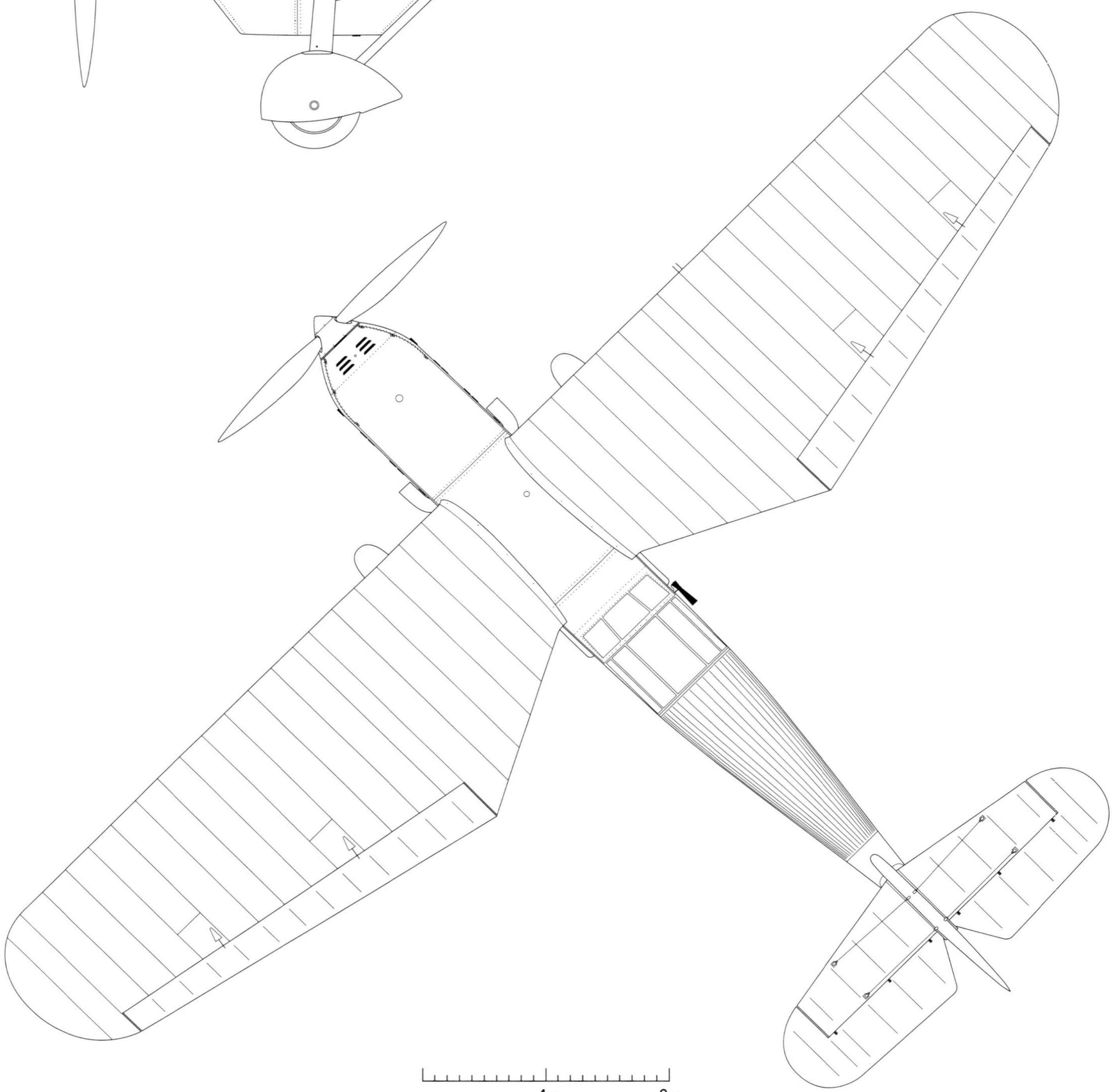

1m 2m

SCALE 1:48

Drawings: Branislav Mirkov, 2019

MONOGRAFIE MONOGRAPHS SPECIAL EDITION

**Sheet 7**

# IKARUS IK-2

1st PROTOTYPE

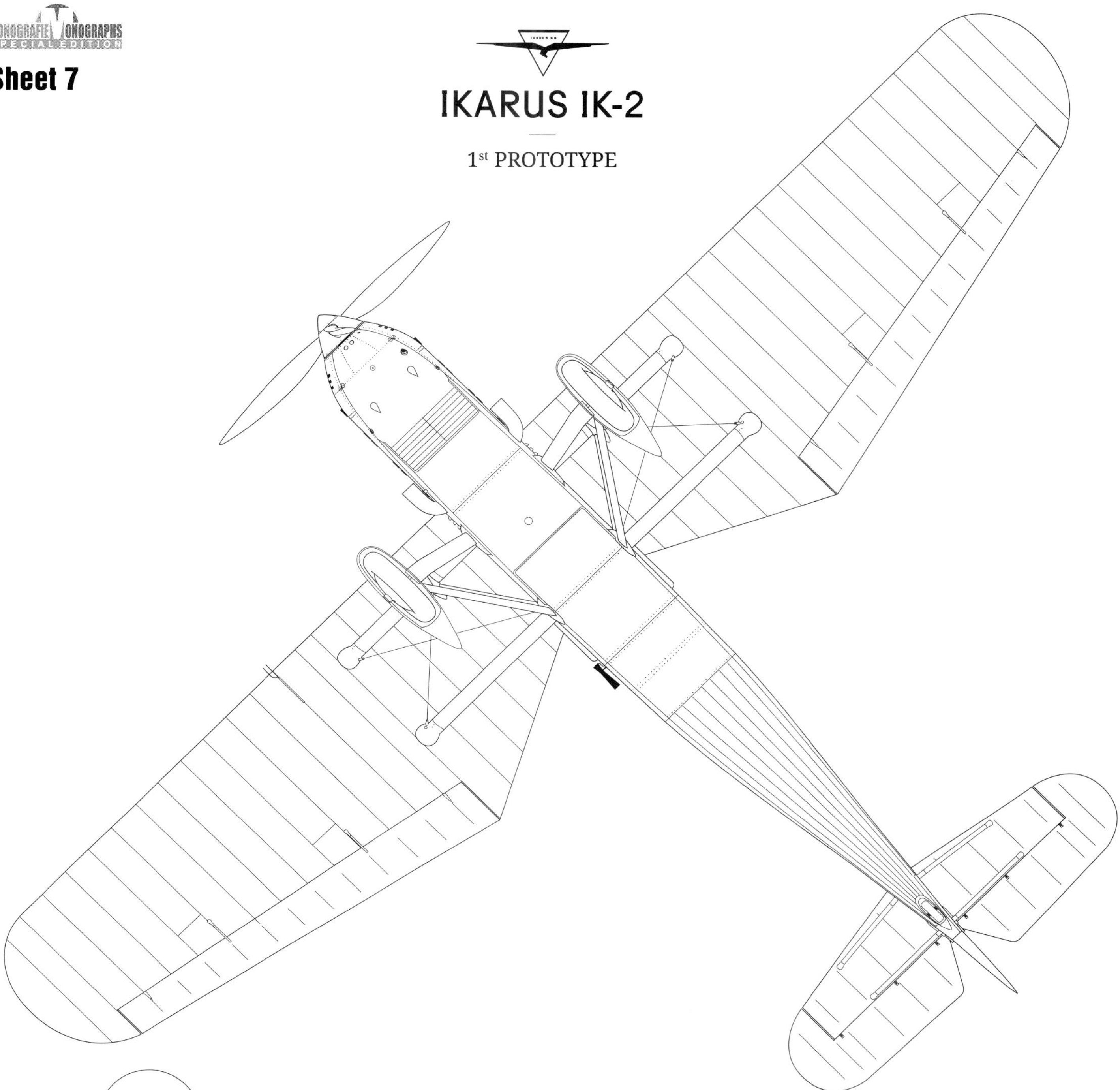

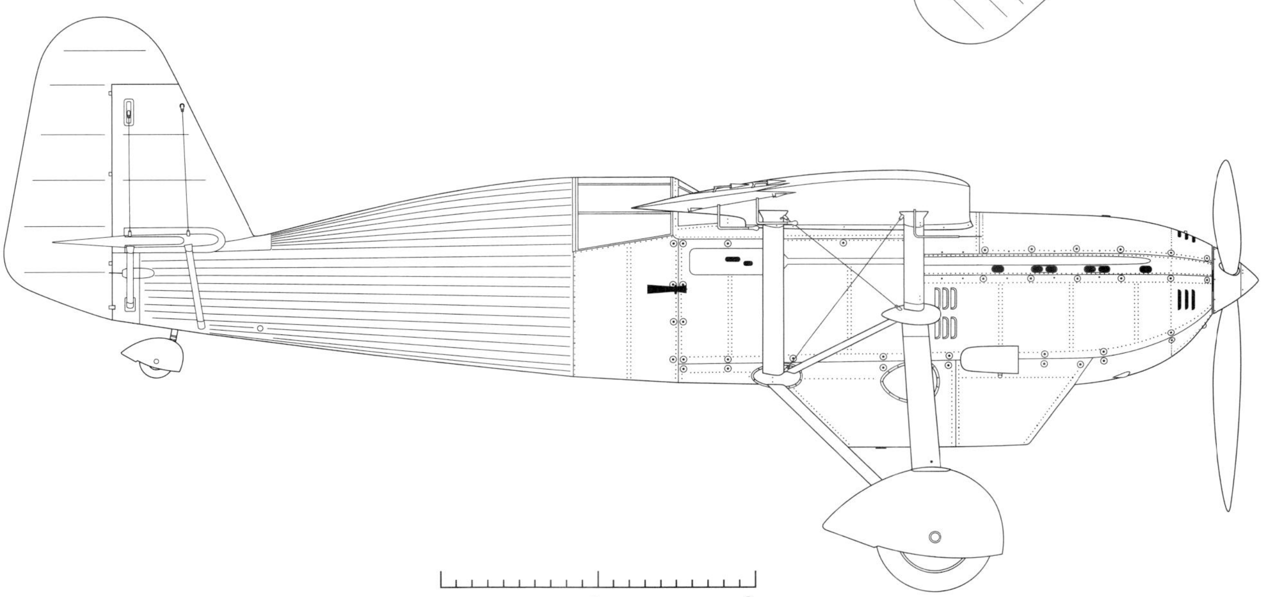

1m 2m

SCALE 1:48

KAGERO

Drawings: Branislav Mirkov, 2019

# IKARUS IK-2

1st PROTOTYPE

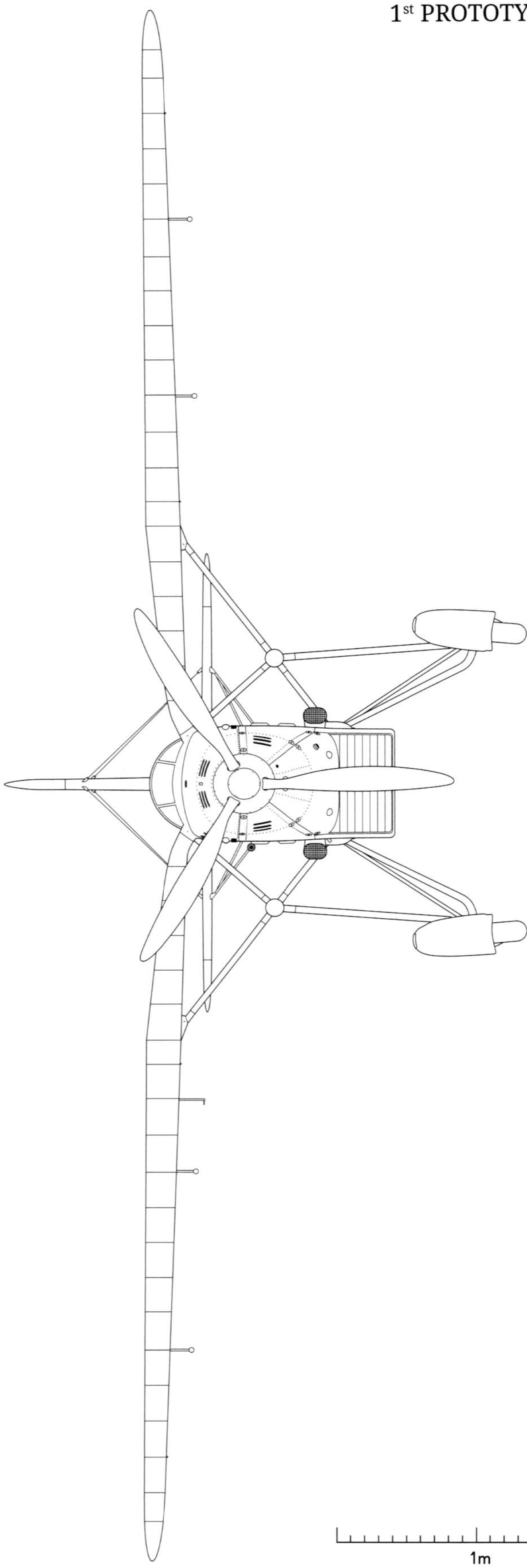

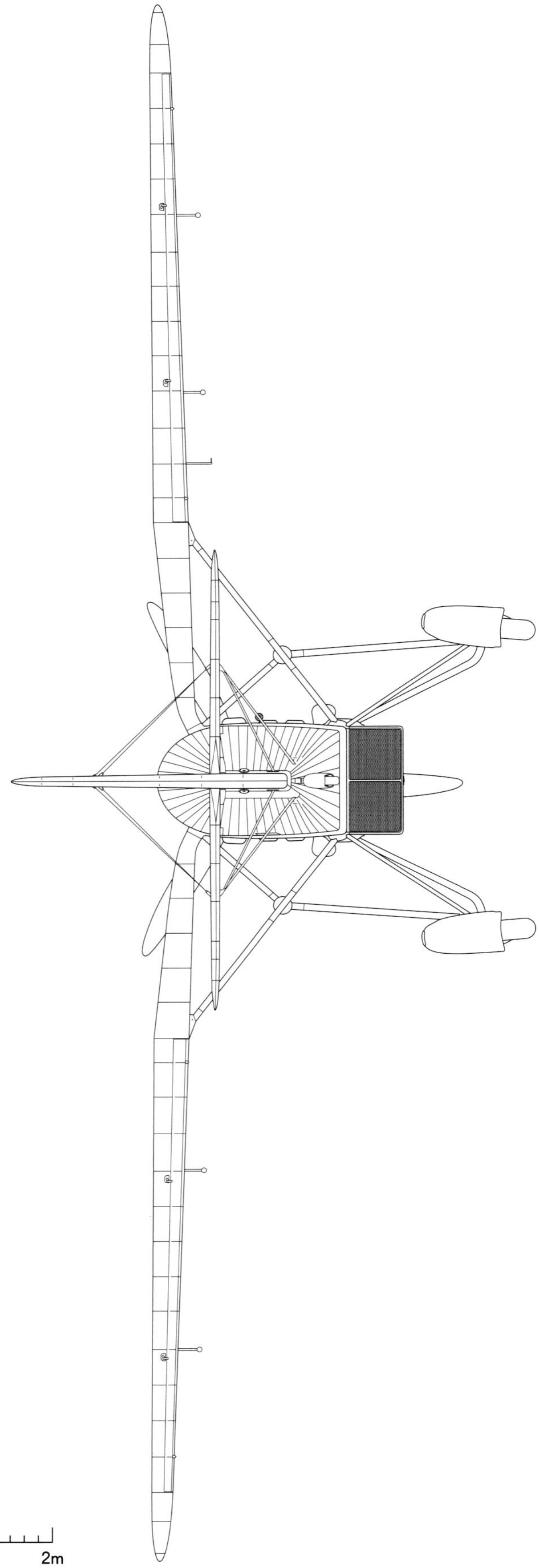

1m 2m

SCALE 1:48



Drawings: Branislav Mirkov, 2019

# IKARUS IK-2

1st PROTOTYPE

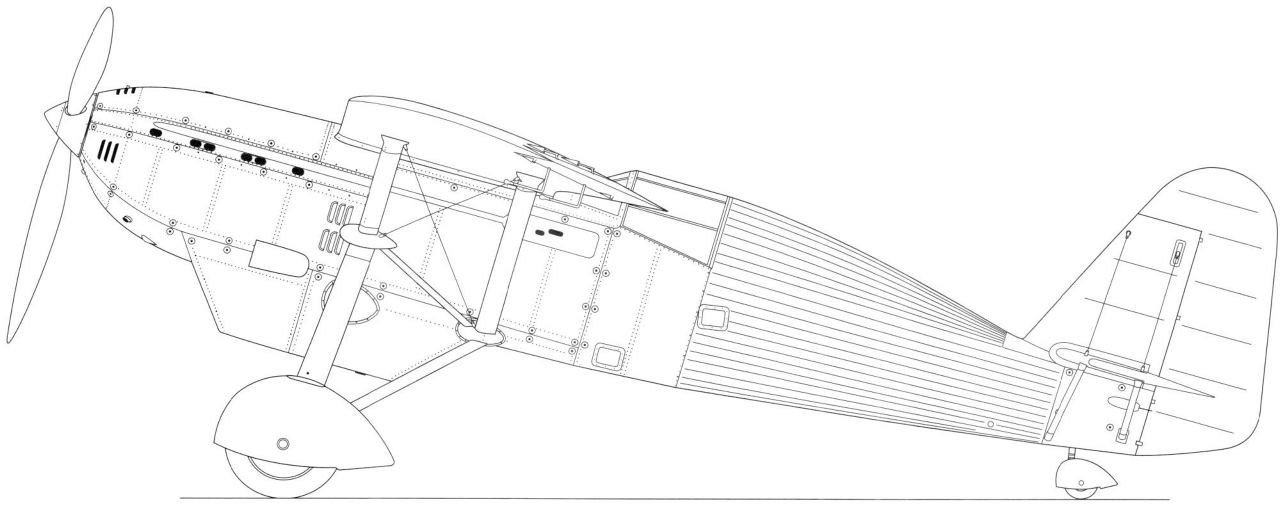

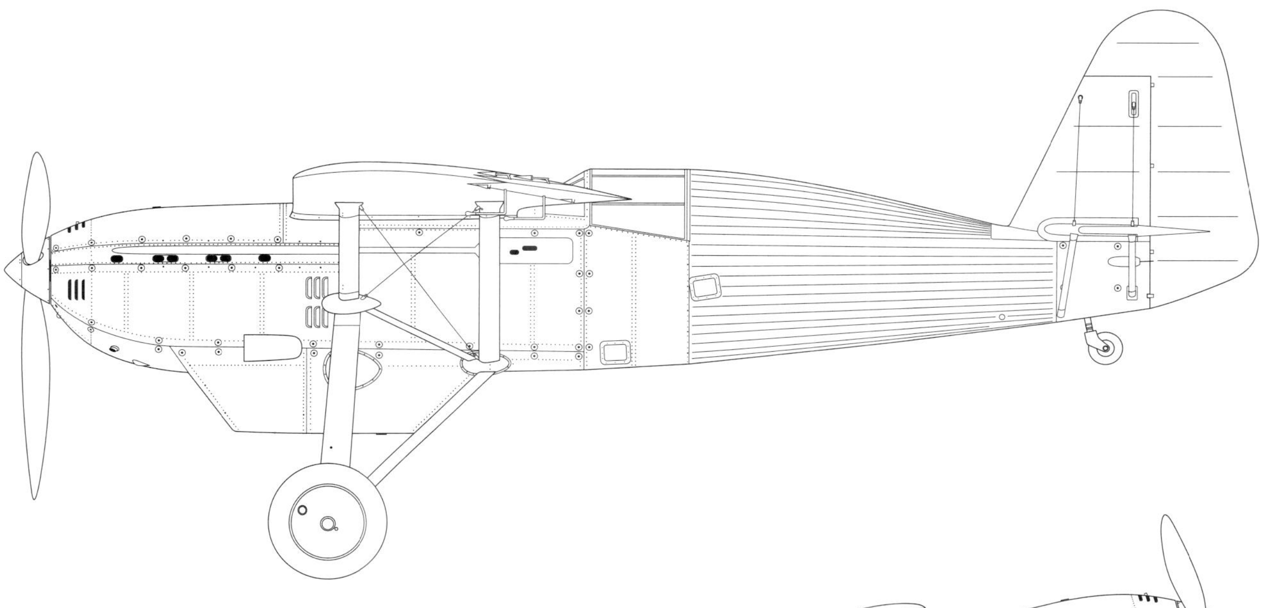

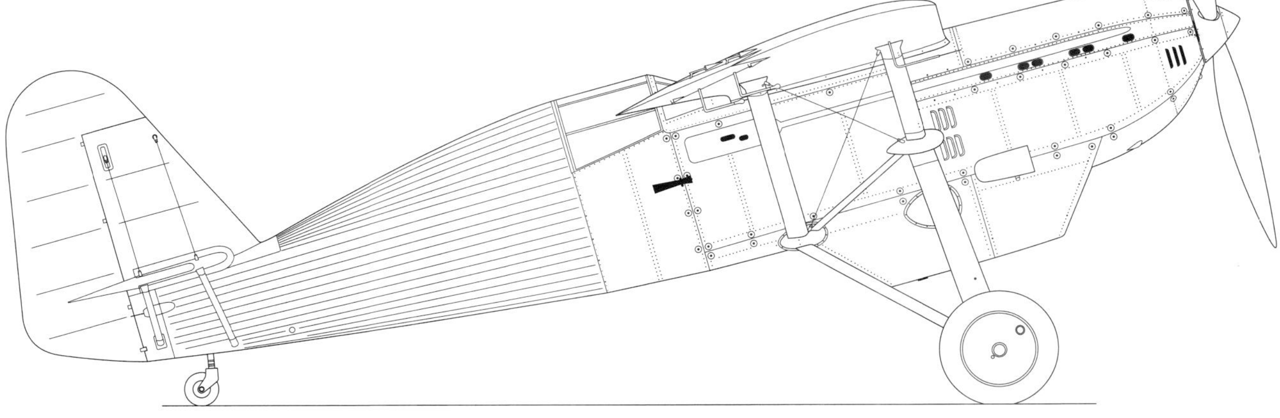

SCALE 1:48



Drawings: Branislav Mirkov, 2019

# IKARUS IK-2

2nd PROTOTYPE

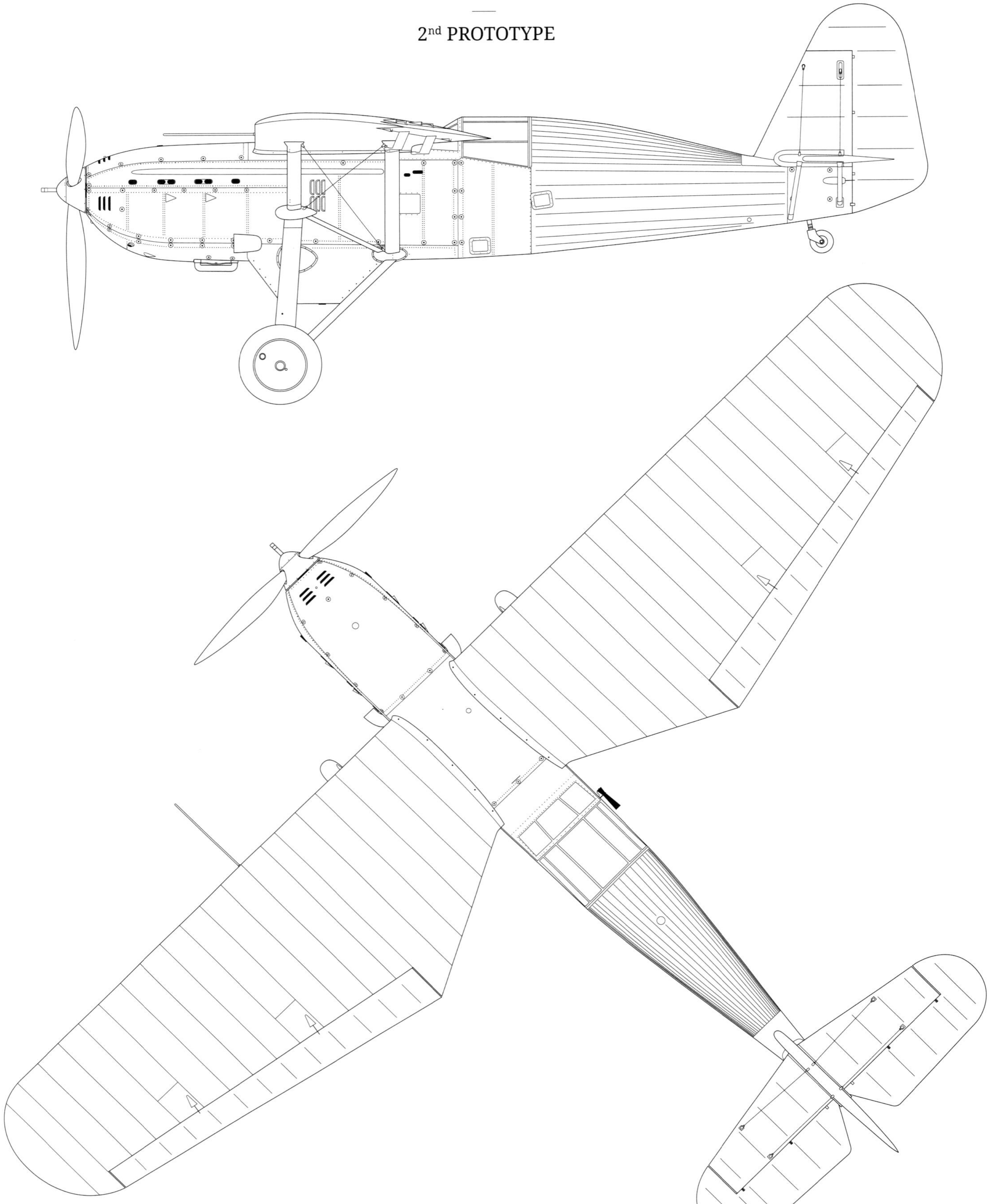

1m 2m

SCALE 1:48

KAGERO

Drawings: Branislav Mirkov, 2019

Sheet 11

# IKARUS IK-2

2nd PROTOTYPE

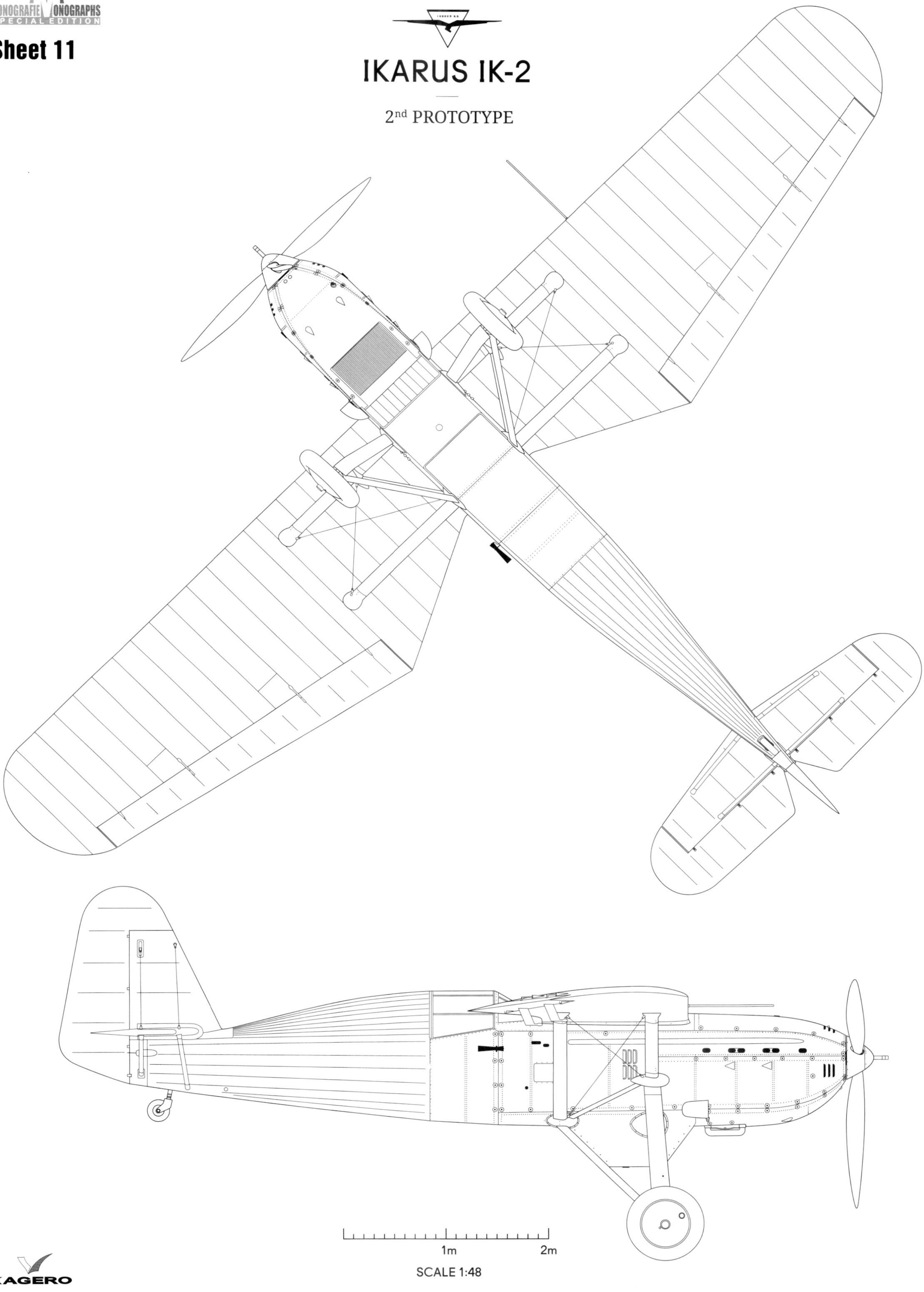


KAGERO

Drawings: Branislav Mirkov, 2019

# IKARUS IK-2

2nd PROTOTYPE

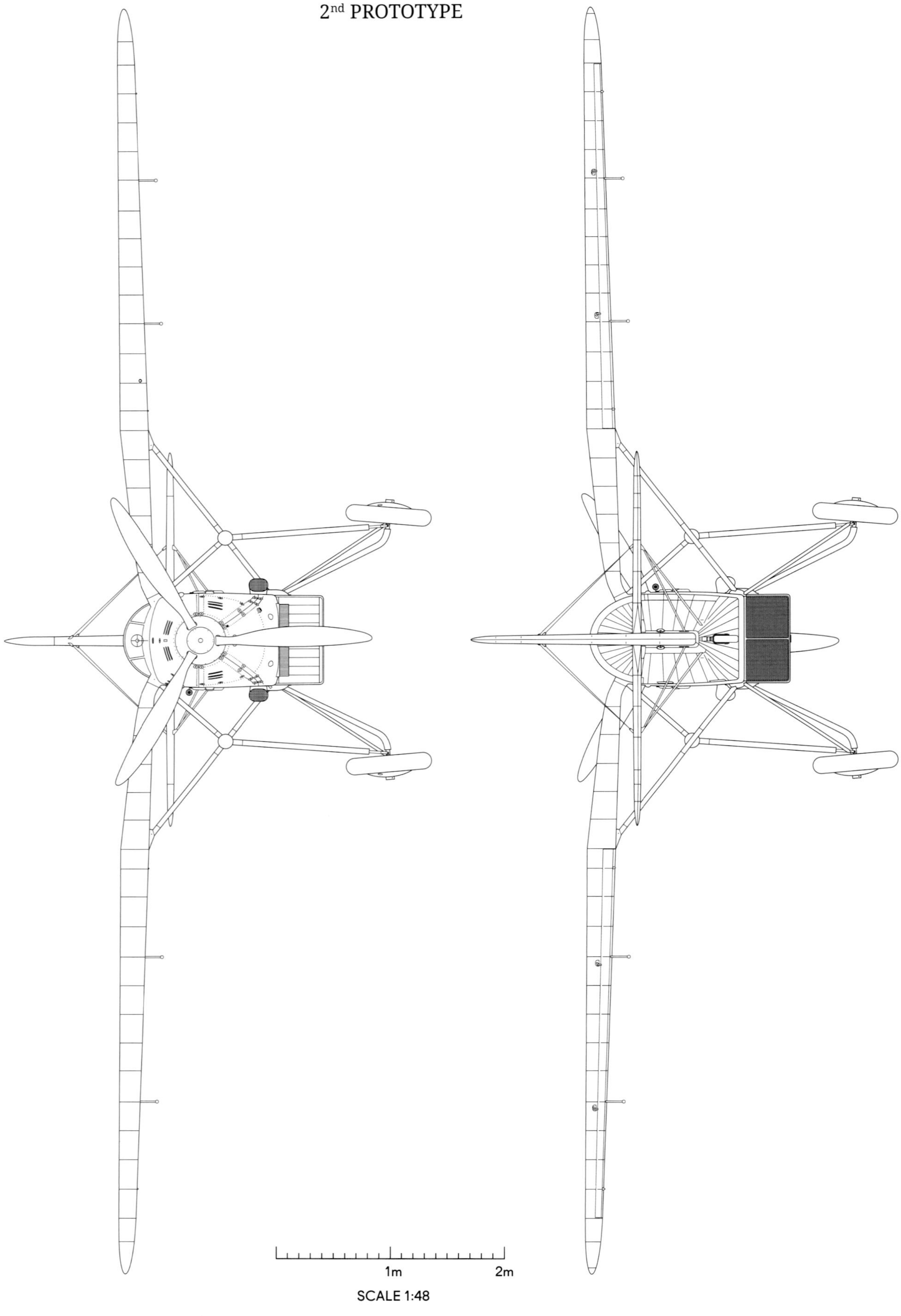

1m 2m

SCALE 1:48

KAGERO

Drawings: Branislav Mirkov, 2019

MONOGRAFIE MONOGRAPHS SPECIAL EDITION

**Sheet 13**

# IKARUS IK-2

PRODUCTION SERIES 1st MODEL

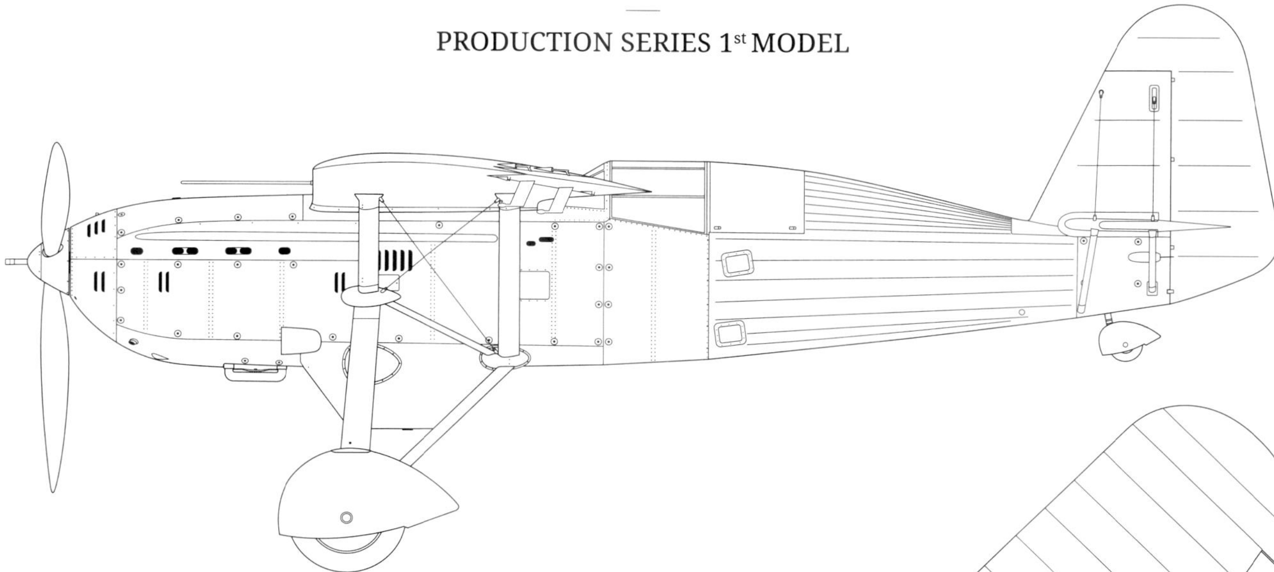

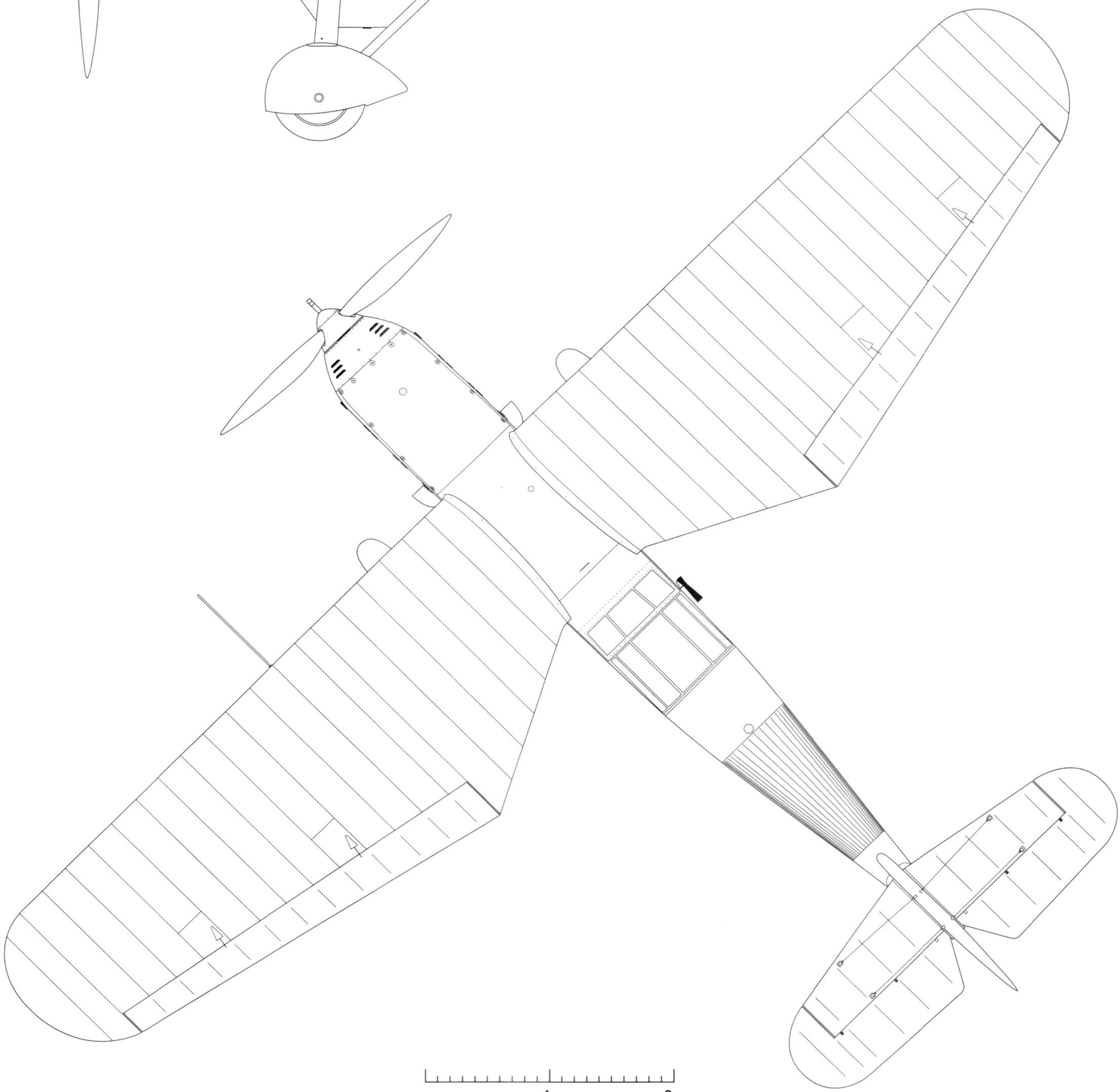


SCALE 1:48

KAGERO

Drawings: Branislav Mirkov, 2019

MONOGRAFIE MONOGRAPHS SPECIAL EDITION

**Sheet 14**

# IKARUS IK-2

PRODUCTION SERIES 1st MODEL

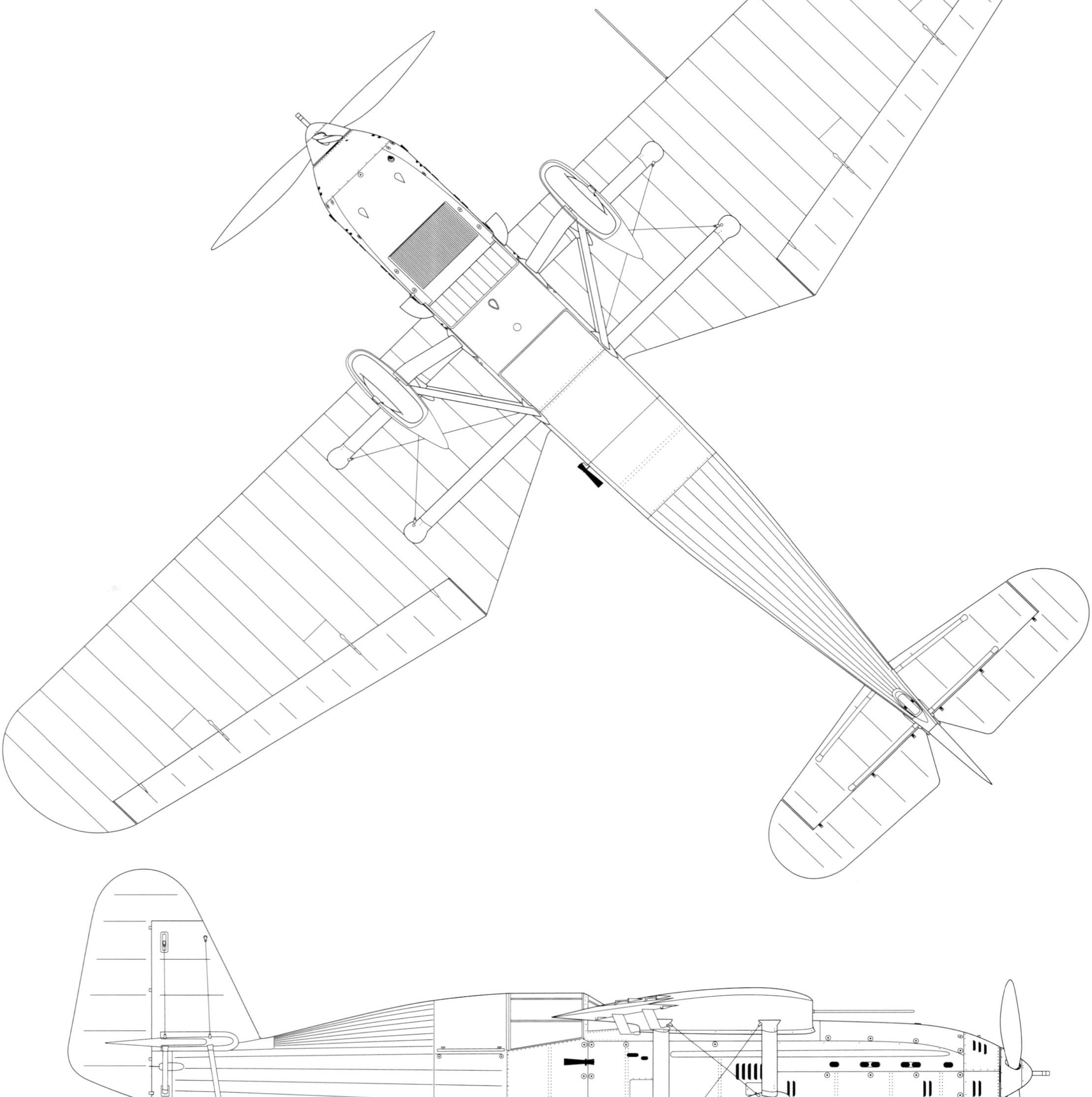

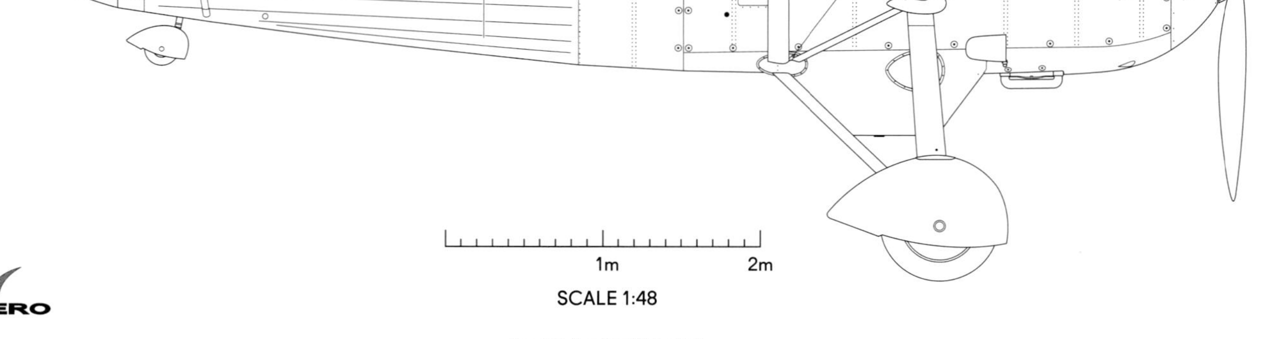

1m 2m

SCALE 1:48

KAGERO

Drawings: Branislav Mirkov, 2019

# IKARUS IK-2

PRODUCTION SERIES 1st MODEL

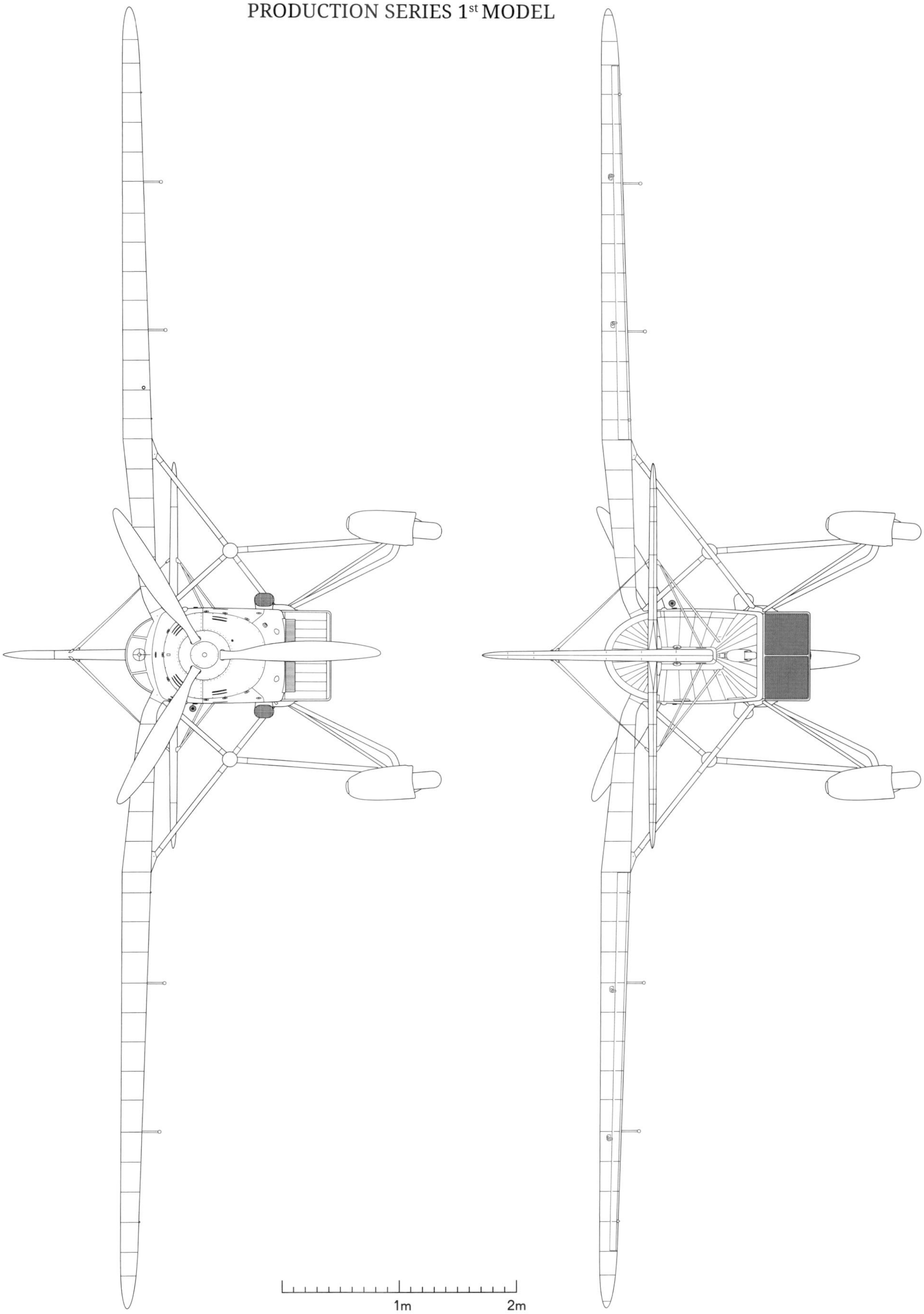

1m 2m

SCALE 1:48

KAGERO

Drawings: Branislav Mirkov, 2019

# IKARUS IK-2

PRODUCTION SERIES UNKNOWN S/N

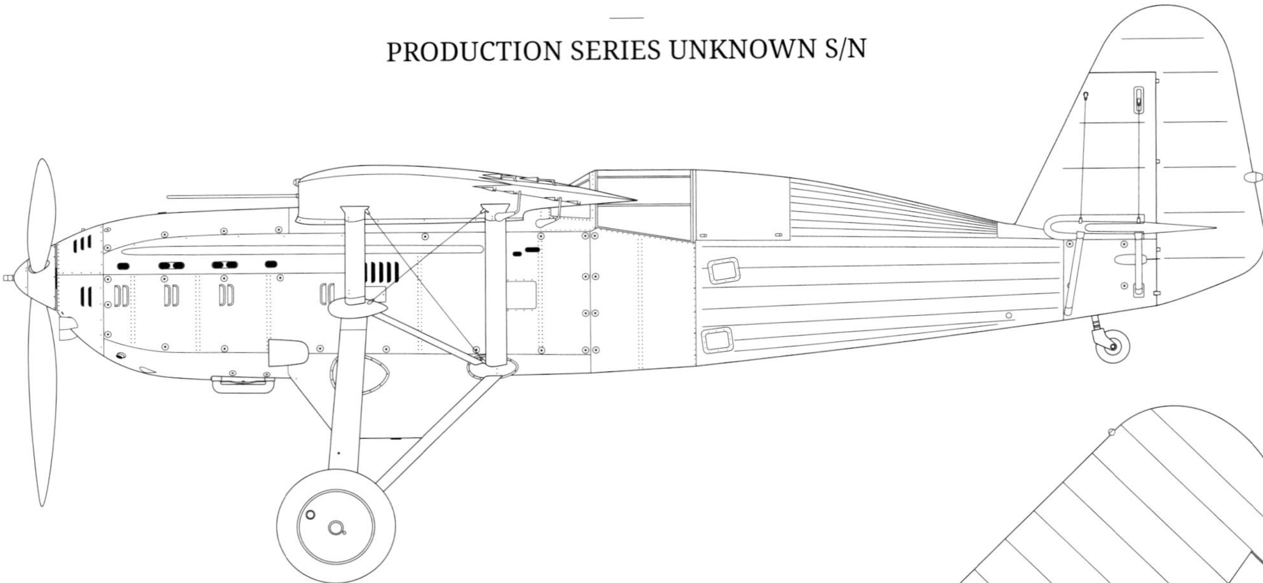

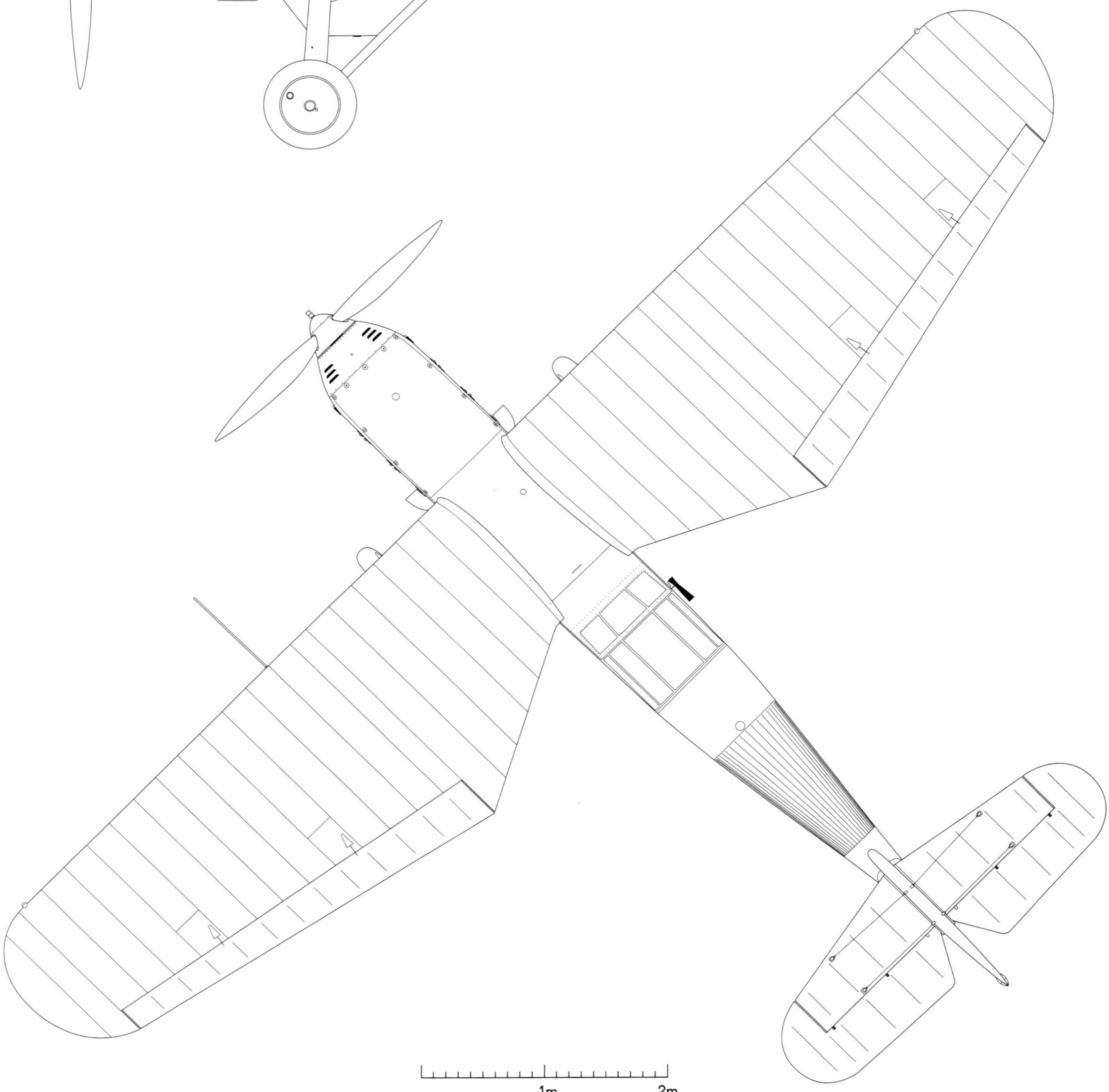





Drawings: Branislav Mirkov, 2019

**Sheet 17**

# IKARUS IK-2

## PRODUCTION SERIES UNKNOWN S/N

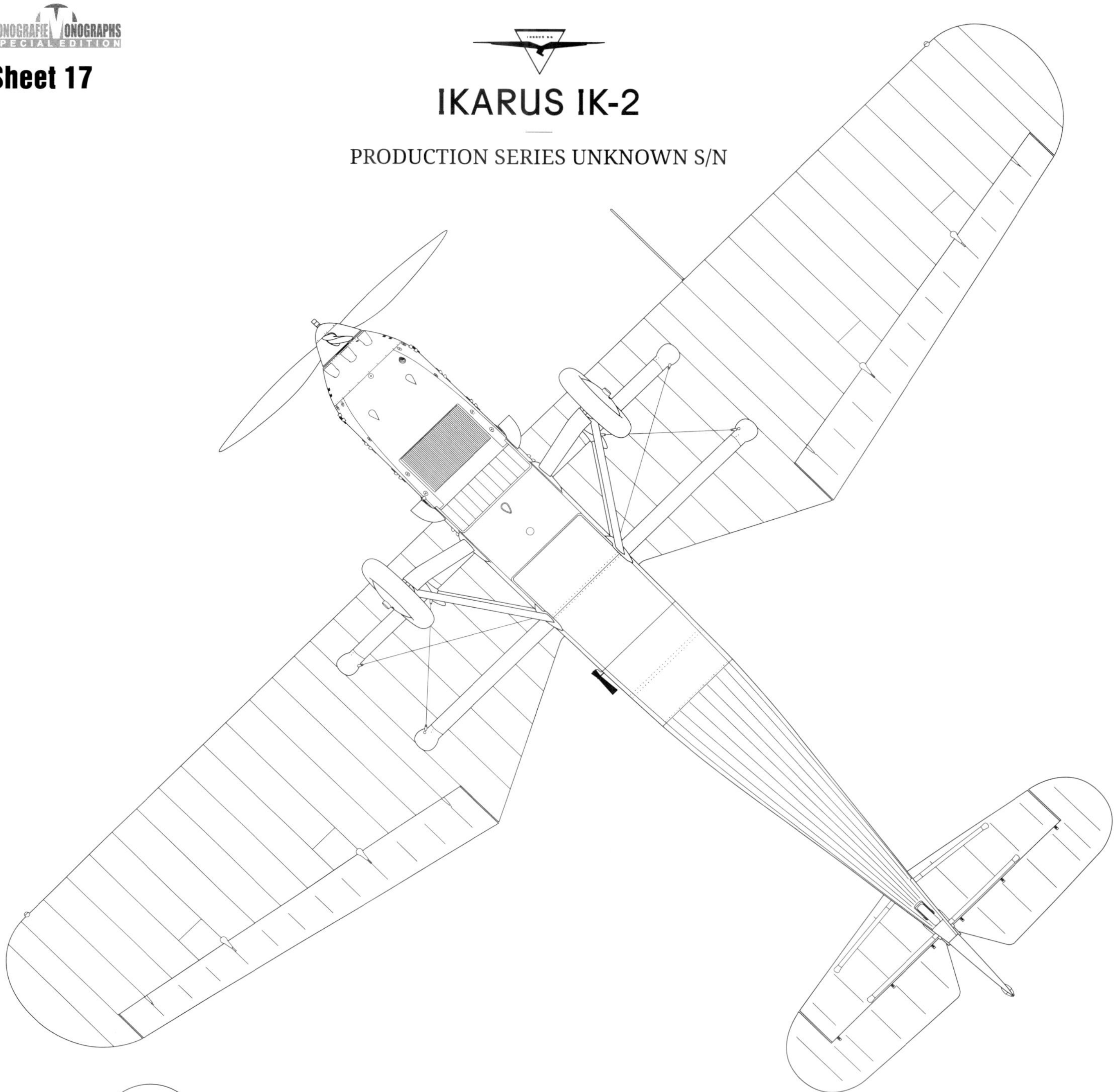

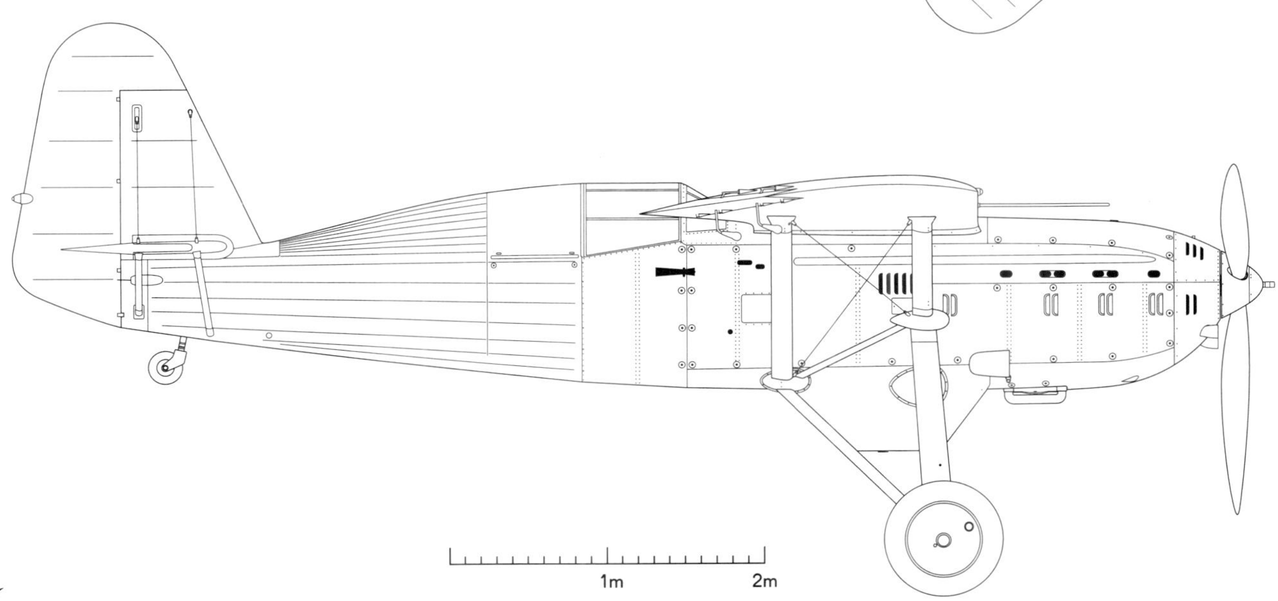

1m 2m

SCALE 1:48

Drawings: Branislav Mirkov, 2019

# IKARUS IK-2

PRODUCTION SERIES UNKNOWN S/N

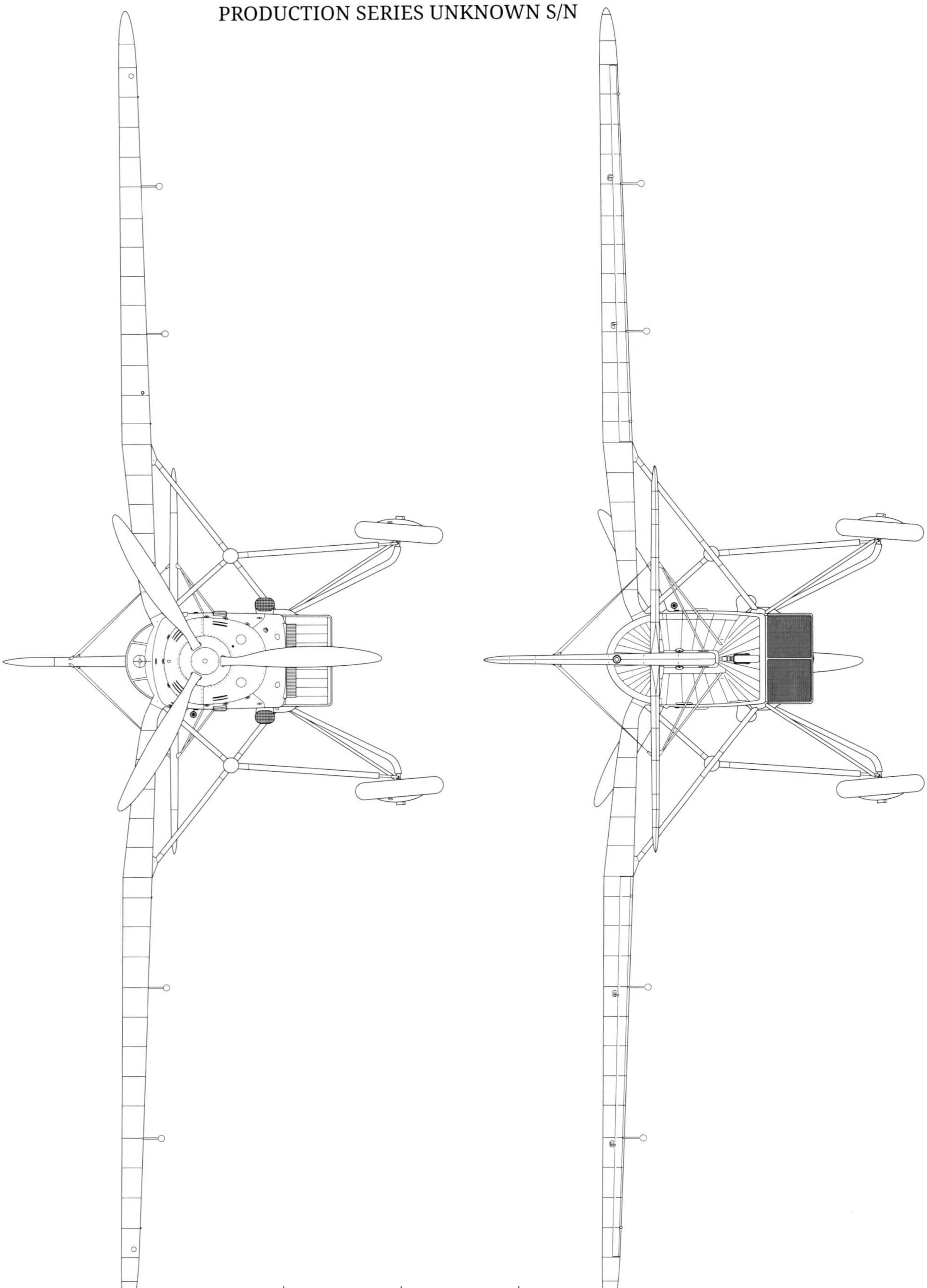

1m 2m

SCALE 1:48



Drawings: Branislav Mirkov, 2019

# IKARUS IK-2

## PRODUCTION SERIES

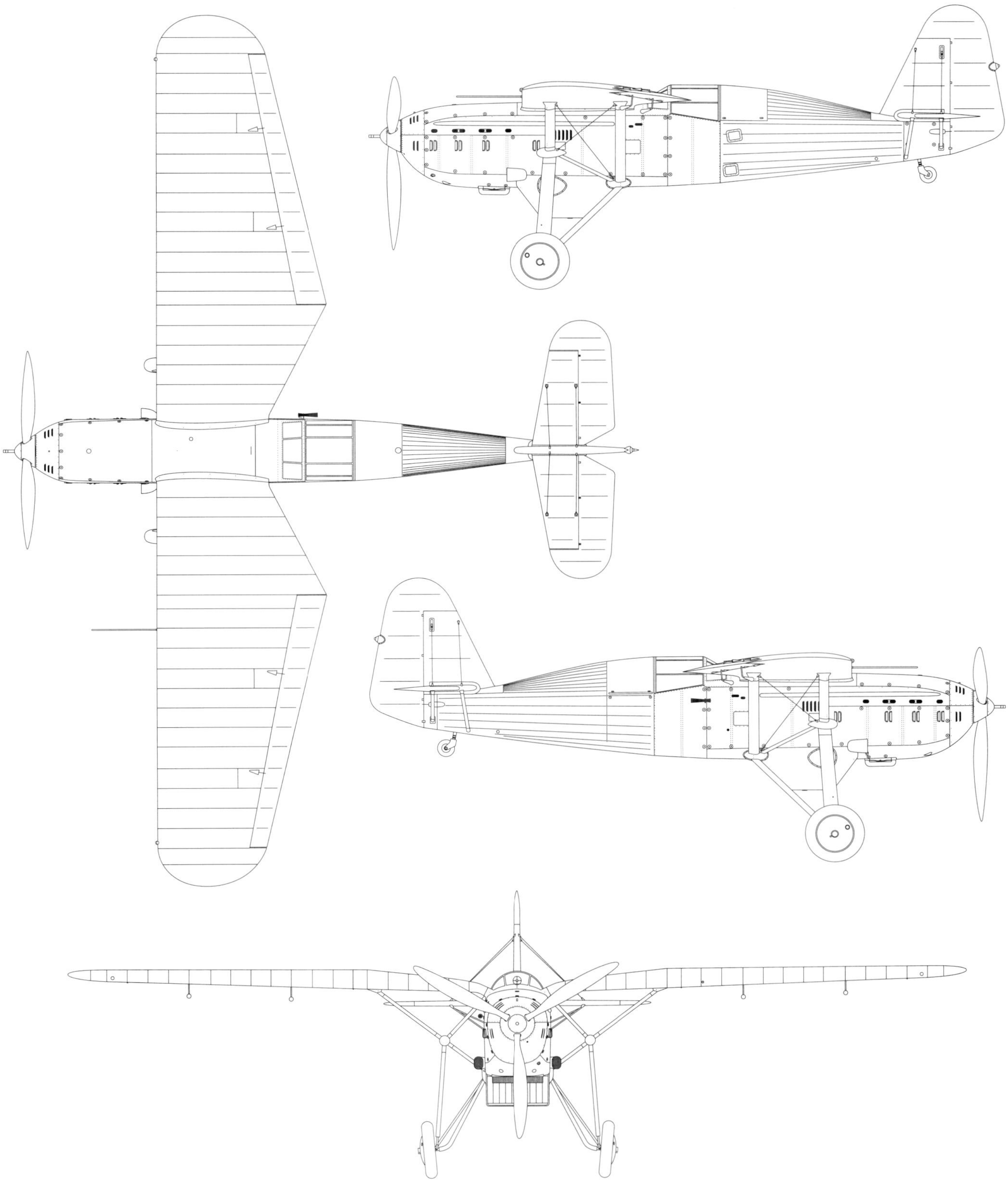

1m 2m

SCALE 1:72

Drawings: Branislav Mirkov, 2019

# IKARUS IK-2

## PRODUCTION SERIES

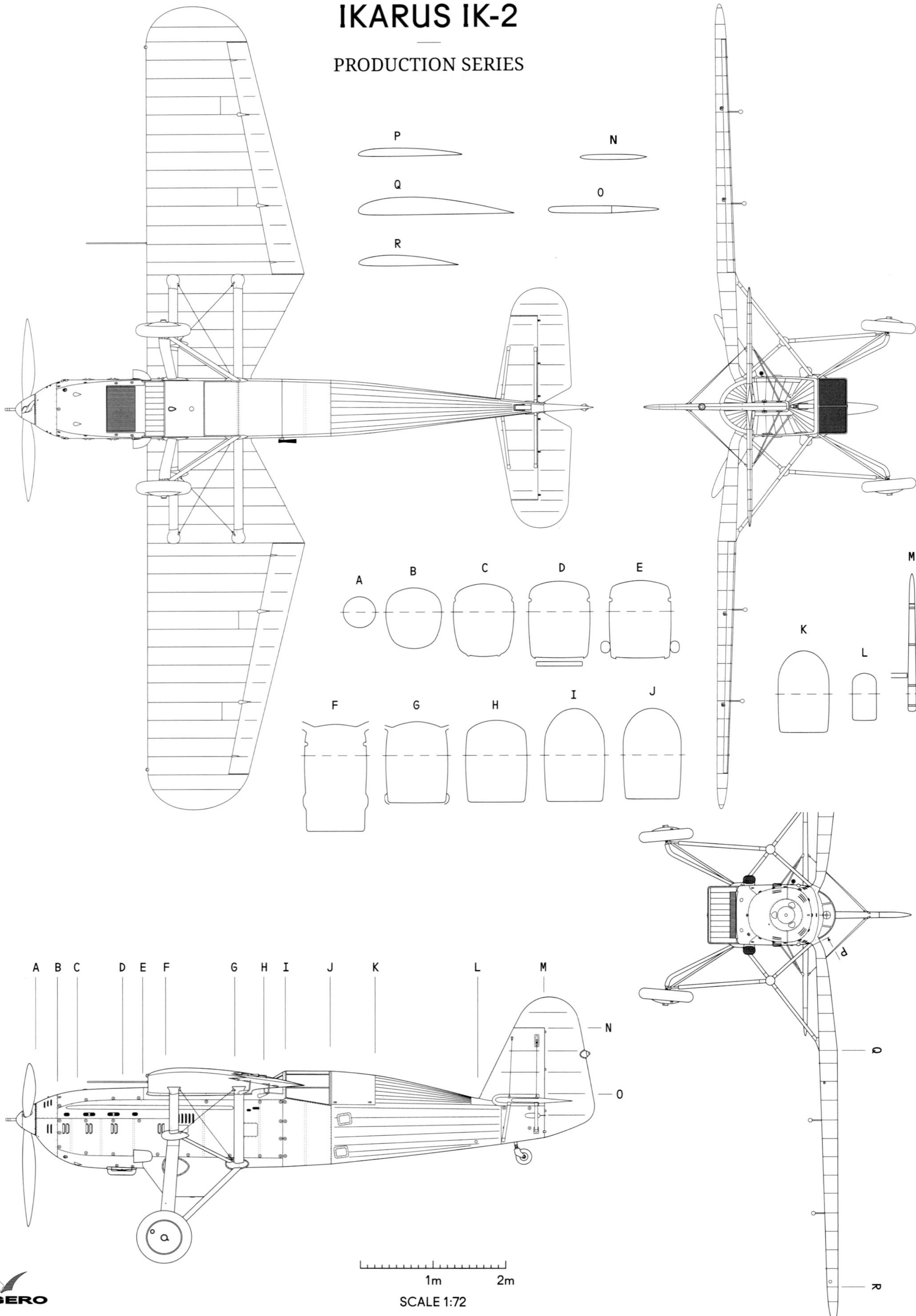


1m 2m

SCALE 1:72



Drawings: Branislav Mirkov, 2019

# IKARUS IK-2

## 1st PROTOTYPE

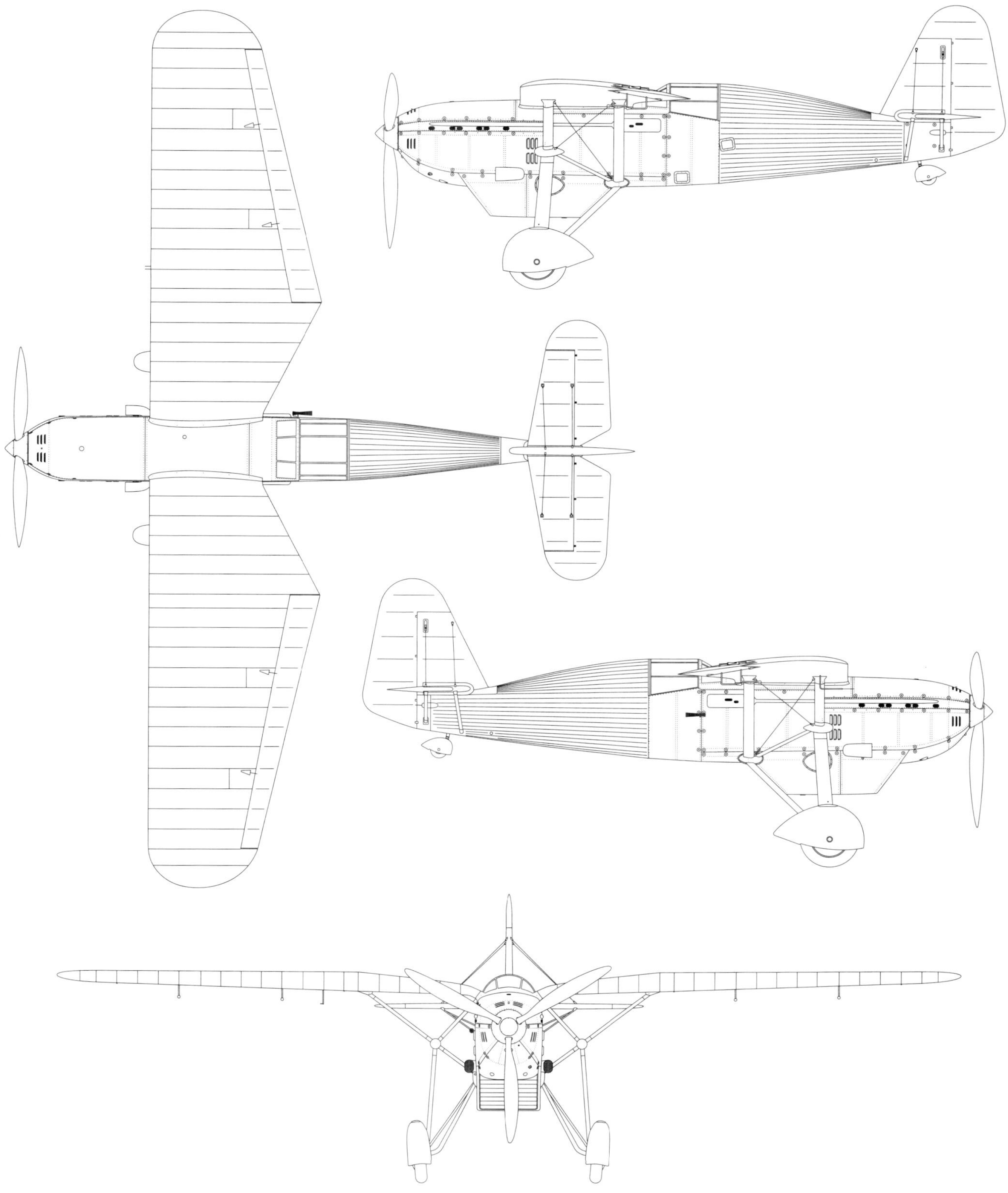

1m 2m

SCALE 1:72

Drawings: Branislav Mirkov, 2019

# IKARUS IK-2

1st PROTOTYPE

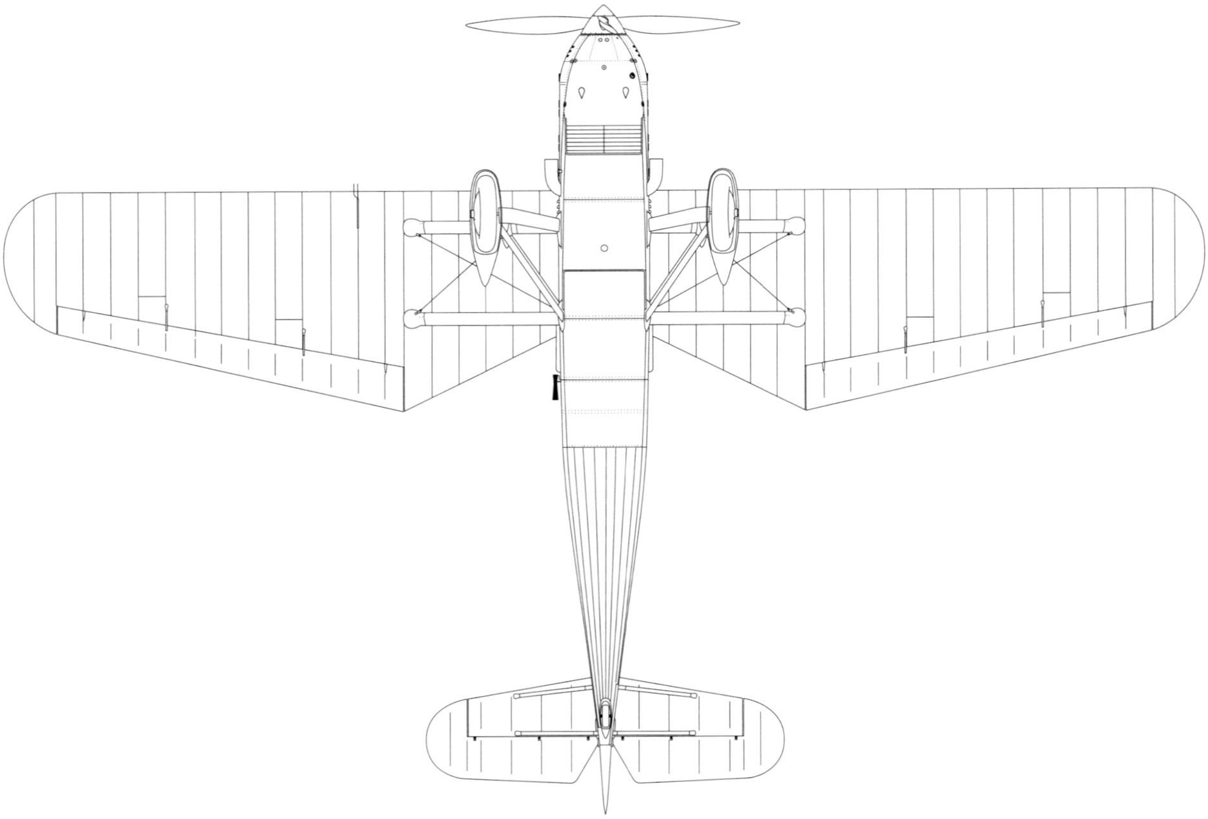

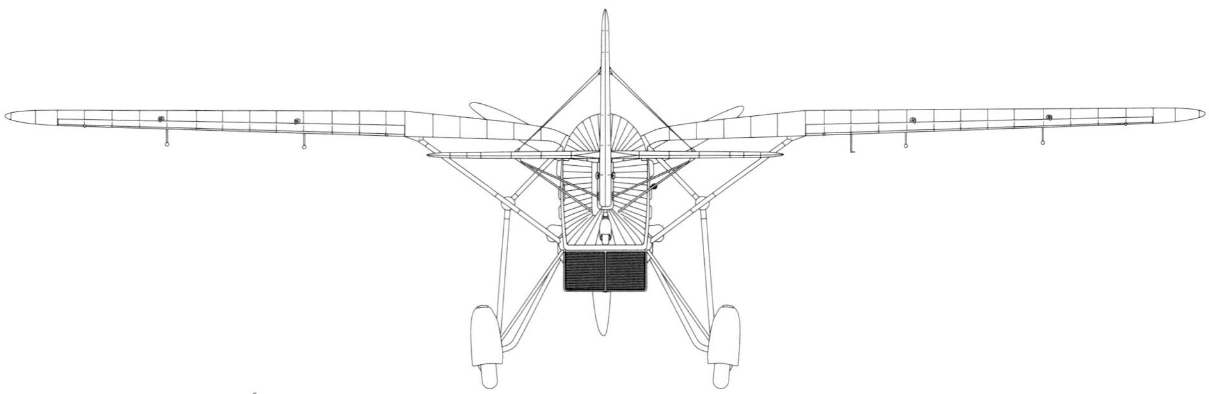

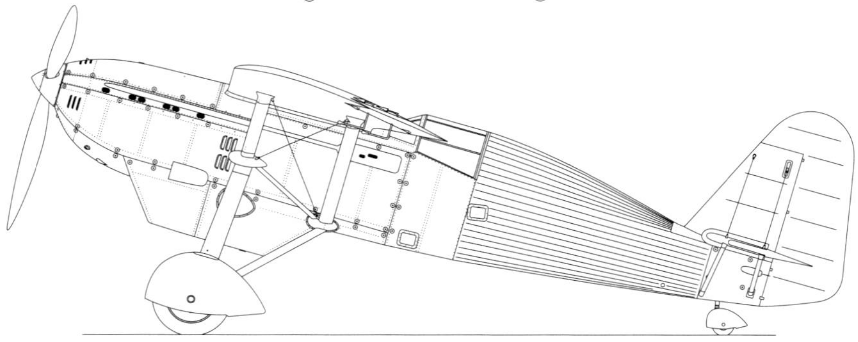

1m 2m

SCALE 1:72

Drawings: Branislav Mirkov, 2019

# IKARUS IK-2

1st PROTOTYPE

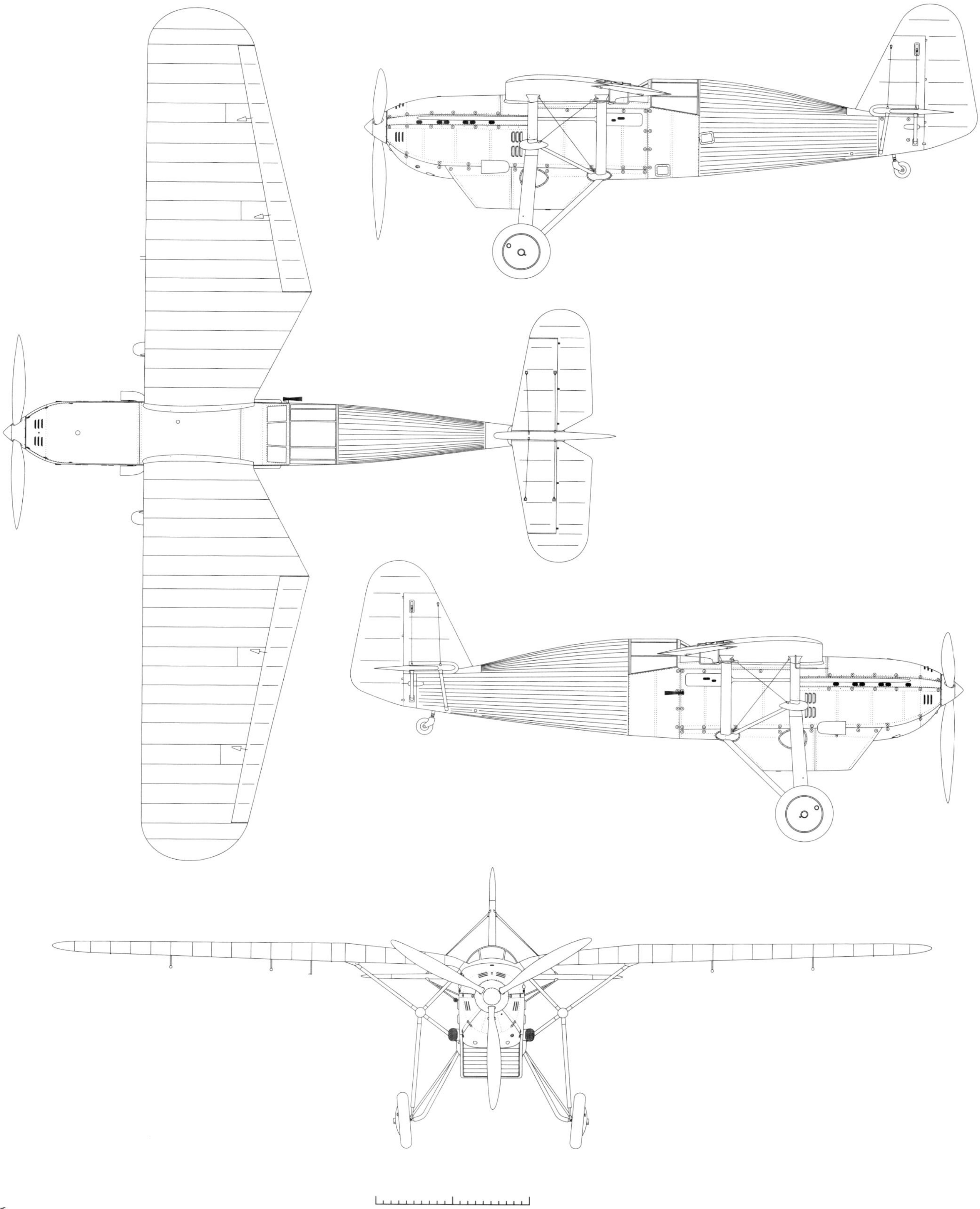


Drawings: Branislav Mirkov, 2019

# IKARUS IK-2

1st PROTOTYPE

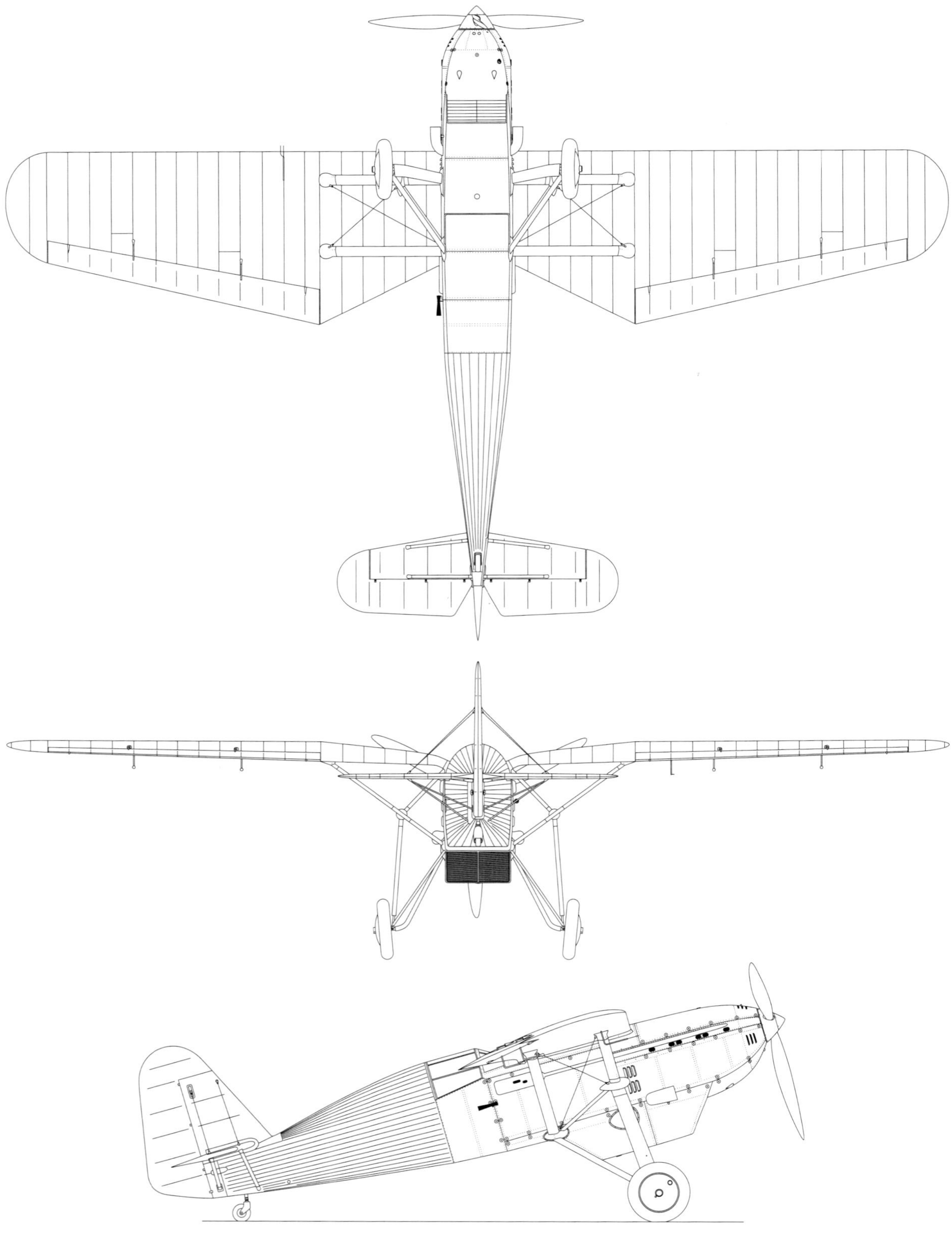

1m 2m

SCALE 1:72

KAGERO

Drawings: Branislav Mirkov, 2019

# IKARUS IK-2

CONSTRUCTION MATERIALS

Aluminium    Fabric

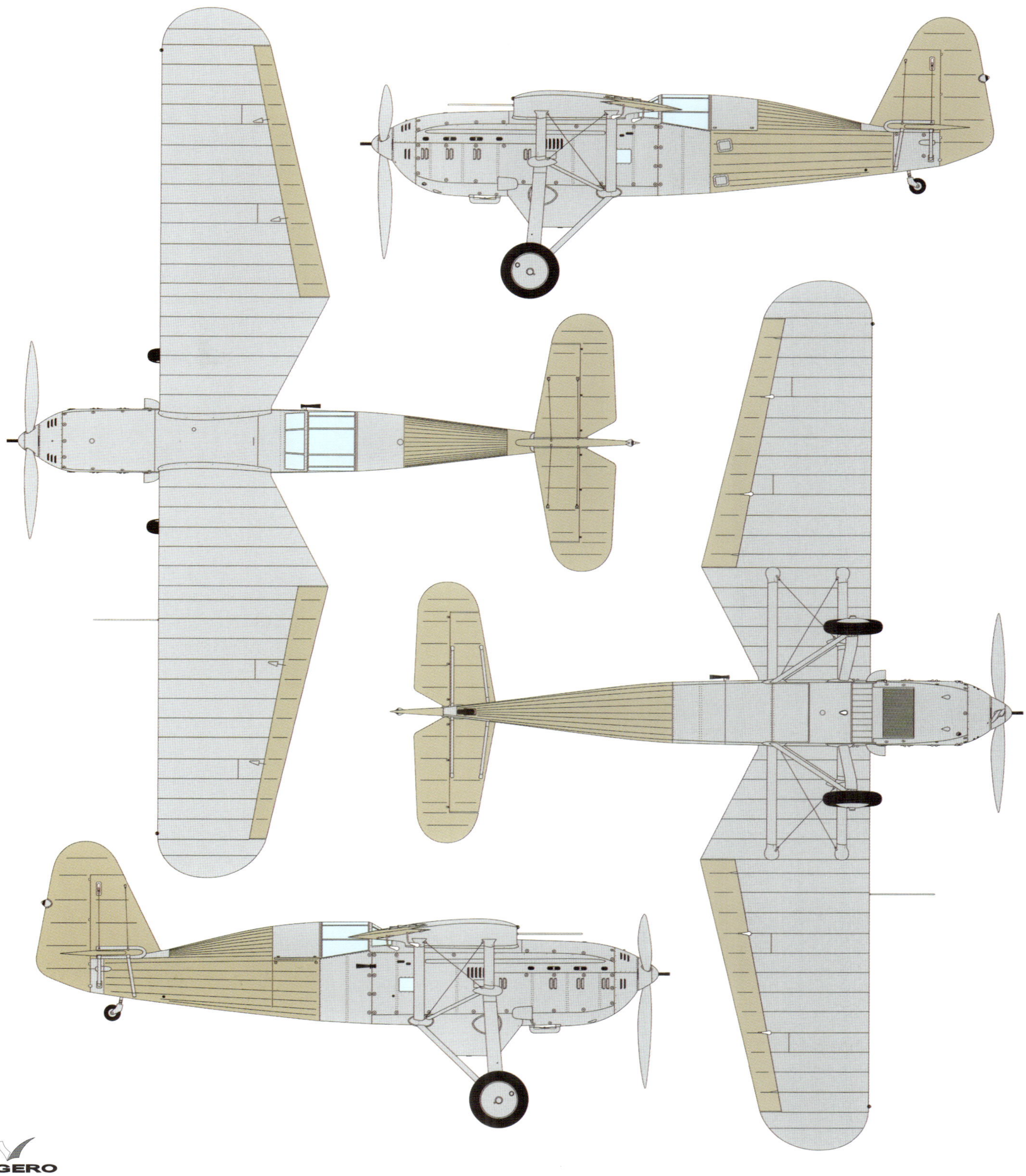

3D illustrations: Branislav Mirkov

Port view of IK-2 showing fuselage and wing structure along with the engine, fuel tanks and cockpit arrangement.

Starboard view of IK-2 basic structure. Note fuel tanks stacked between the engine and the cockpit.

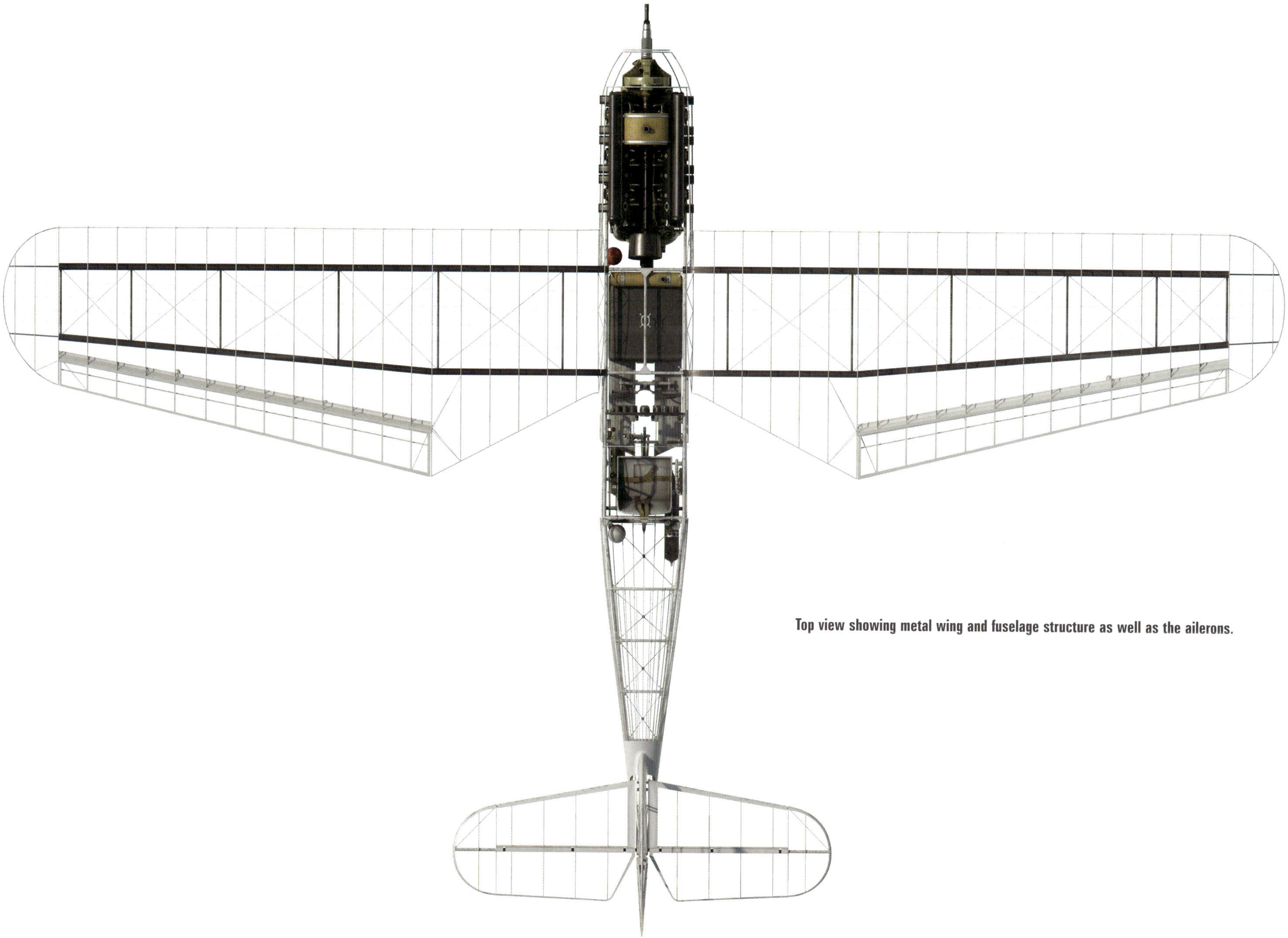

Top view showing metal wing and fuselage structure as well as the ailerons.

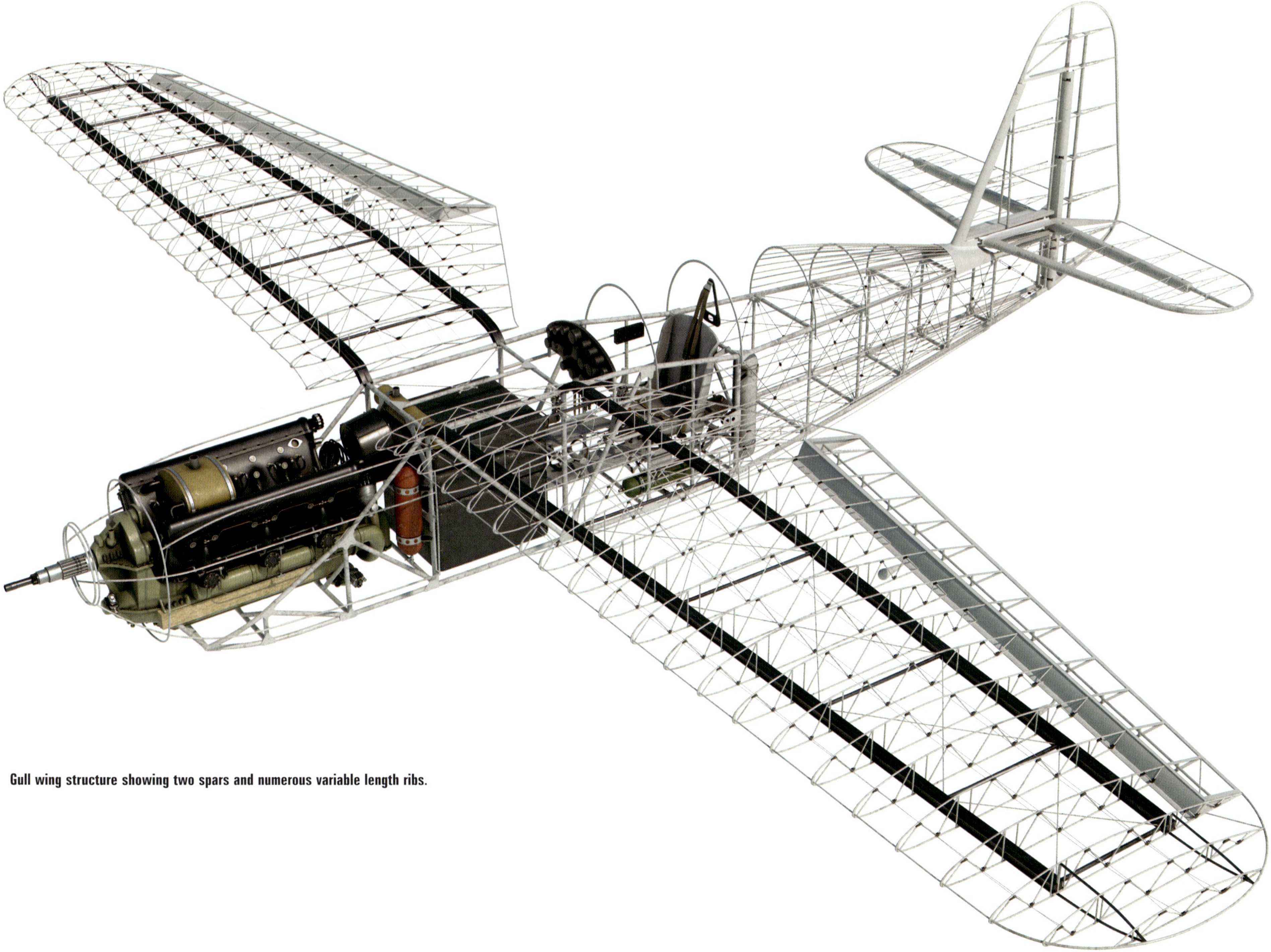

Gull wing structure showing two spars and numerous variable length ribs.

Front view showing detail of the engine within the fuselage frame.

Close up of the engine with the engine cylinders, oil and cooling tanks, and cannon installation.

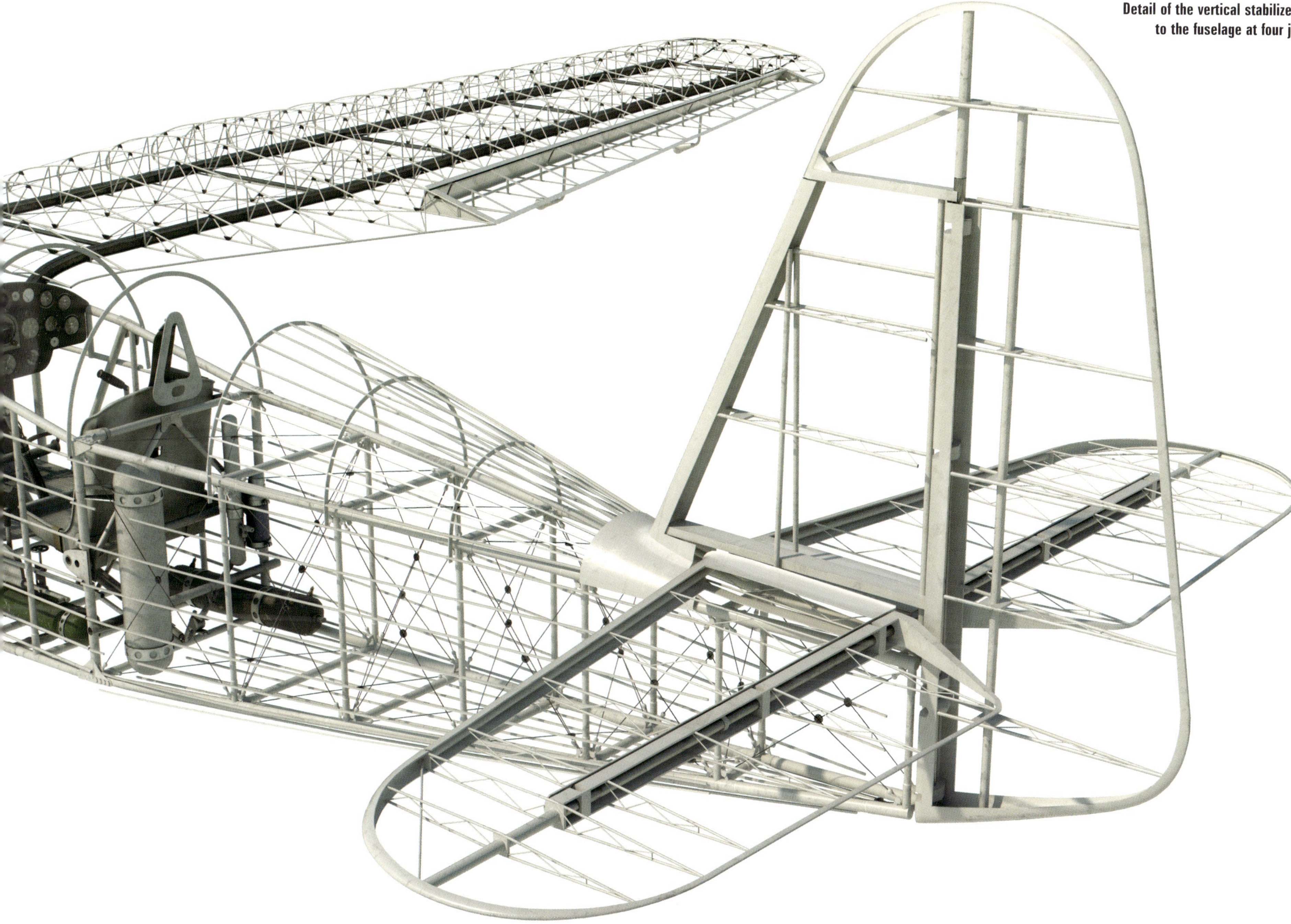

Detail of the vertical stabilizer, which were bolted to the fuselage at four junction points.

Aft view of IK-2 structure.

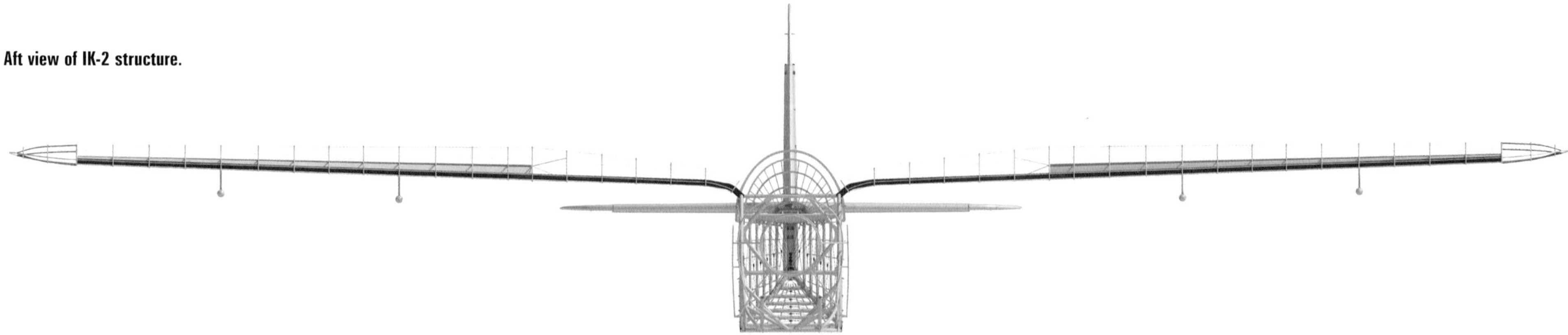

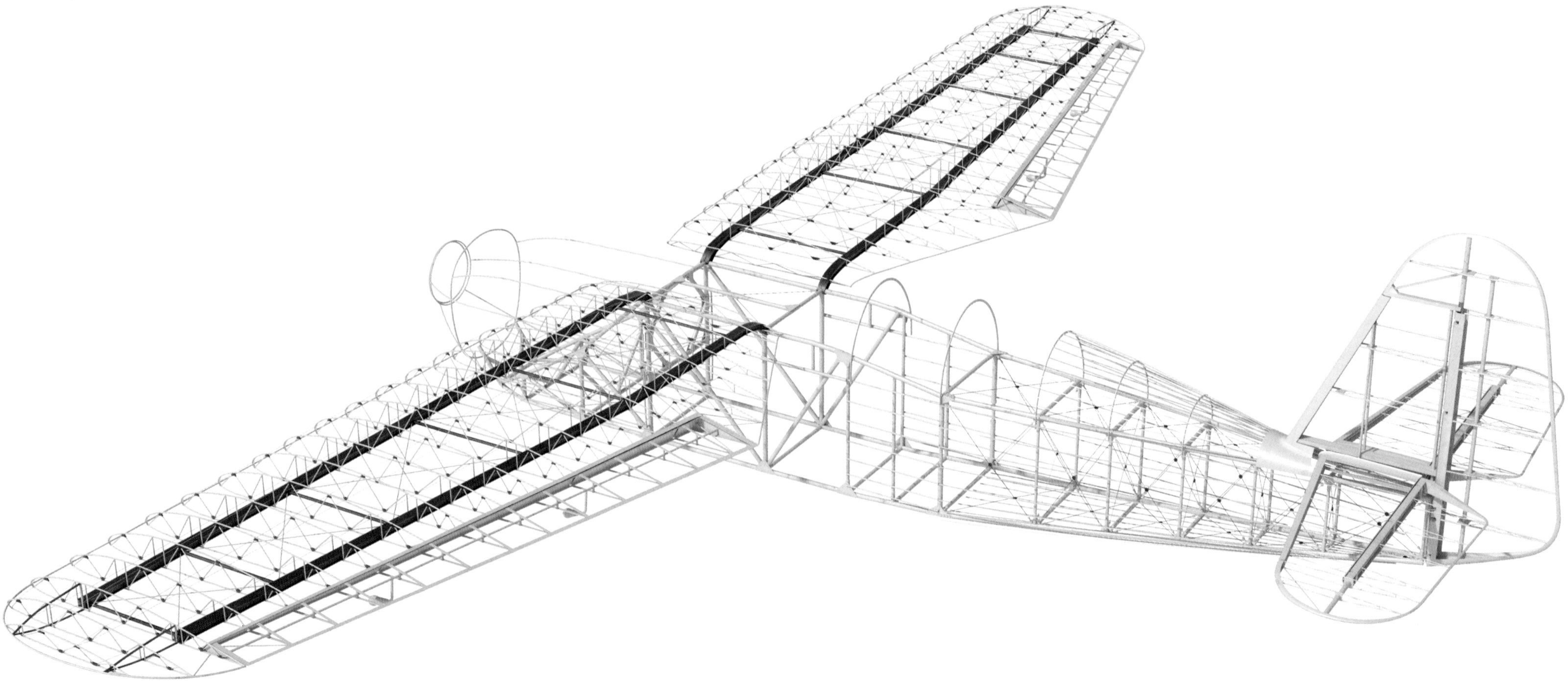

IK-2 tubular fuselage structure and metal wings are clearly visible.

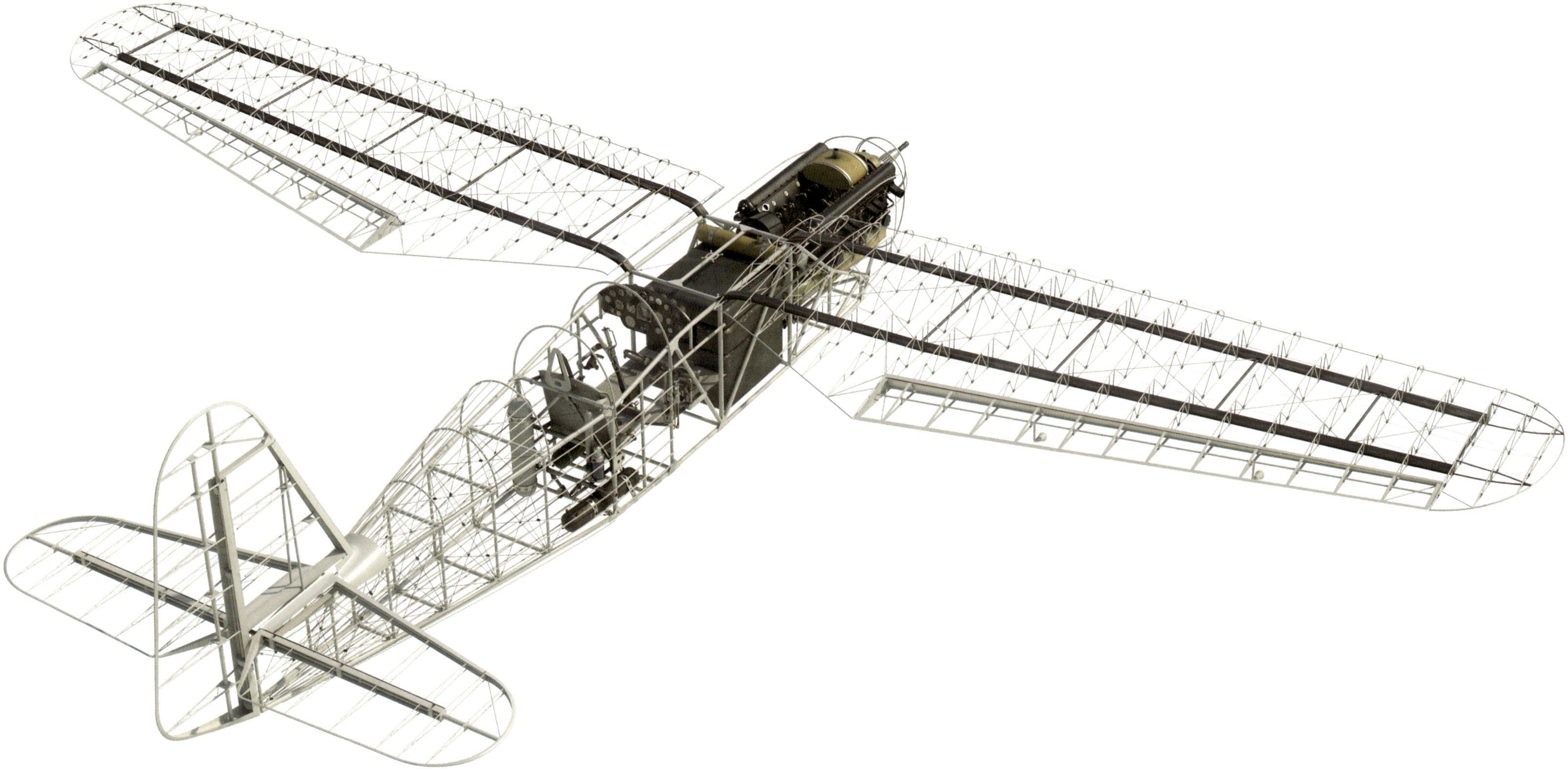

Large ailerons dominate the wing trailing edge.

Detail of construction around Czechoslovak built Avia Hispano-Suiza HS 12YCrs engine.

IK-2 Instrument panel.

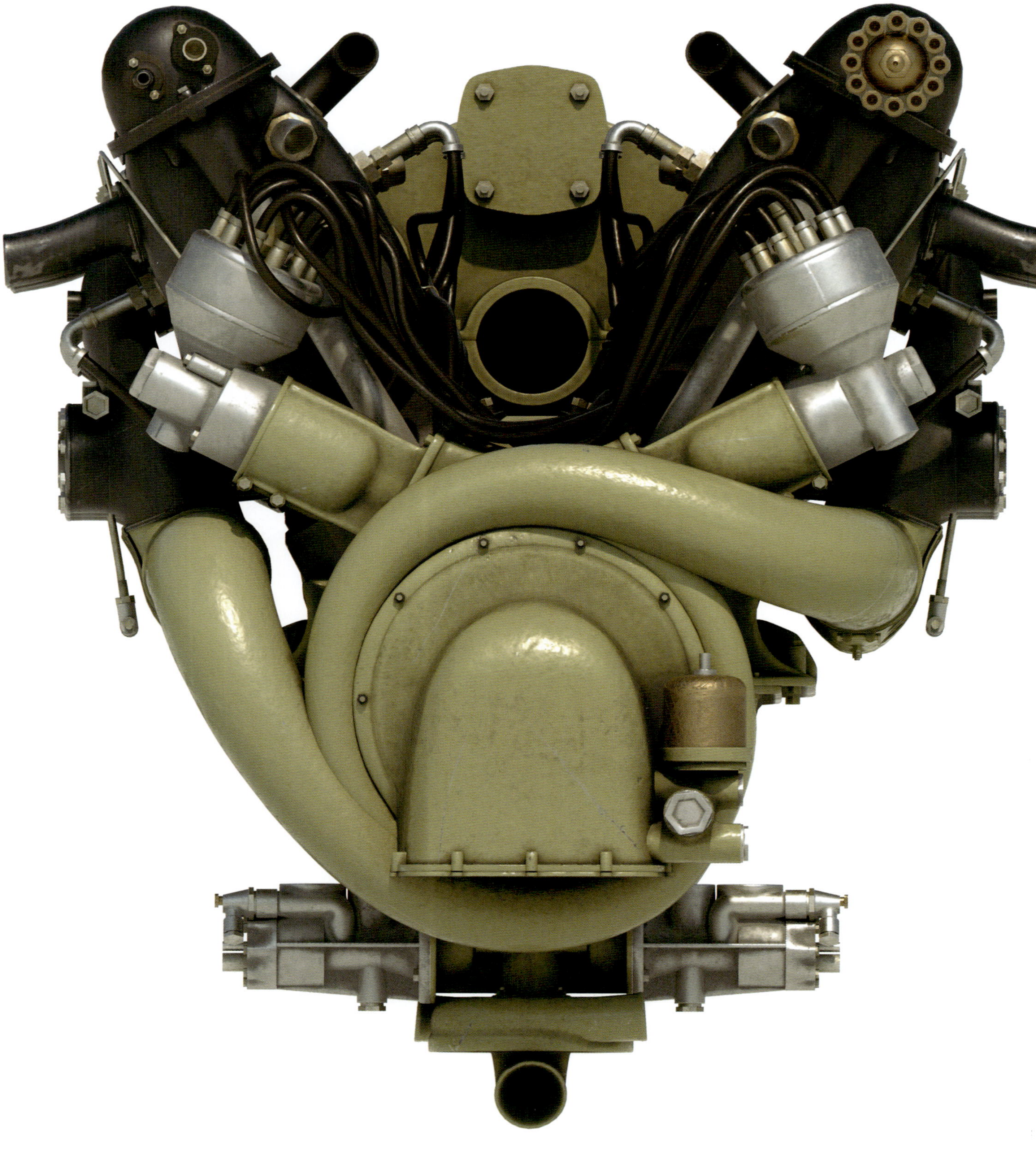

Aft view of the engine.

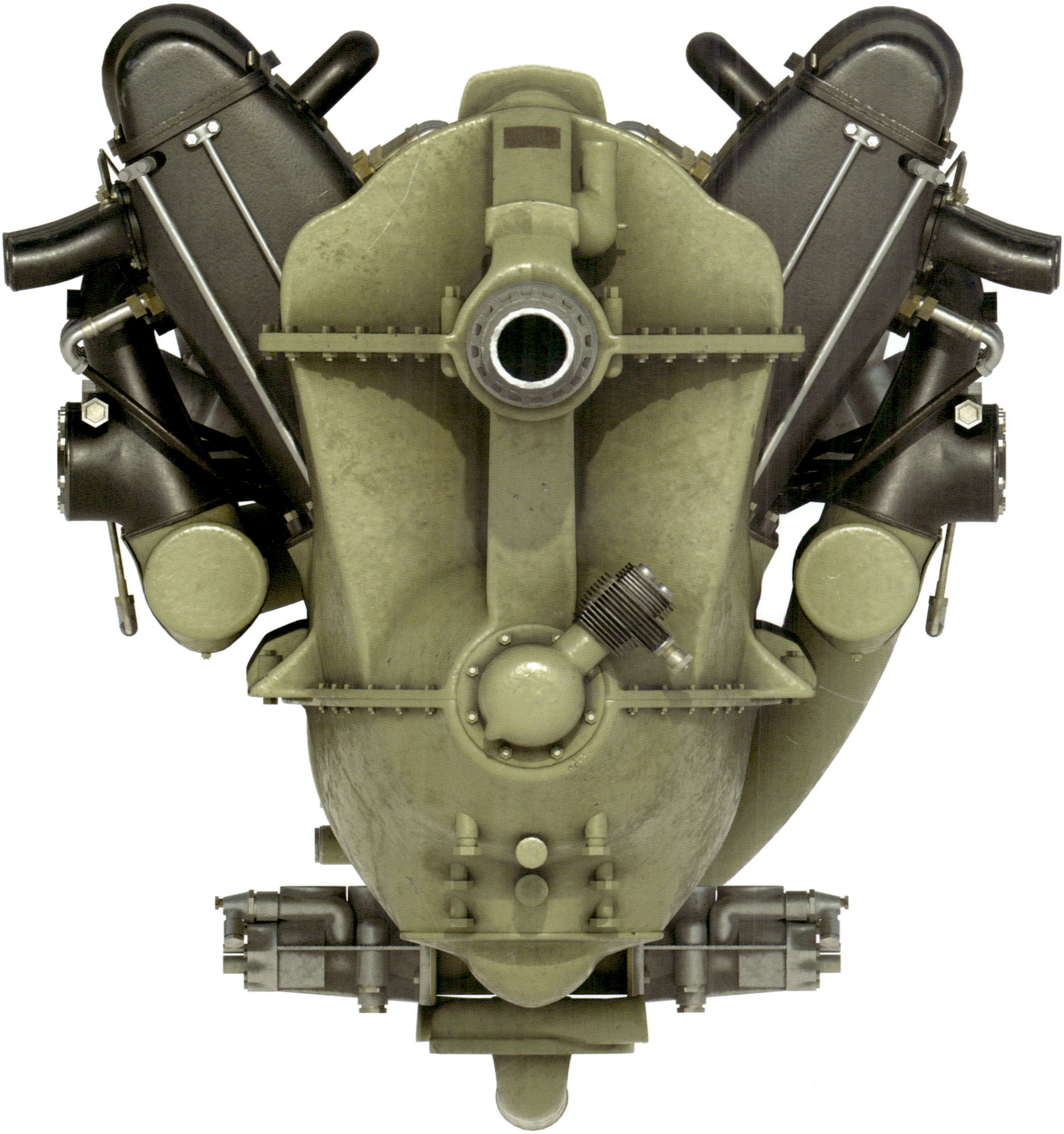

Front view showing the cannon muzzle.

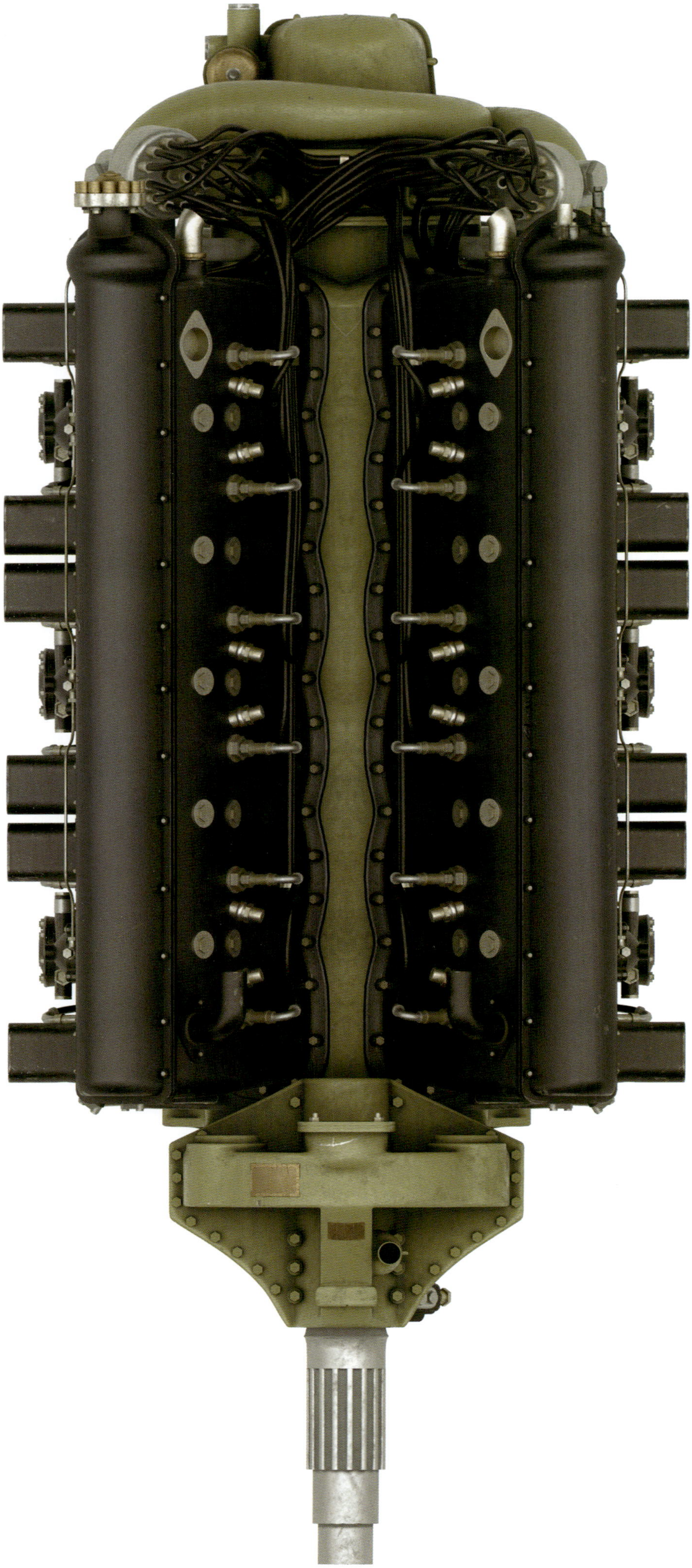

Engine top view.

Port view of the engine. Note the six cylinder exhausts.

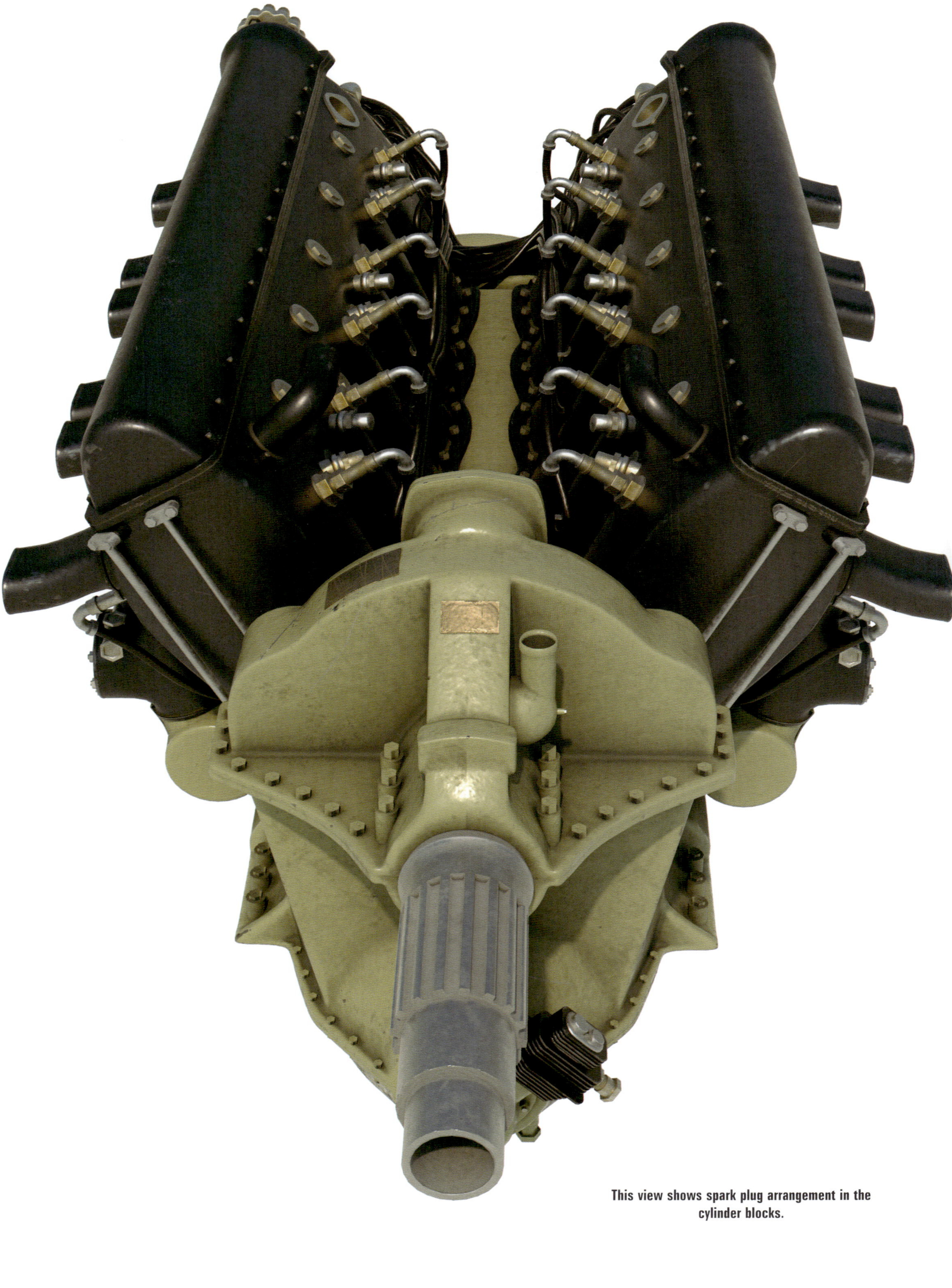

This view shows spark plug arrangement in the cylinder blocks.

Aft view with spark plug distributor caps.

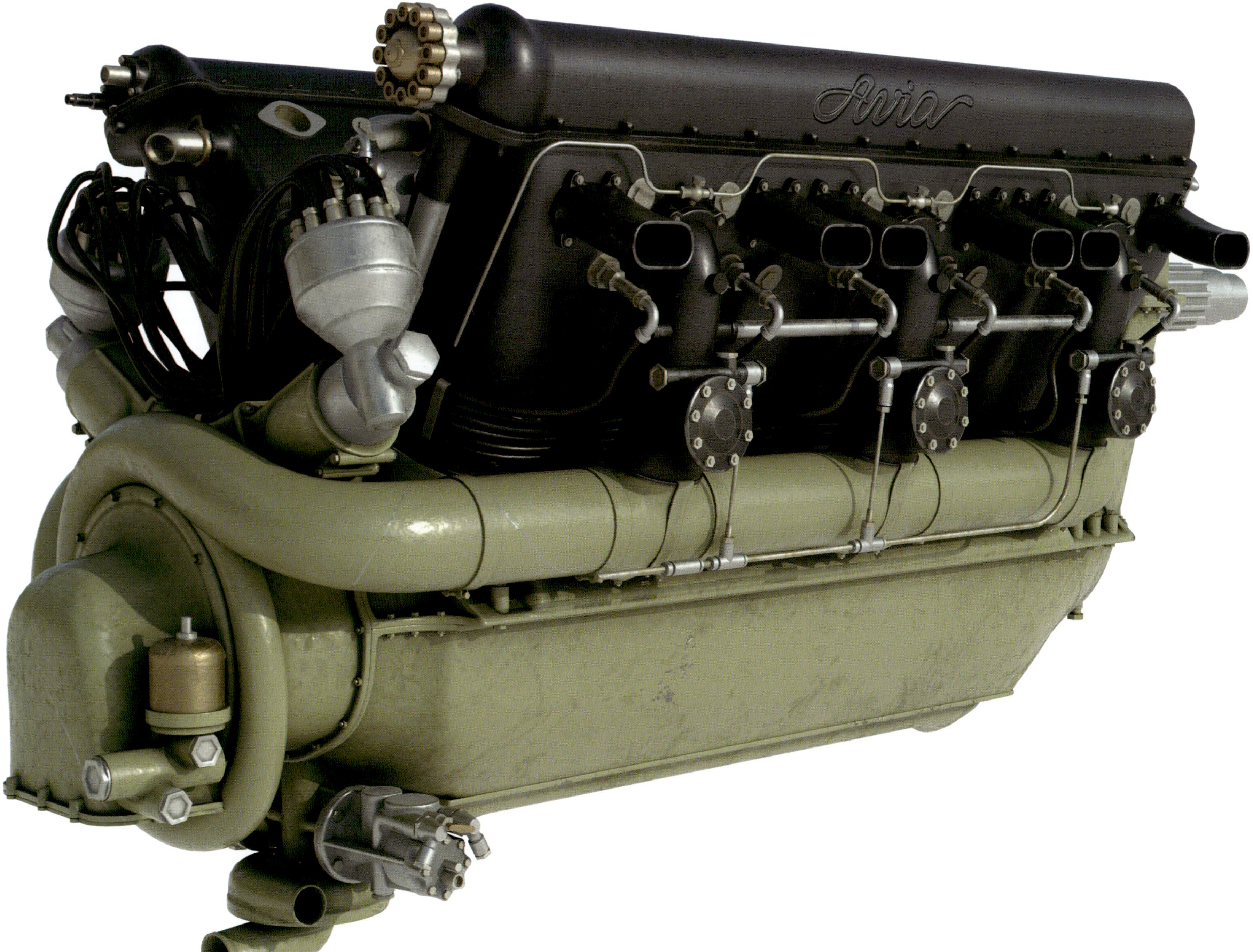


Aft view showing the supercharger arrangement.

Cylinder block had a cast Avia factory logo.

HS 12YCrs engine with 20mm HS9 cannon installed.

Note that the cannon muzzle protruded past the propeller crown wheel.

Aft engine view showing the supercharger and the cannon ammo drum arrangement.

Side view of the engine and cannon arrangement.

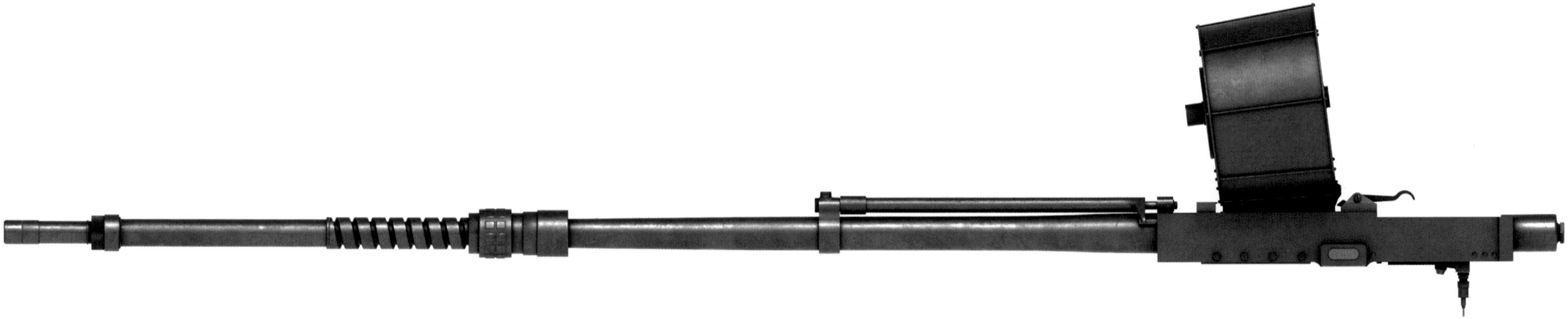

Side view of 20 mm HS9 cannon.

Cannon top view.

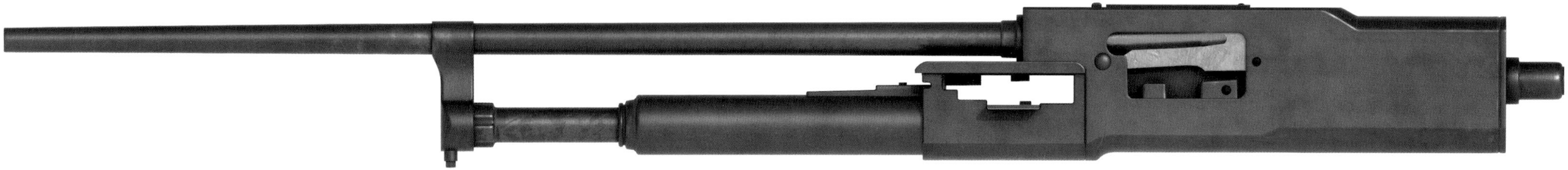

Saint Étienne Darne M.30 7.7 mm machine gun port view.

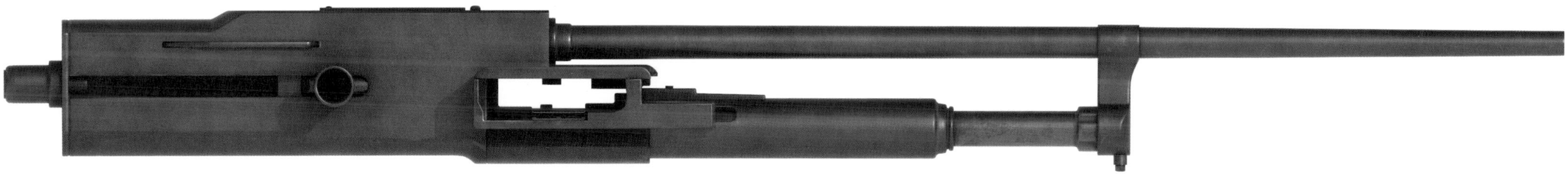

Saint Étienne Darne M.30 7.7 mm machine gun starboard view.

**Cannon ammo drum stored with 60 incendiary and tracer rounds.**

Detail view of the cannon ammo drum front.

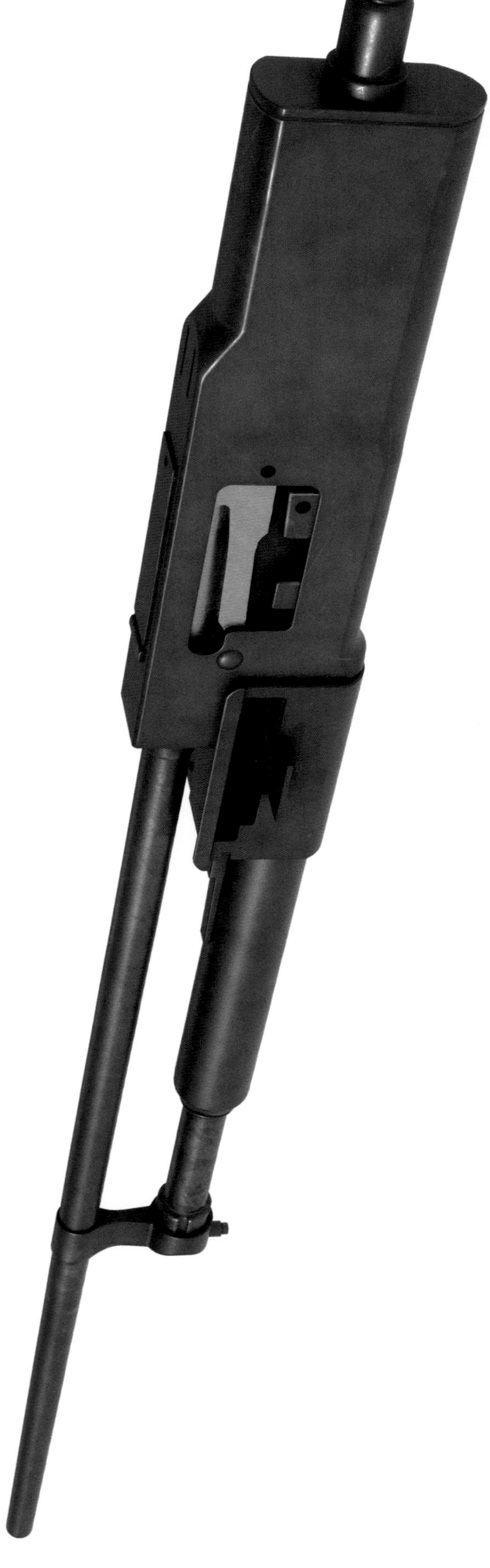

M.30 machine gun detail view.

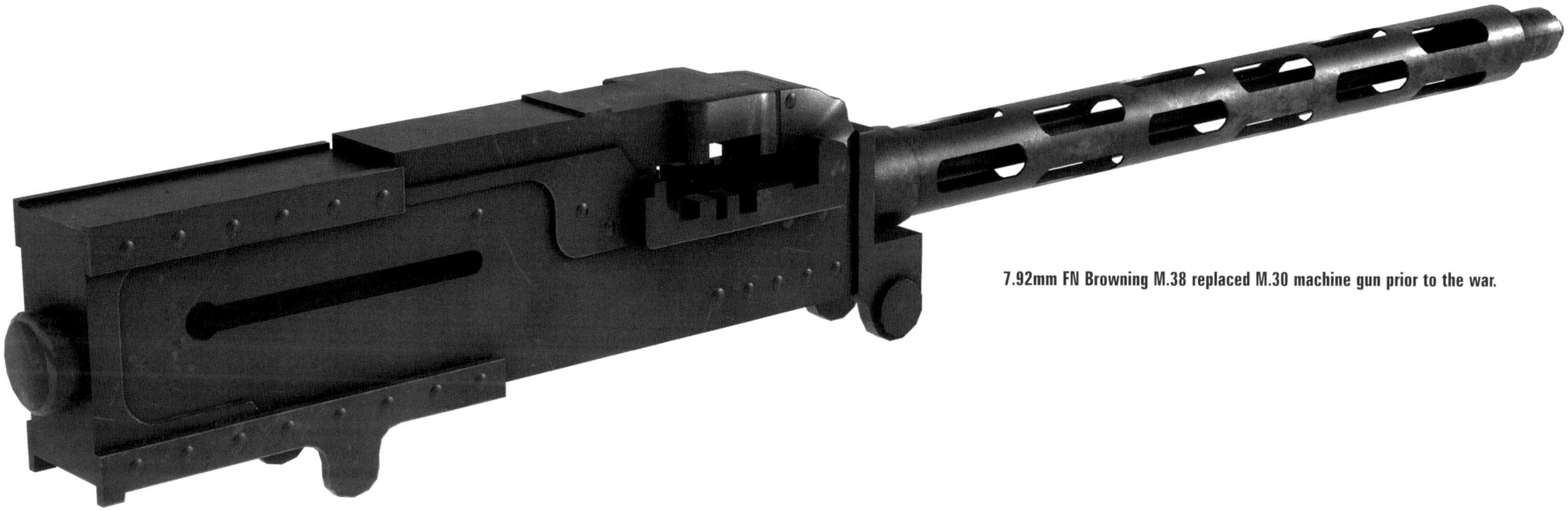

7.92mm FN Browning M.38 replaced M.30 machine gun prior to the war.

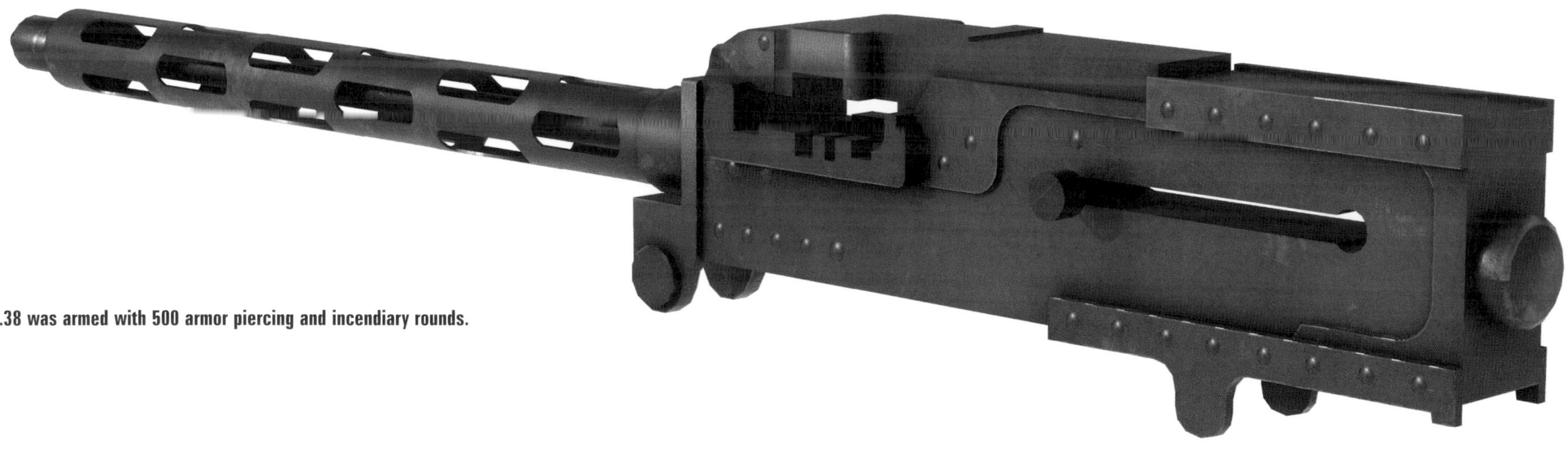

M.38 was armed with 500 armor piercing and incendiary rounds.

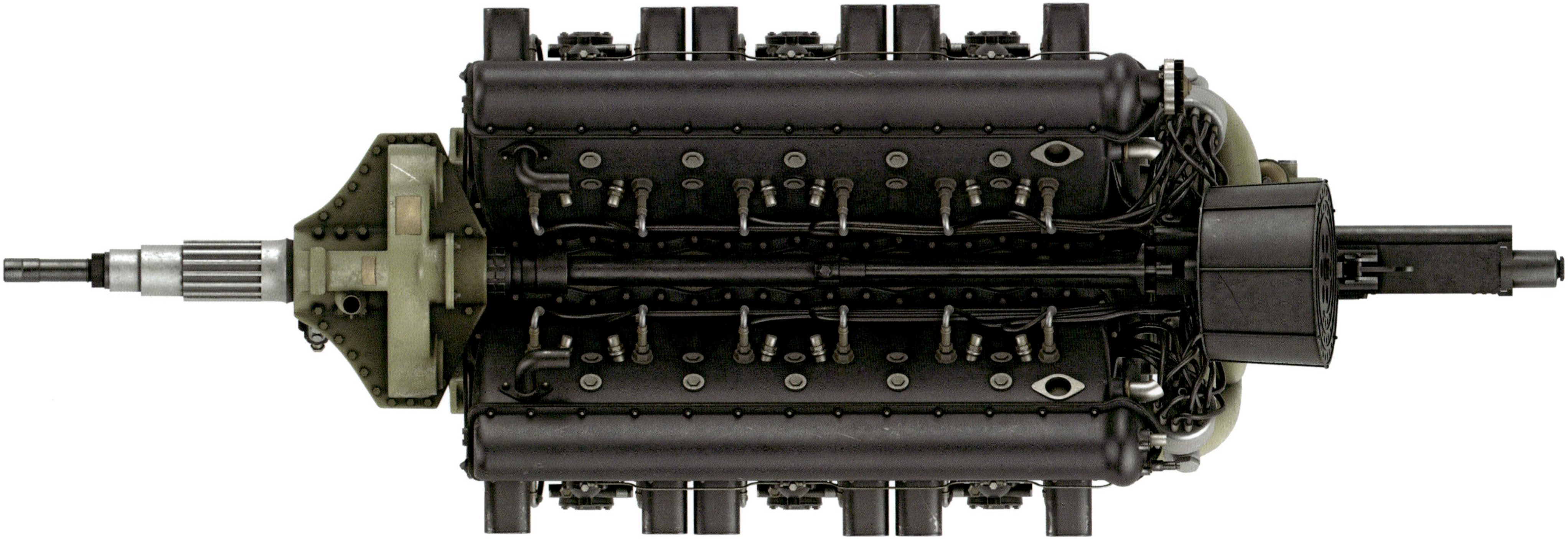

Engine top view with cannon arrangement.

IK-L1 front view.

IK-L1 aft view.

IK-L1 with two large “Kosovo cross” insignia.

Aft view shows the IK-L1 landing gear arrangement.

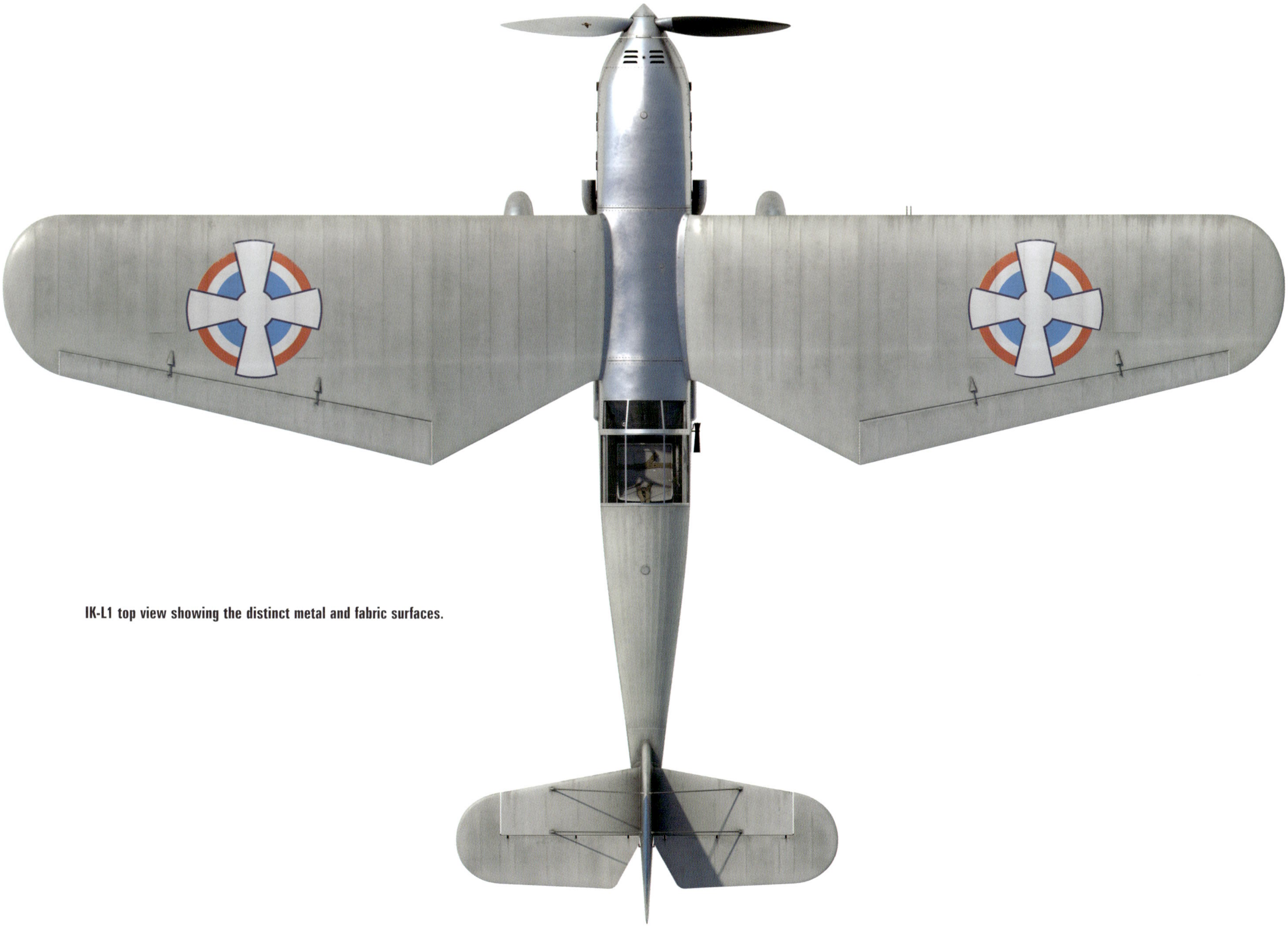

IK-L1 top view showing the distinct metal and fabric surfaces.

IK-L1 undersize view.

Side view showing the distinct metal and fabric surfaces. The tail had a large state flag on the rudder.

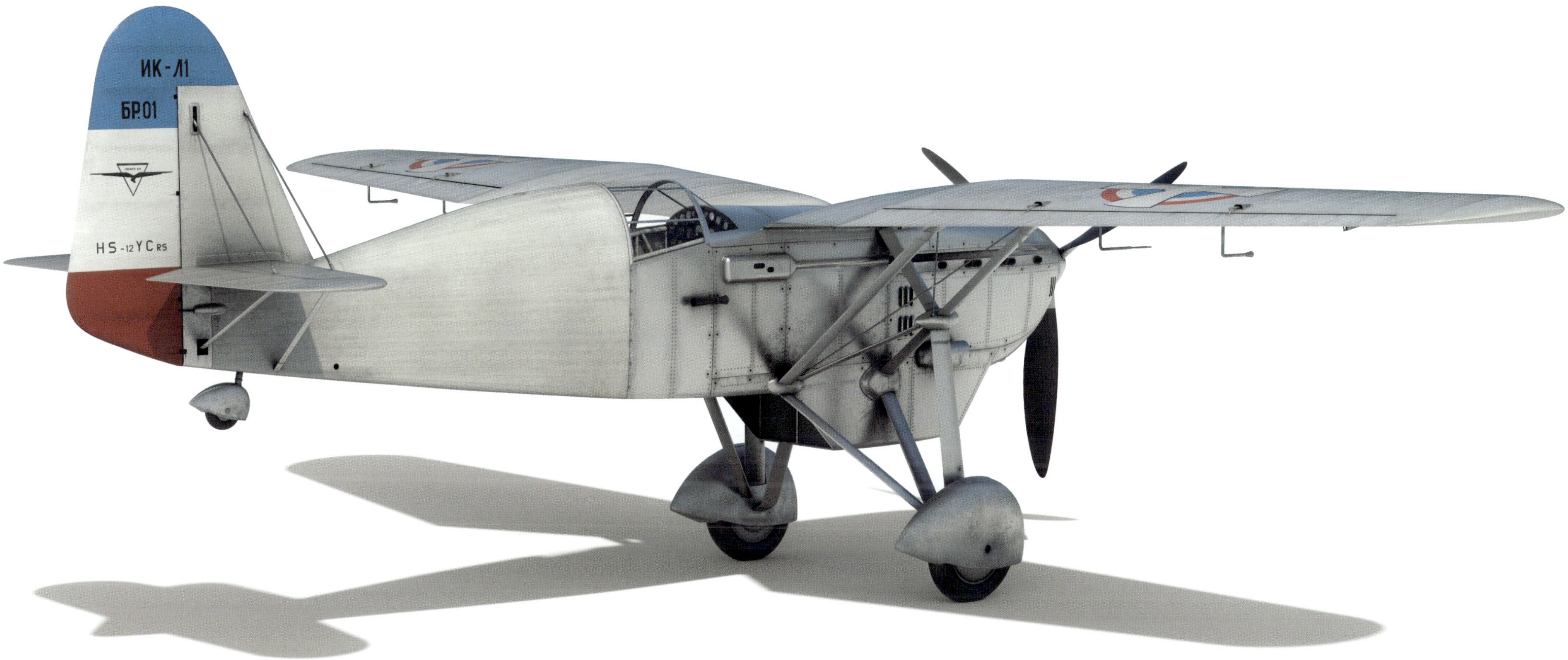


Rudder carried airplane type, number and engine inscriptions along with the factory logo.

IK-L1 with tail up in take off position.

IK-L1 starboard view.

Large radiator was prominent below the IK-L1 fuselage. Note no wheel spats.

IK-L1 without the wheel spats.

**IK-L1 with the wheel spats.**

**IK-L1 front view with wheel spats.**

Front view showing the metal Messier propeller.

IK-2 No2 aft view. Note the angle of the landing gear tires.

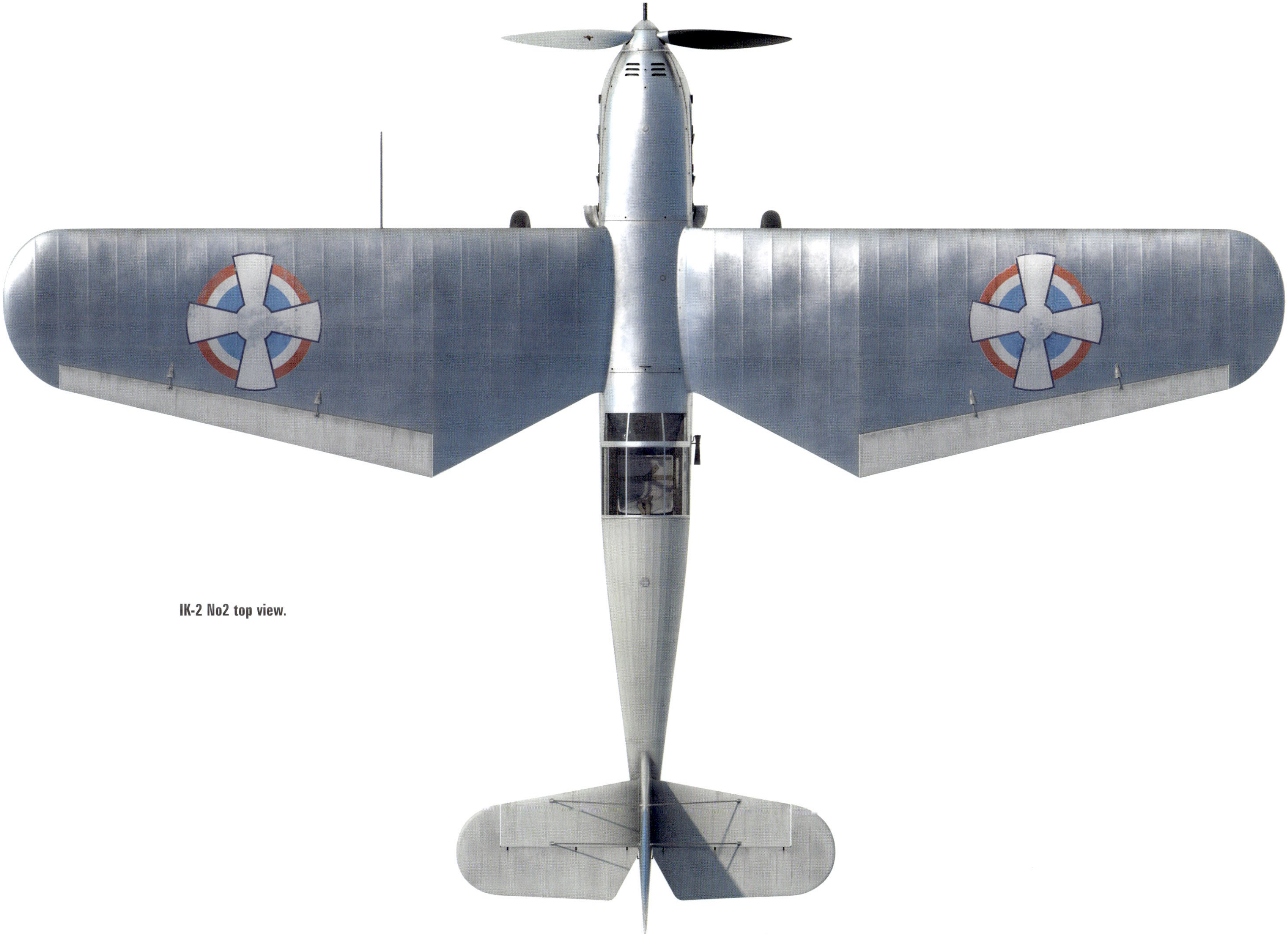

IK-2 No2 top view.

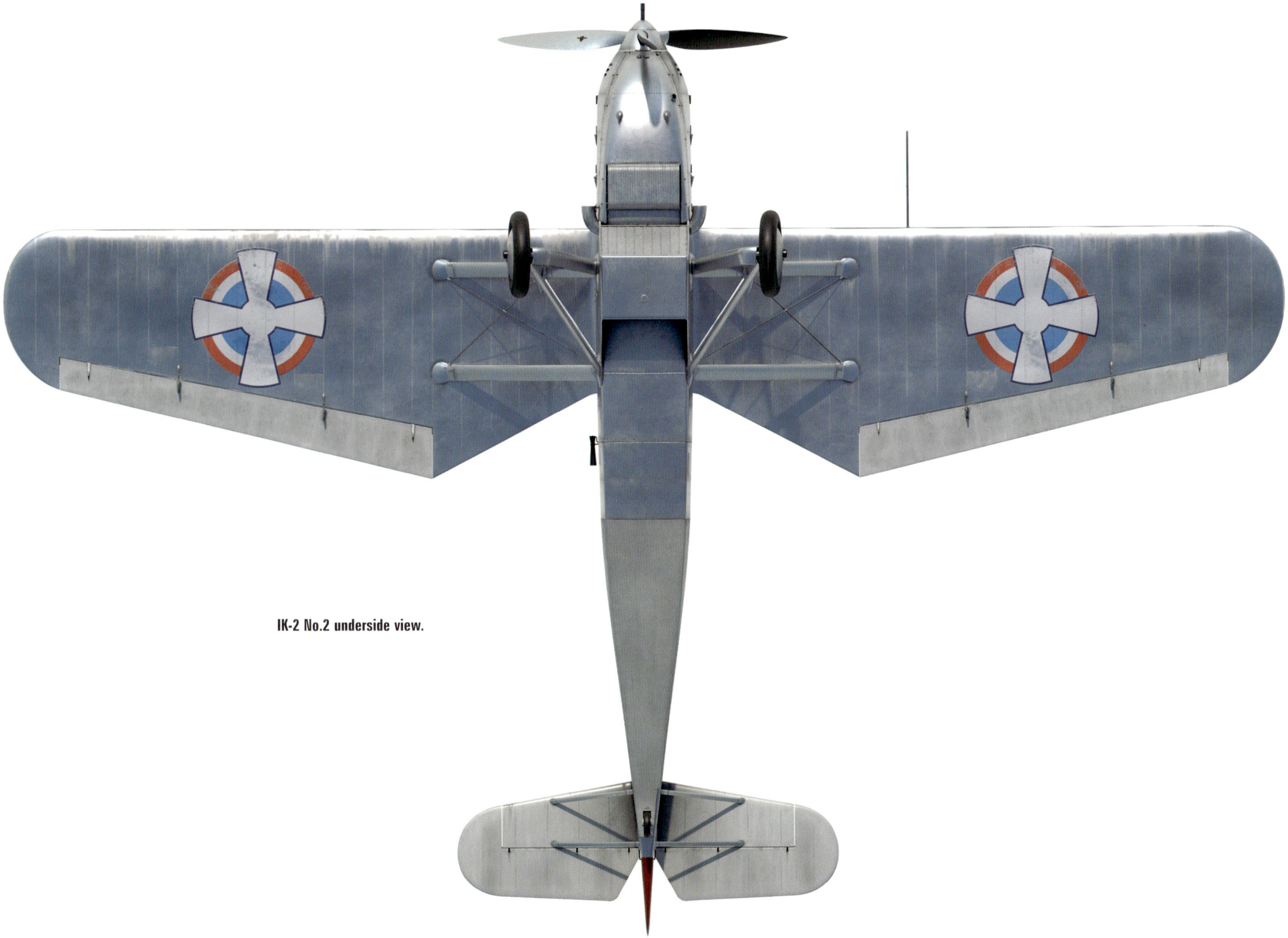

IK-2 No.2 underside view.

IK-2 No.2 with smaller radiator beneath the fuselage.

IK-2 No.2 in take off configuration.

IK-2 No.2 was painted overall silver dope with exception of the metal surfaces which remained in natural aluminum.

IK-2 No.2 aft view showing rudder inscriptions.

IK-2 Br.01 front view.

IK-2 Br.01 aft view.

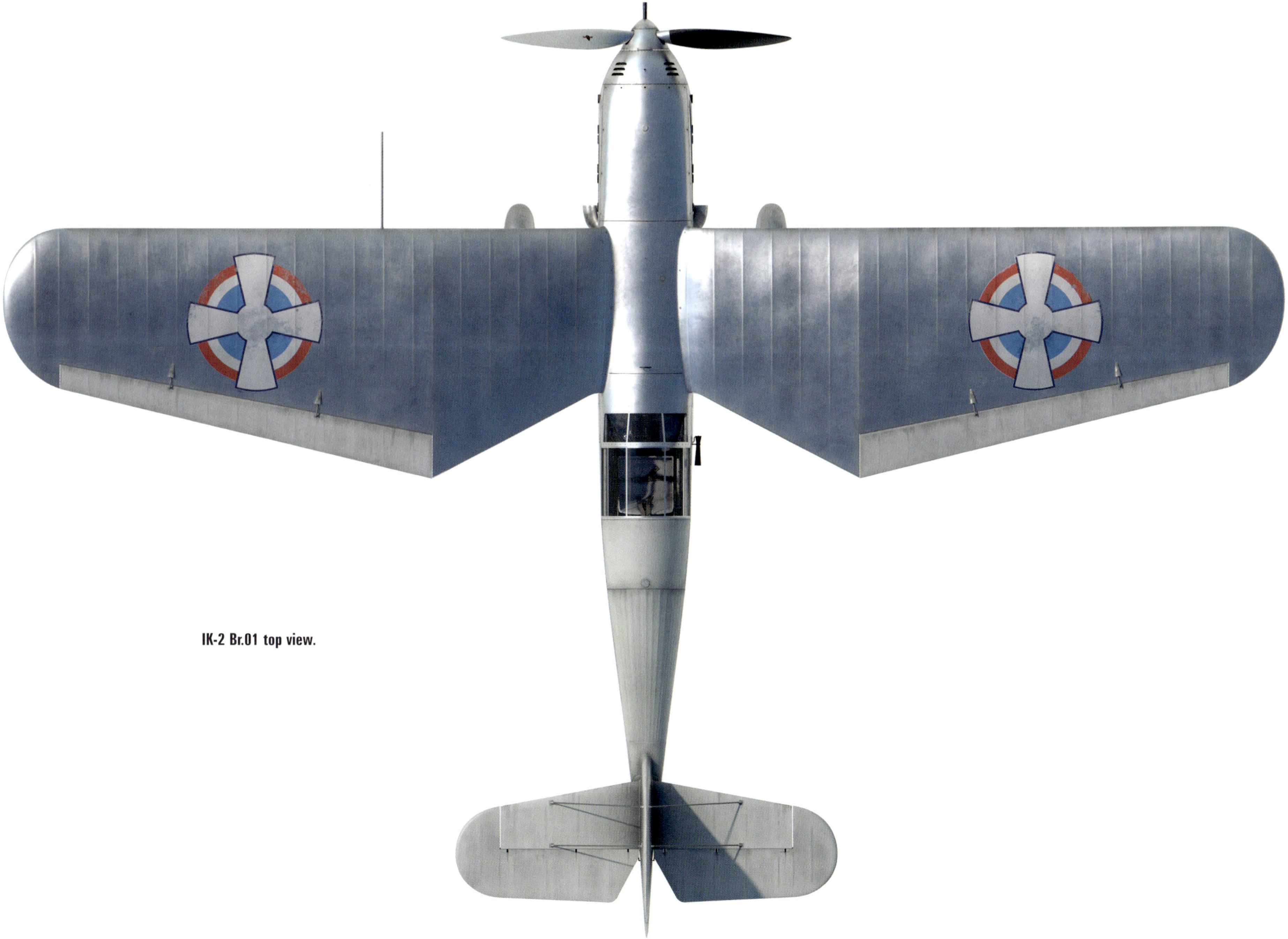

IK-2 Br.01 top view.

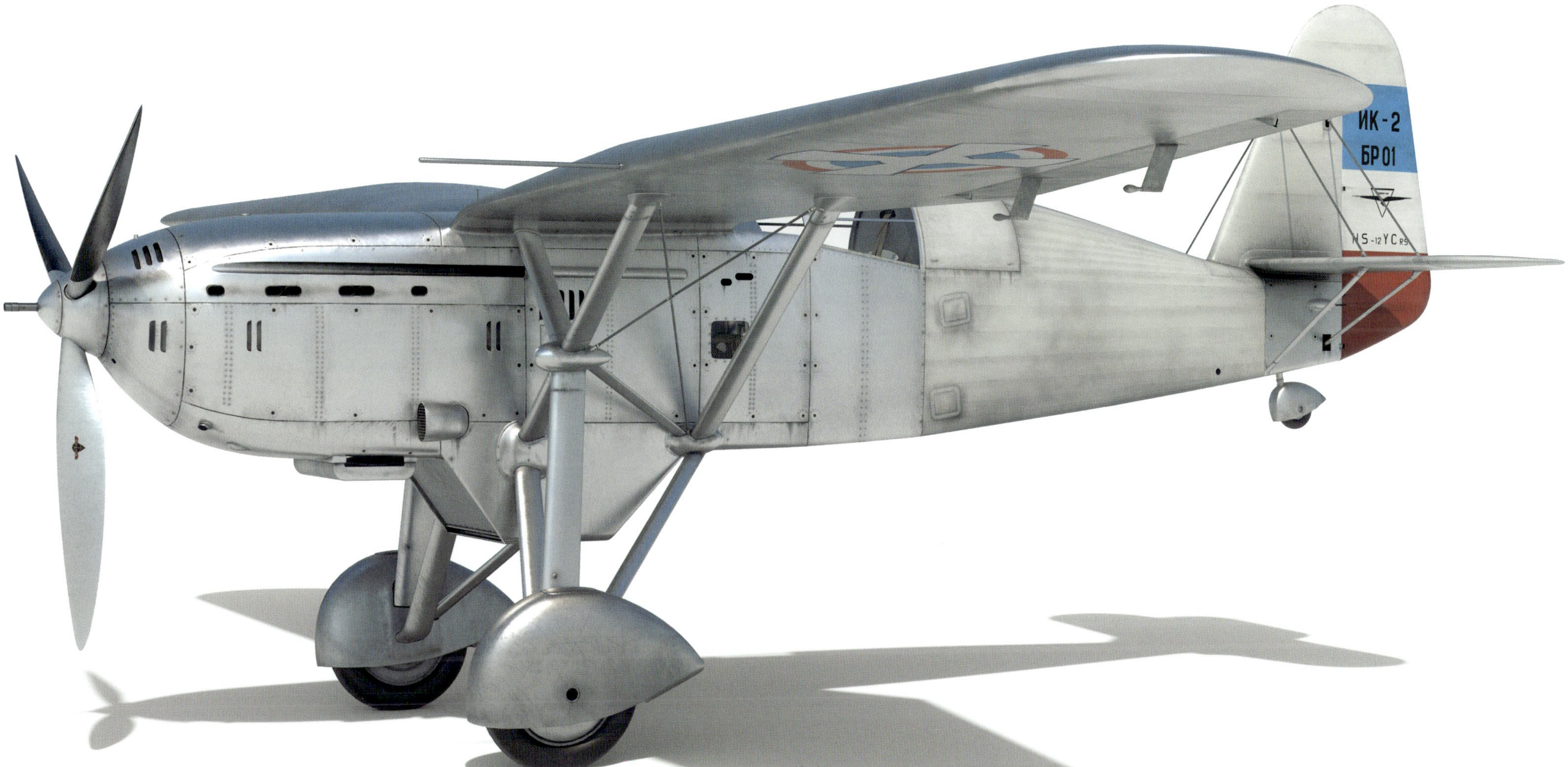


IK-2 Br.01 in take off arrangement.

IK-2 Br.01 with revised painting of the rudder.

Note the HS9 cannon muzzle protruding past the propeller hub.

IK-2 Br.01 aft view showing the horizontal stabilizer bracing cables.

IK-2 BR.2110 front view.

IK-2 BR.2110 aft view.

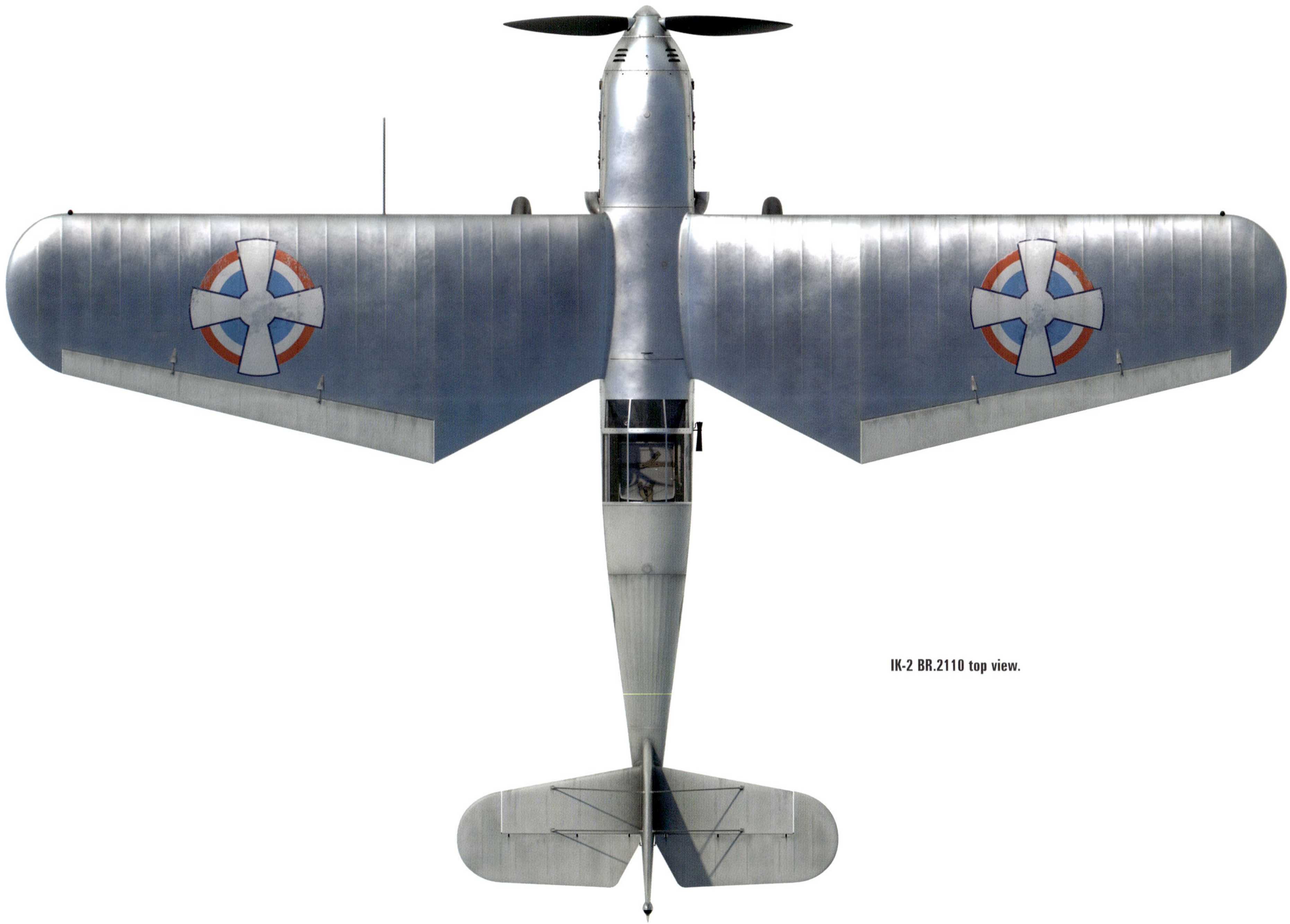

IK-2 BR.2110 top view.

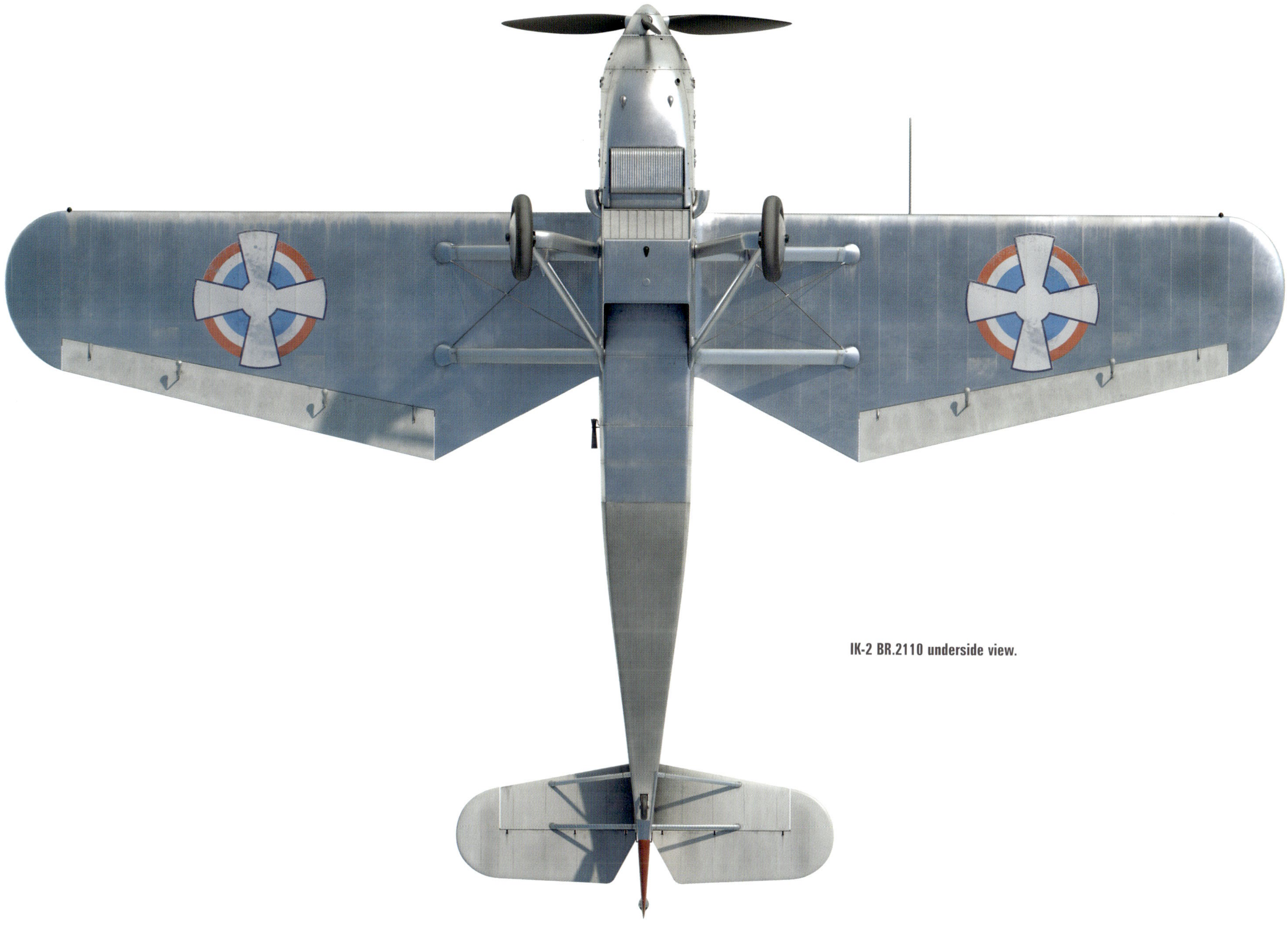

IK-2 BR.2110 underside view.

IK-2 BR.2110 carried large black number 2 on the fuselage.

IK-2 BR.2110 in take off configuration.

IK-2 BR.2110 had two large "Kosovo cross" insignia beneath the wings.

Two "Kosovo cross" insignia were applied on top of the wings as well.

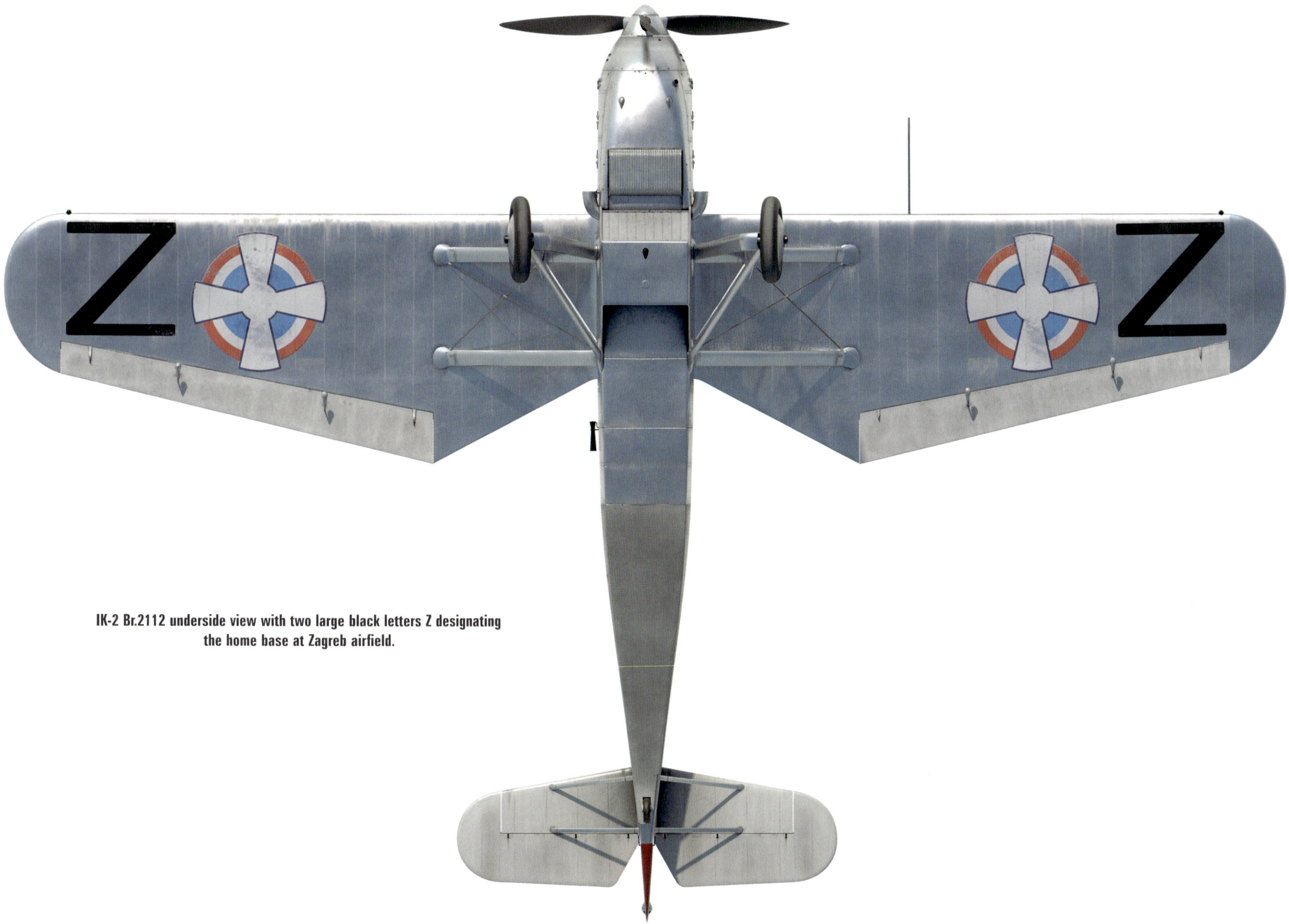

IK-2 Br.2112 underside view with two large black letters Z designating the home base at Zagreb airfield.

IK-2 Br.2112 carried large black number 4 on the fuselage.

IK-2 Br.2112 in take off configuration.

IK-2 Br.2112 showing the large black letter Z towards the wing tips.

Front view of IK-2 No.2104.

Aft view of IK-2 No.2104.

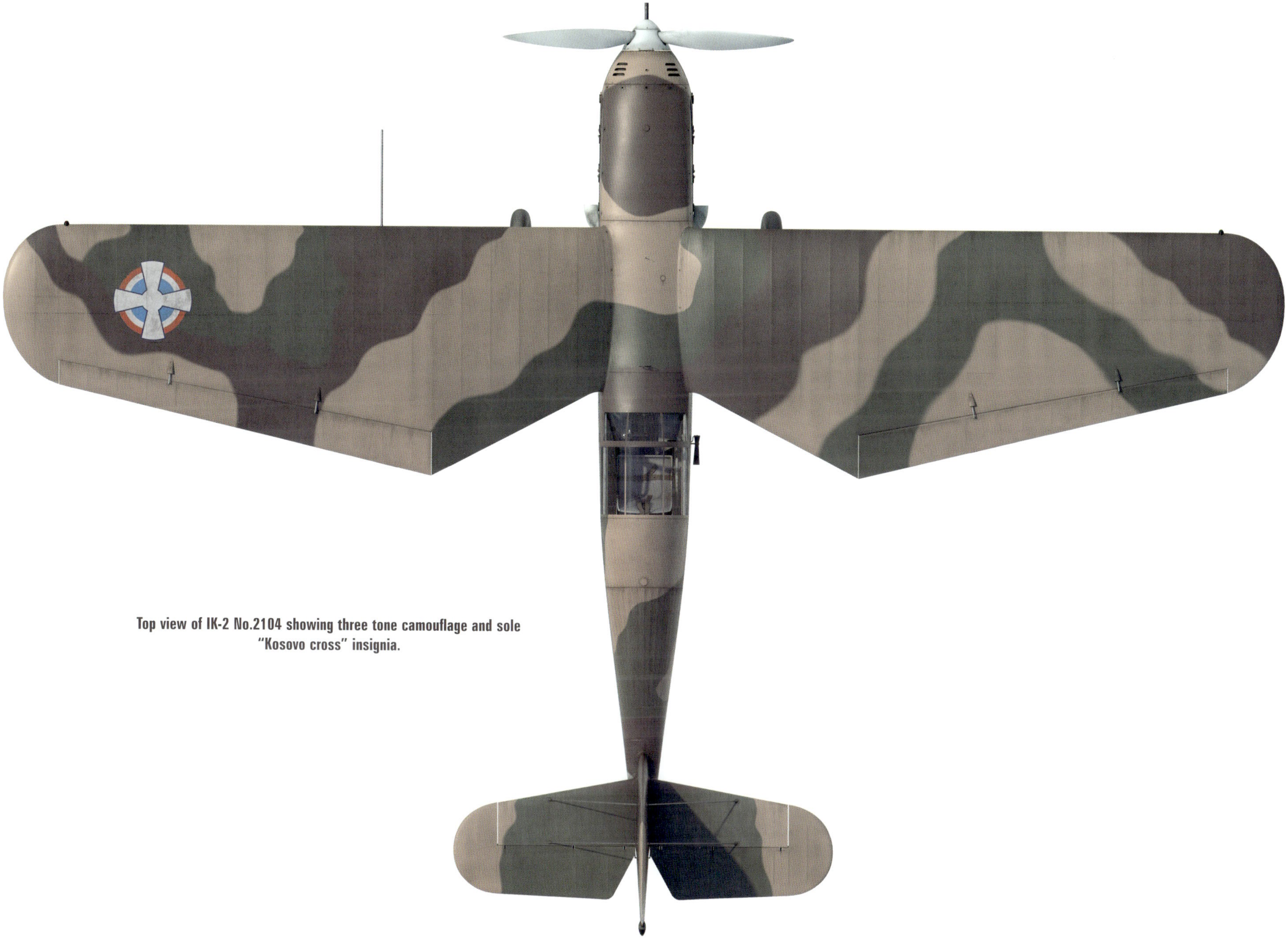

Top view of IK-2 No.2104 showing three tone camouflage and sole "Kosovo cross" insignia.

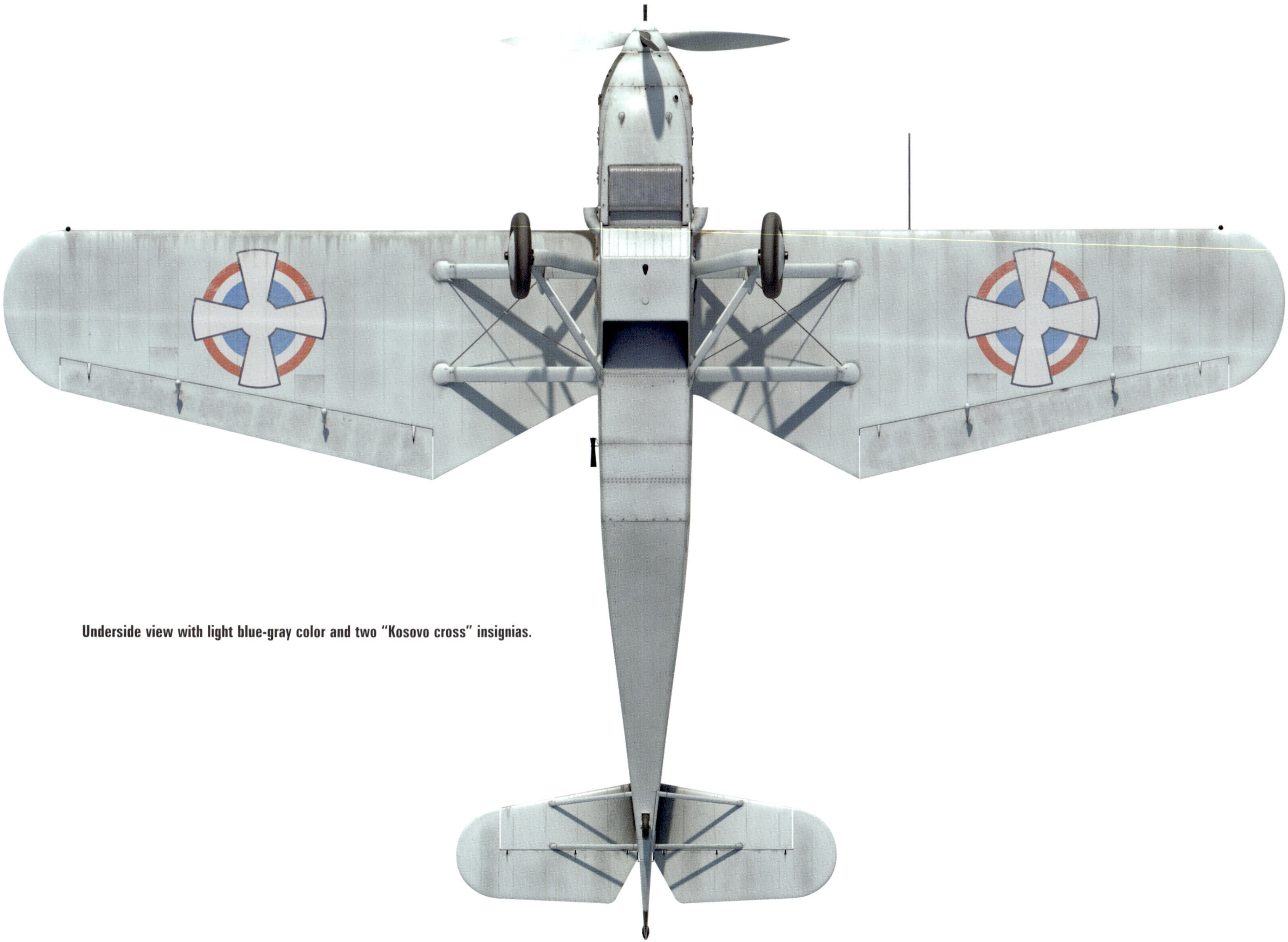

Underside view with light blue-gray color and two "Kosovo cross" insignias.

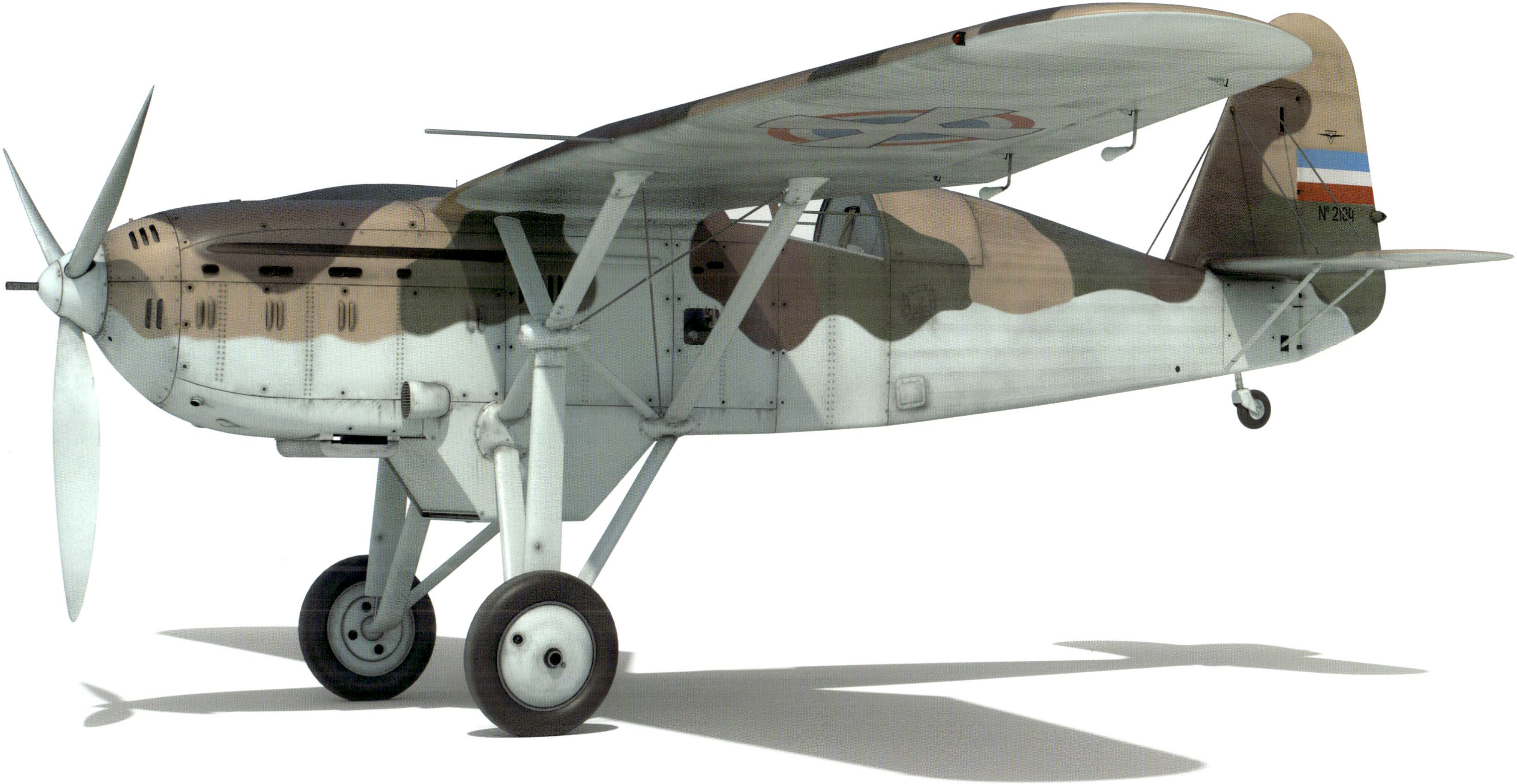


IK-2 No.2104 in take off configuration,

IK-2 No.2104 aft view showing "war flag" on the rudder, factory logo and No.2104.

Front view showing interesting color demarcation on the fuselage.

Aft view of IK-2 No.2104.

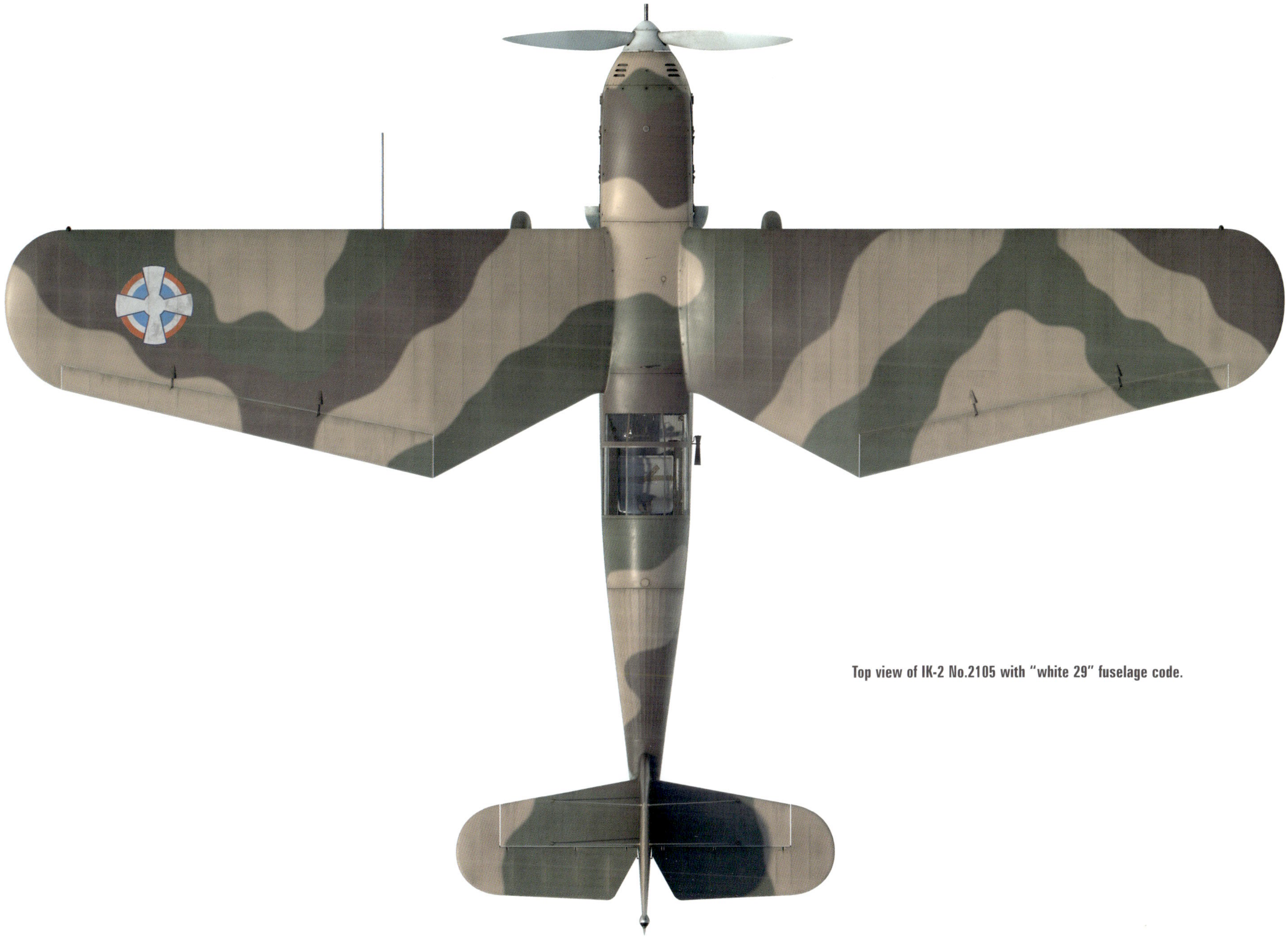

Top view of IK-2 No.2105 with "white 29" fuselage code.

IK-2 No.2105 in take off configuration.

IK-2 No.2105 aft view.

IK-2 BR.2105 had two large "Kosovo cross" insignia beneath the wings.

The vertical stabilizer had a larger "war flag" on the rudder than No. 2104.

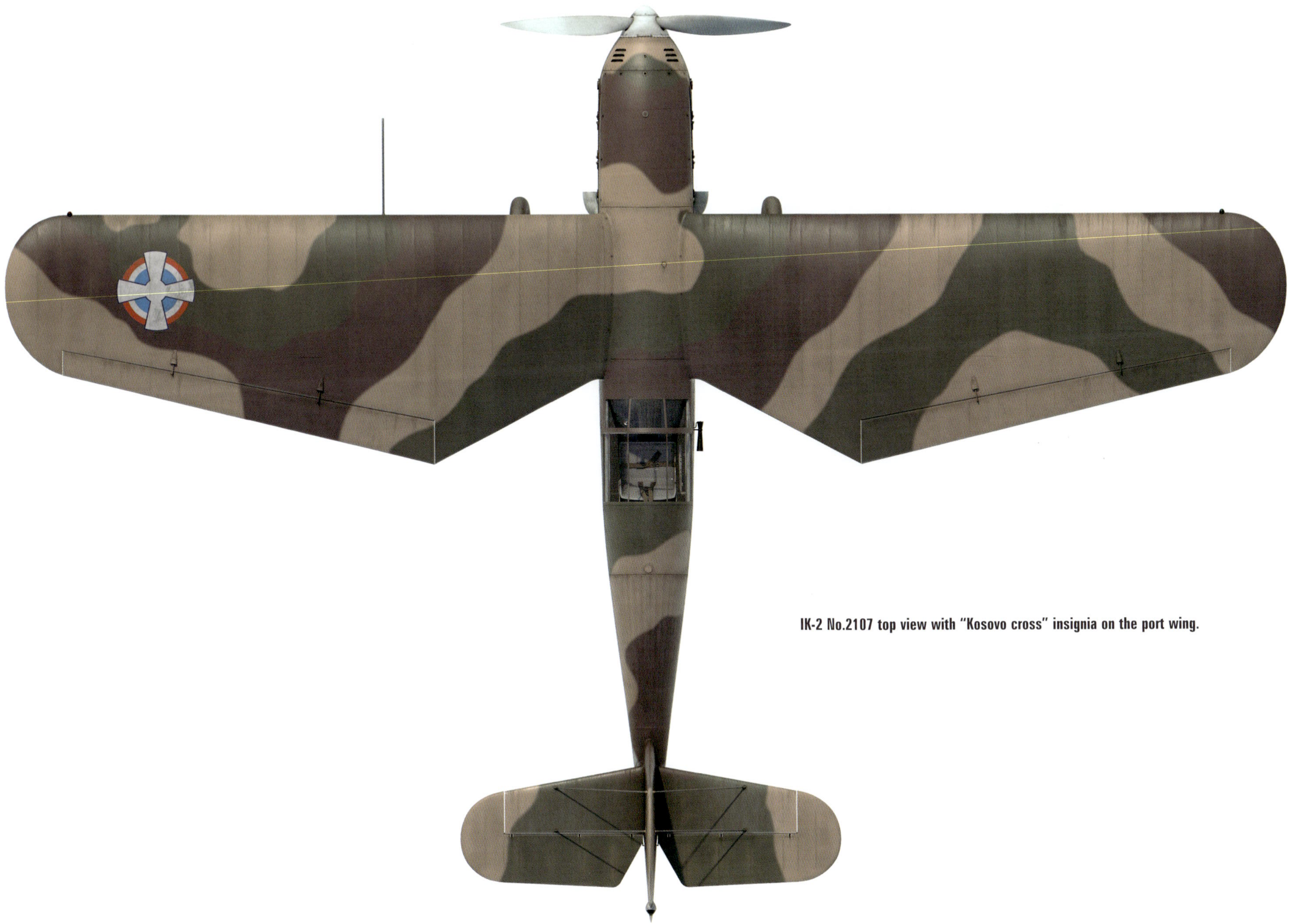

IK-2 No.2107 top view with "Kosovo cross" insignia on the port wing.

IK-2 No.2107 had "white 31" fuselage code.

IK-2 No.2107 aft view.

Front view of unknown IK-2 captured at Bosanski Aleksandrovac airfield.

Aft view of the unknown IK-2.

Wing undersides had two "Kosovo cross" insignia.

Aft view showing camouflage on the wings and horizontal stabilizers.

Note that the underside of the fuselage is painted in dark green color.

Underside view of IK-2.

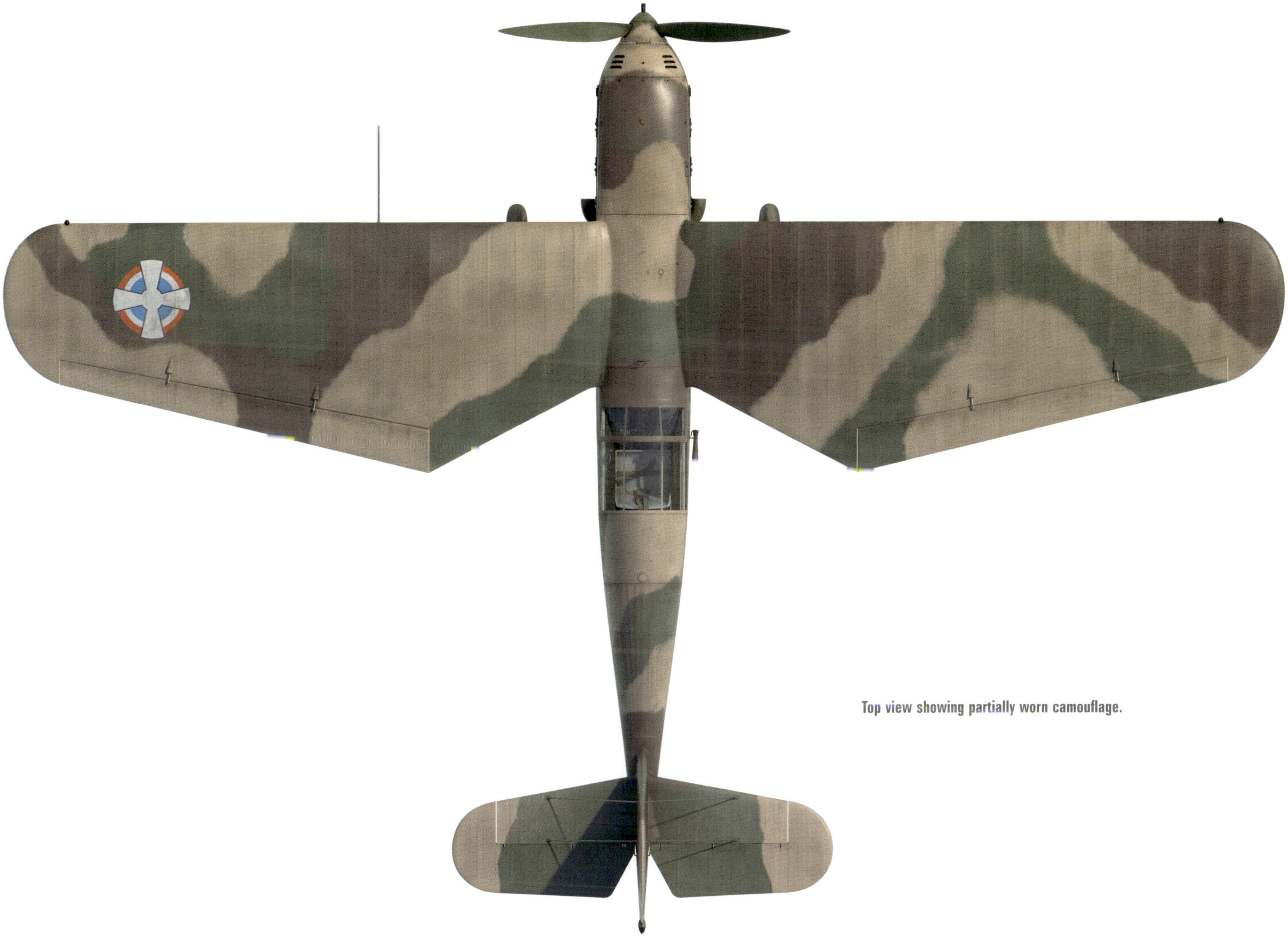

Top view showing partially worn camouflage.

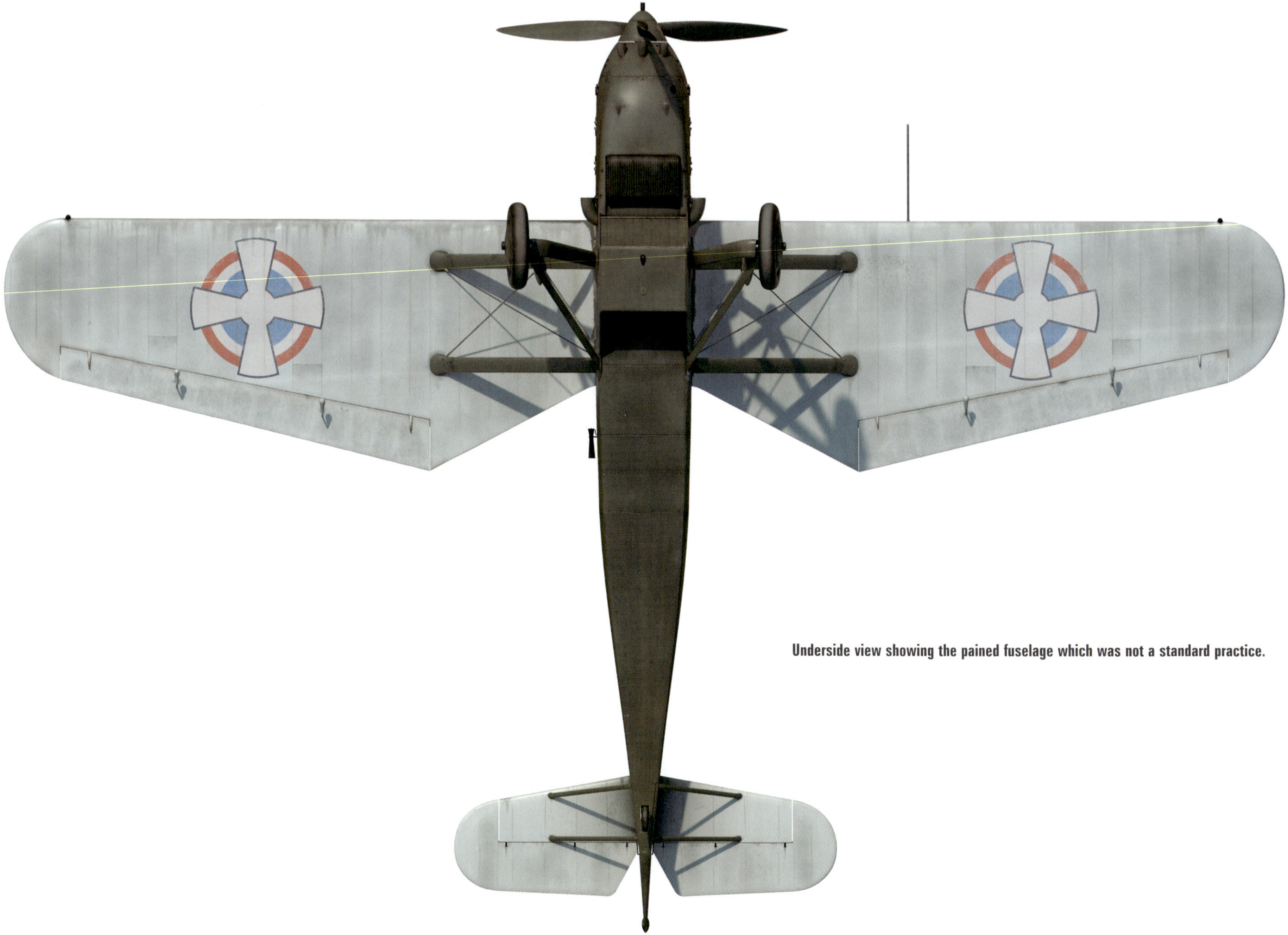

Underside view showing the pained fuselage which was not a standard practice.

Side view showing interesting ad hoc camouflage and no visible markings.

Aft view showing the “war flag”.

Note that the landing gear struts have also been painted with dark green color.

Aft starboard view of IK-2.

Port view of the unusual IK-2.

Side view with engine panels removed.

Engine and some of the wing underside access hatches to the aileron ball bearings removed.

Nose detail with engine cover removed. Note the unusual and non-standard intake vents behind the propeller.

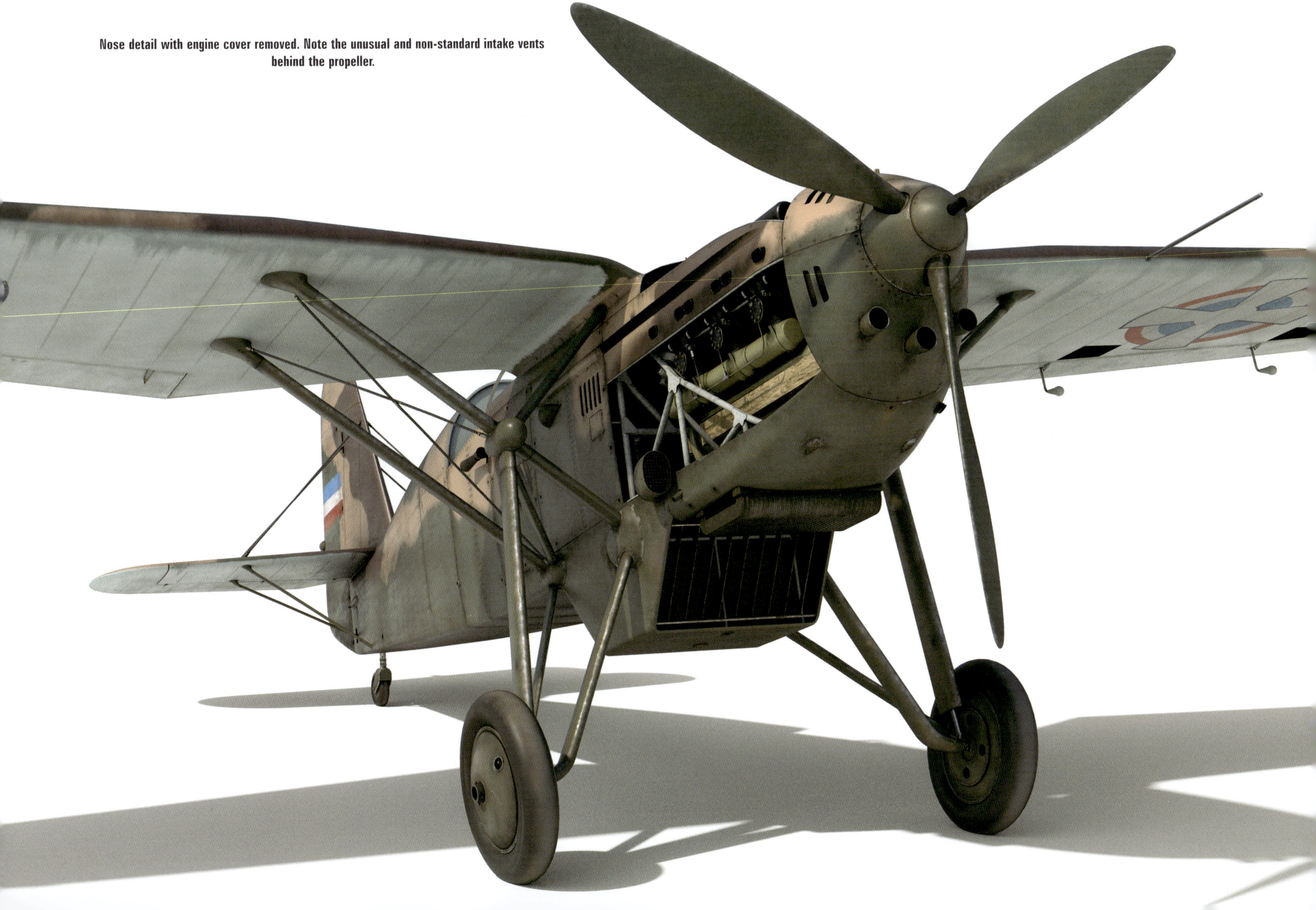

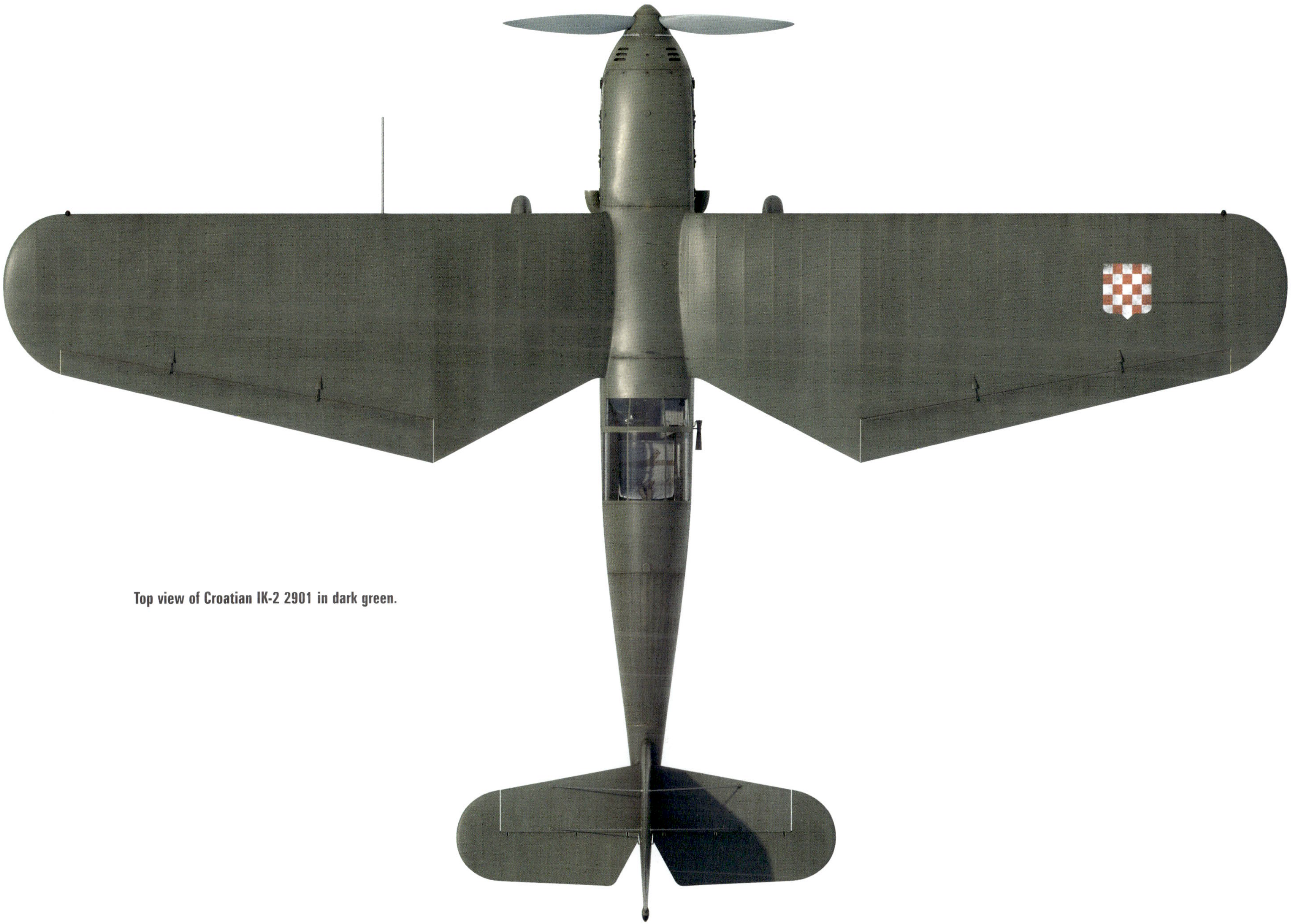

Top view of Croatian IK-2 2901 in dark green.

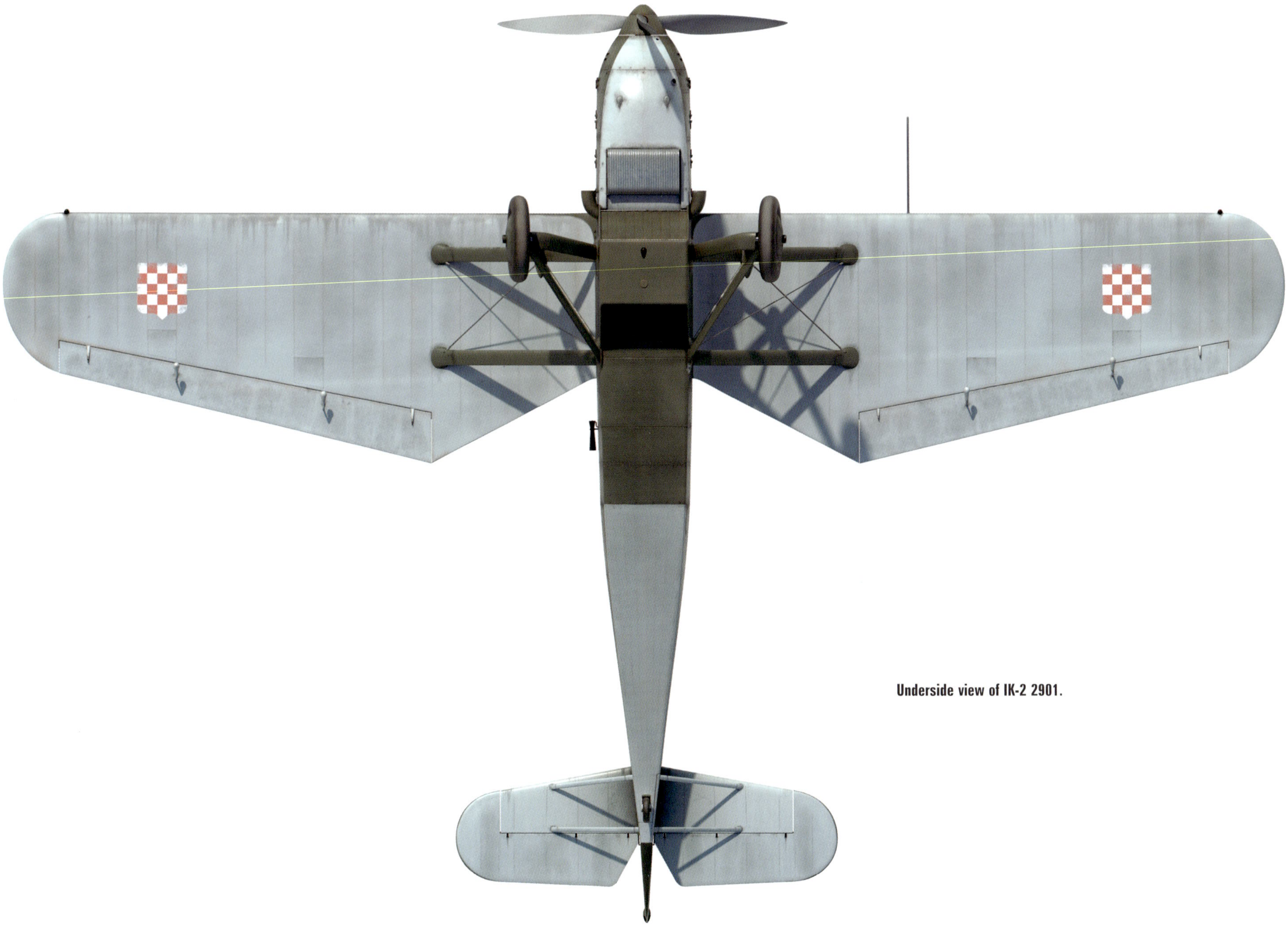

Underside view of IK-2 2901.

Side view of IK-2 2901 with large Croat flag on the rudder and black fuselage number 2901.

Starboard wing only had the Croat flag.

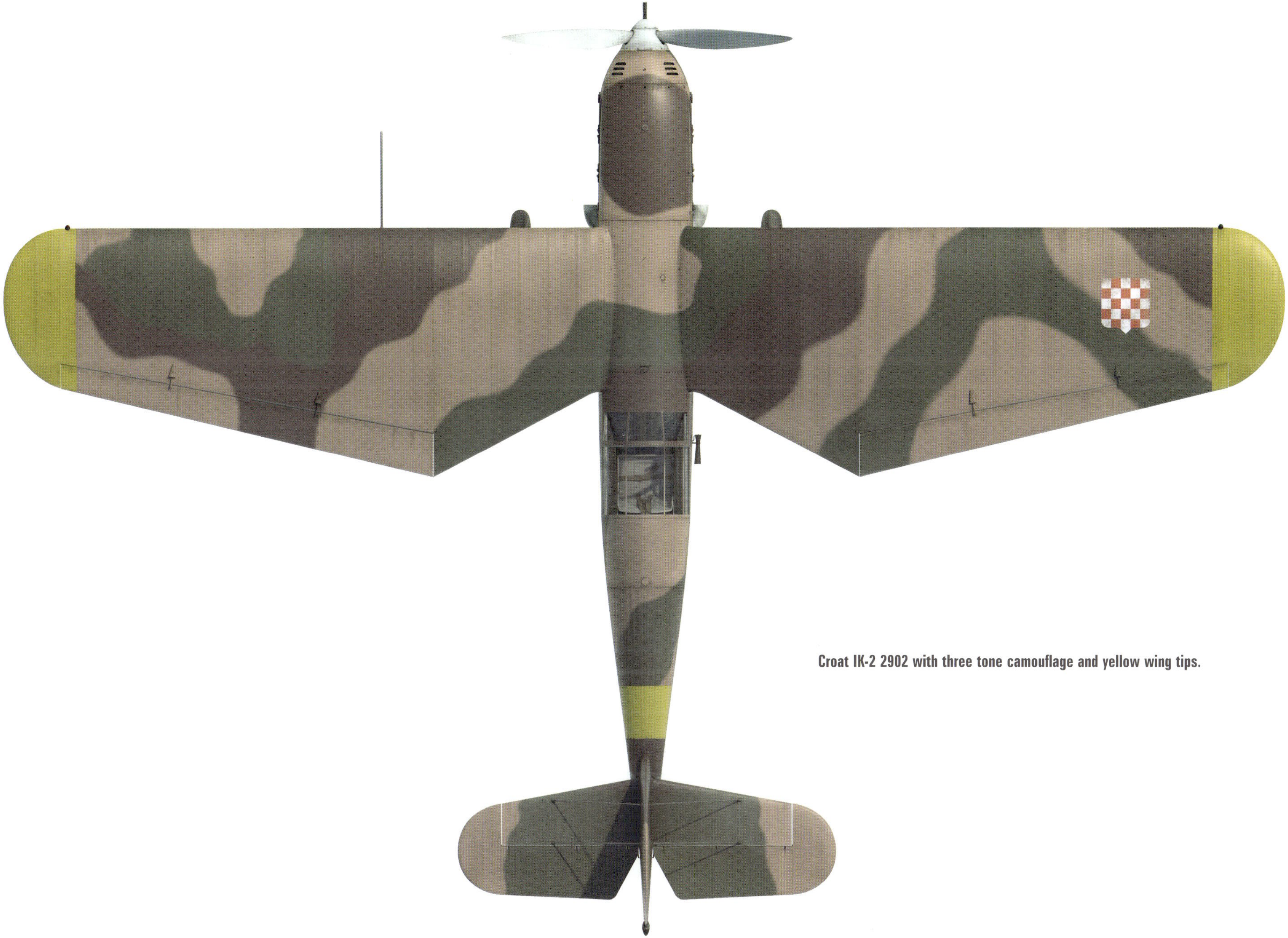

Croat IK-2 2902 with three tone camouflage and yellow wing tips.

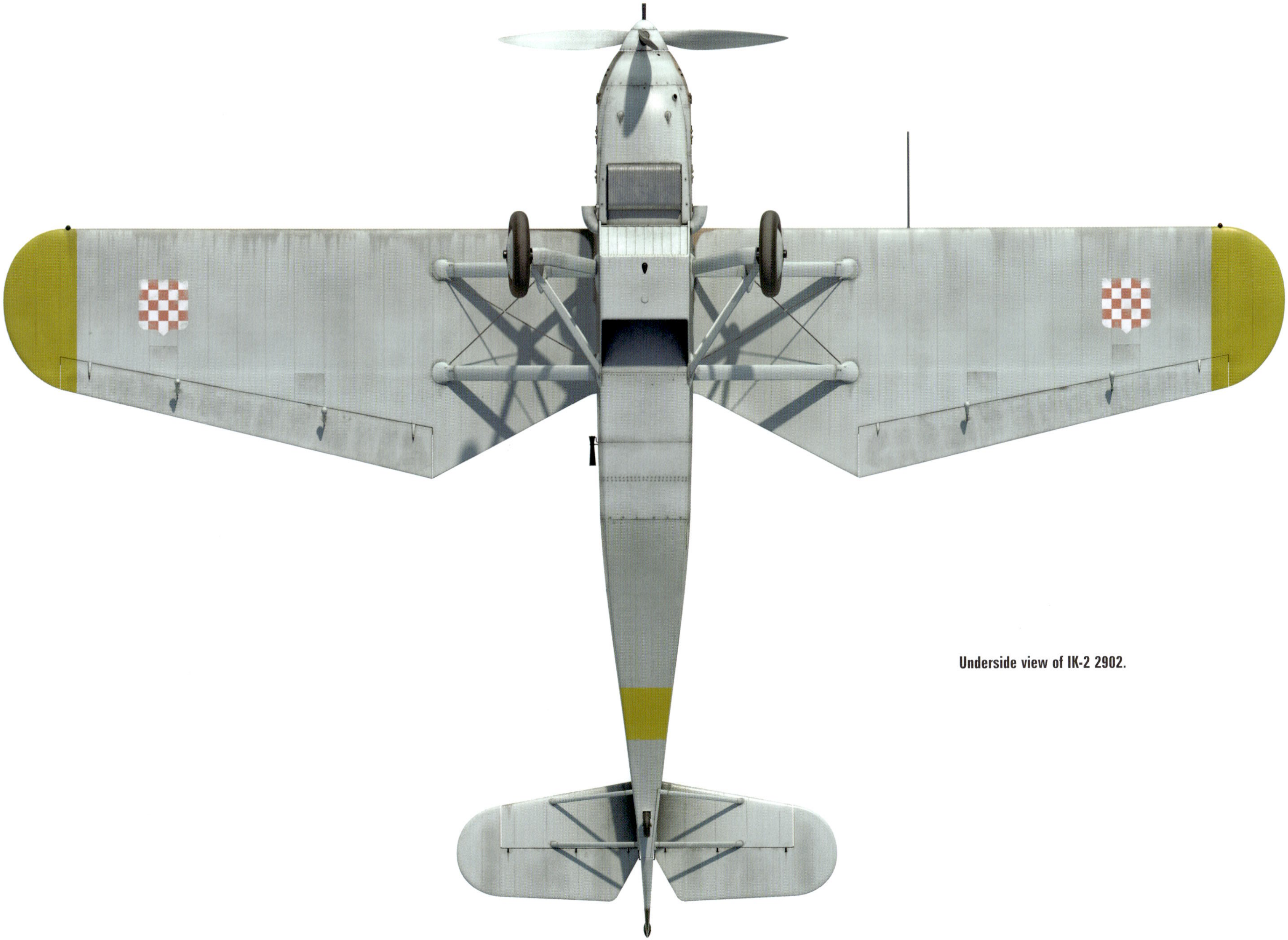

Underside view of IK-2 2902.

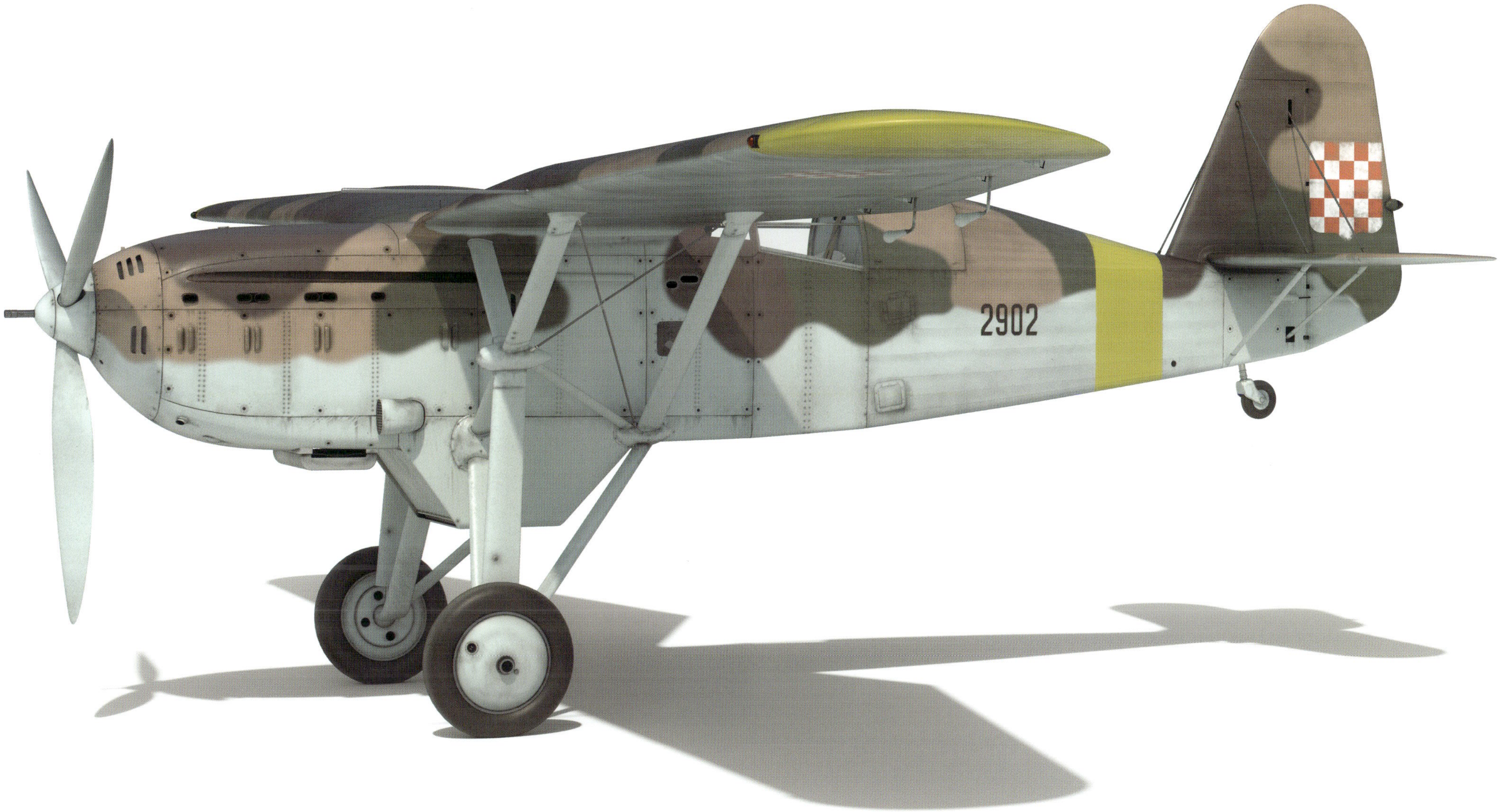


2902 in a take off configuration.

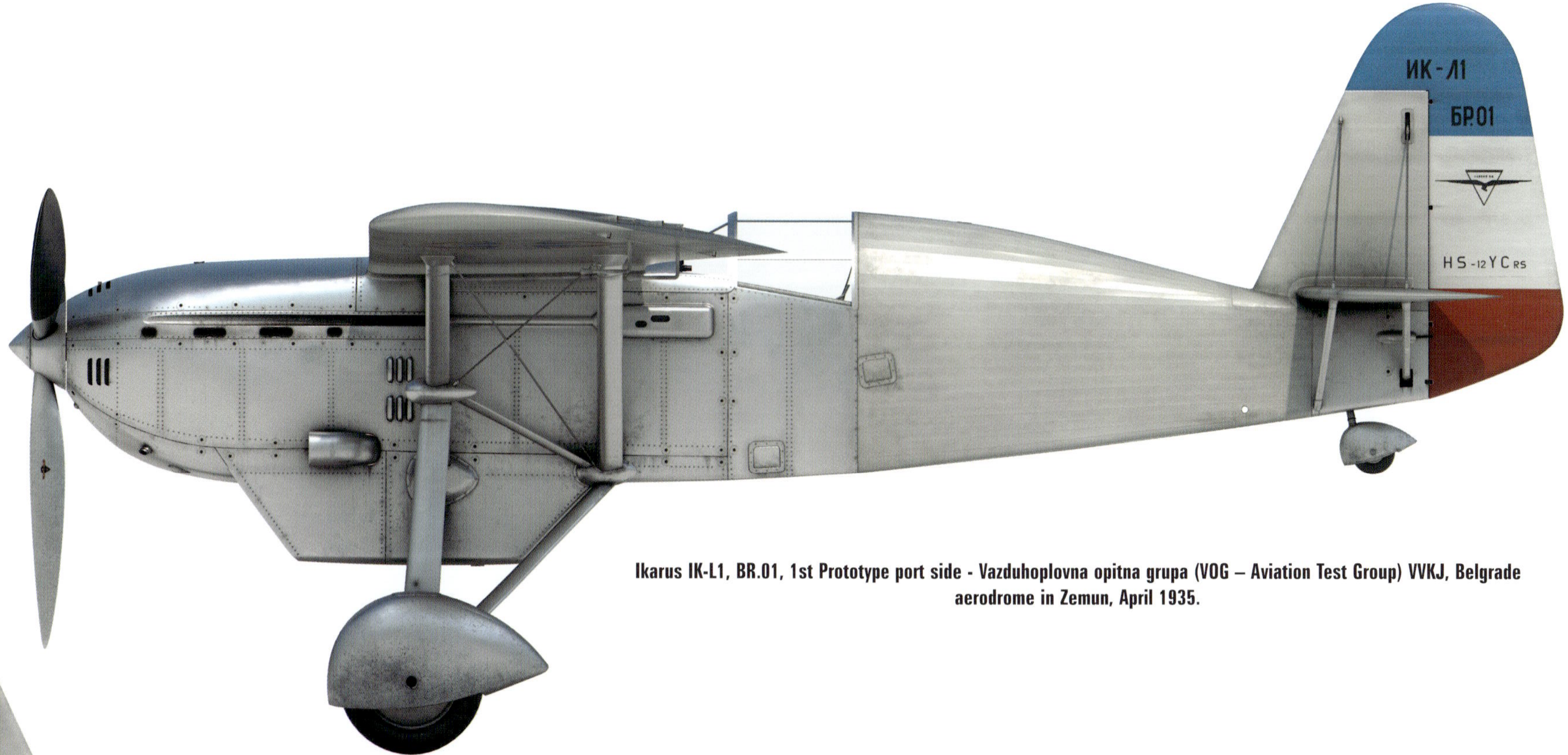


Ikarus IK-L1, BR.01, 1st Prototype port side - Vazduhoplovna opitna grupa (VOG – Aviation Test Group) VVKJ, Belgrade aerodrome in Zemun, April 1935.

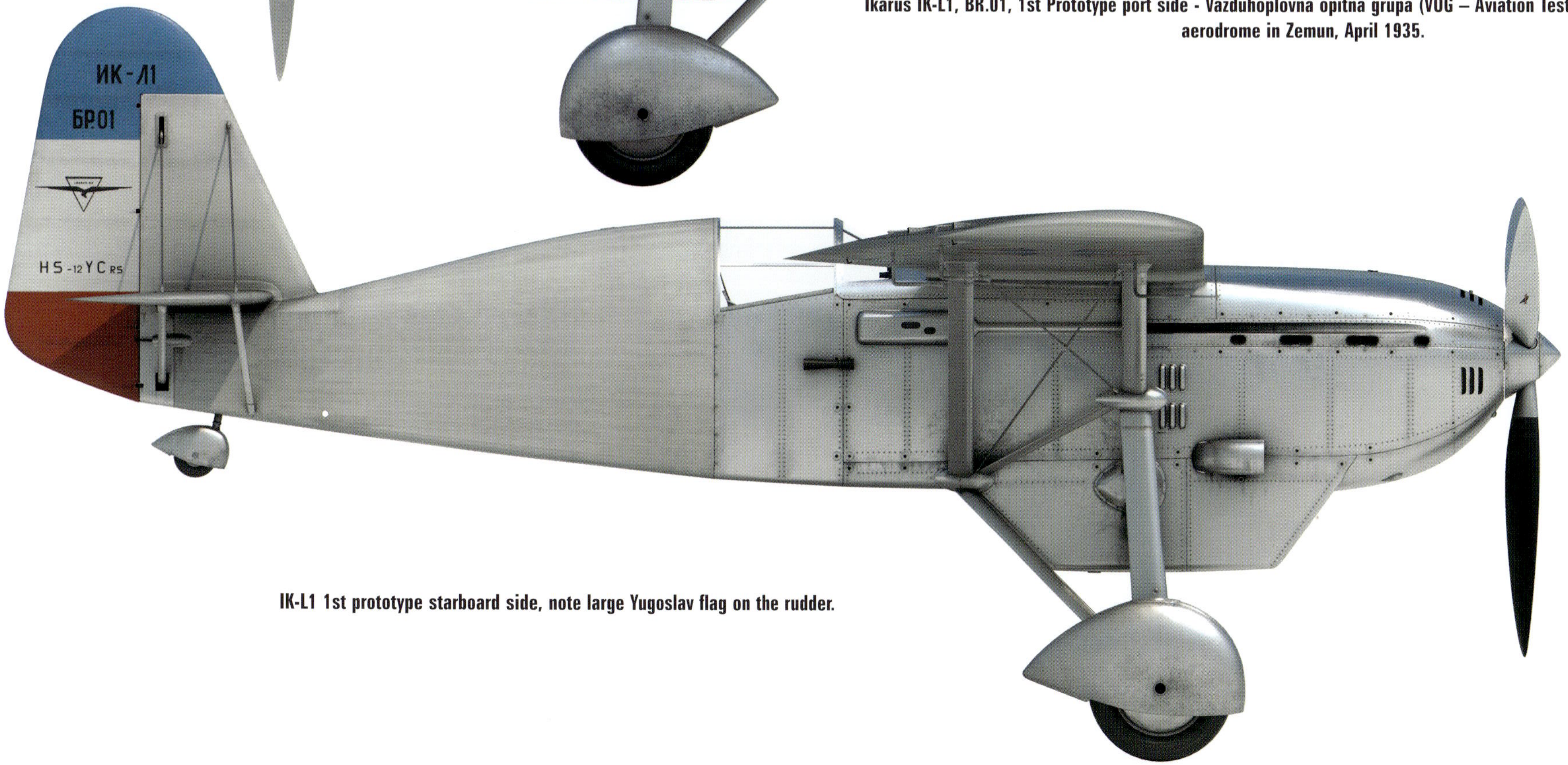


IK-L1 1st prototype starboard side, note large Yugoslav flag on the rudder.

Ikarus IK-L1, BR.01, 1st Prototype port side. Originally mounted main and tail wheel spats were removed during testing. Belgrade aerodrome in Zemun, April 1935.

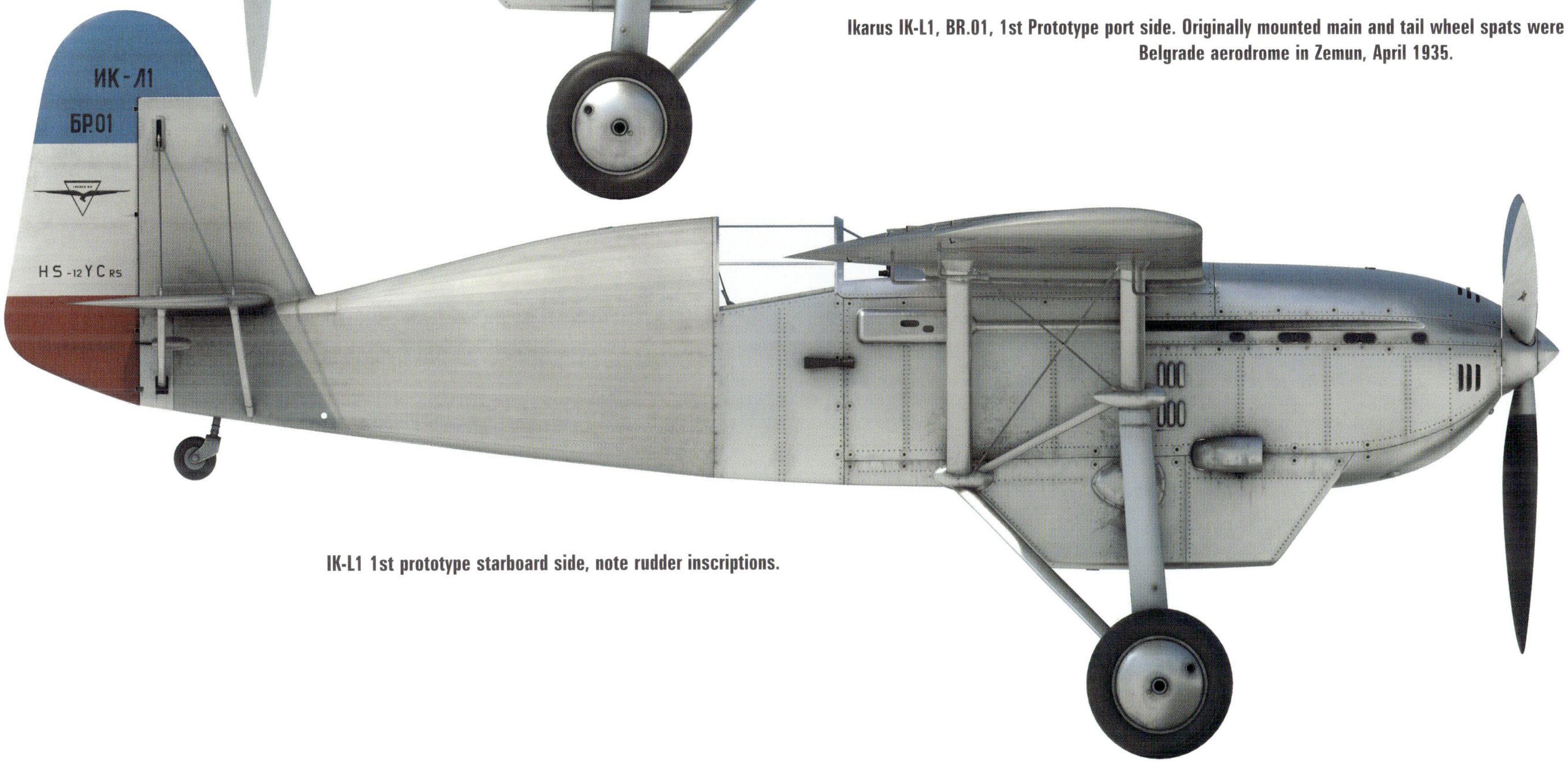


IK-L1 1st prototype starboard side, note rudder inscriptions.

Ikarus IK-2 No2, 2nd prototype port side – VOG, Belgrade aerodrome, summer of 1936.

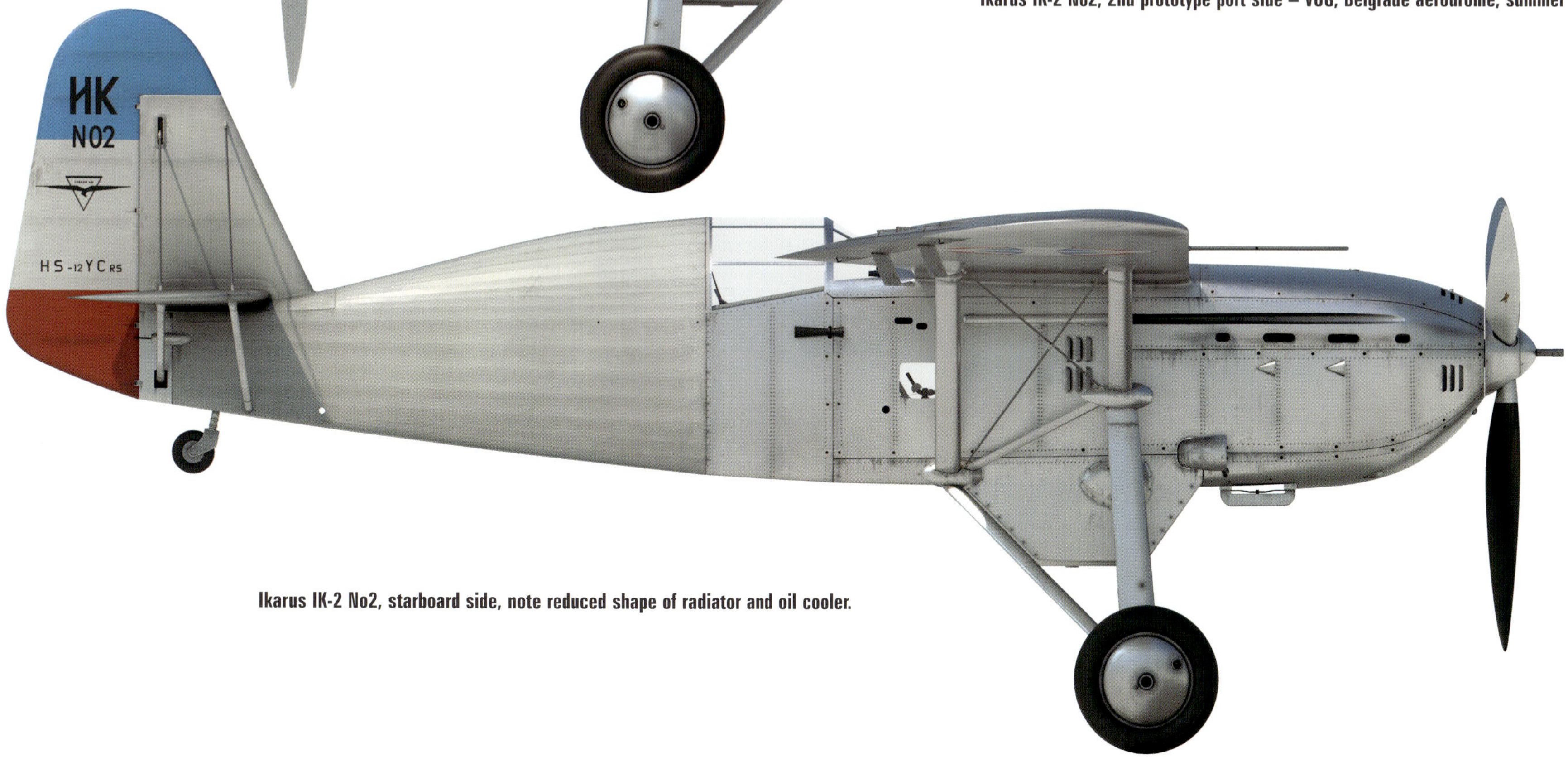

Ikarus IK-2 No2, starboard side, note reduced shape of radiator and oil cooler.

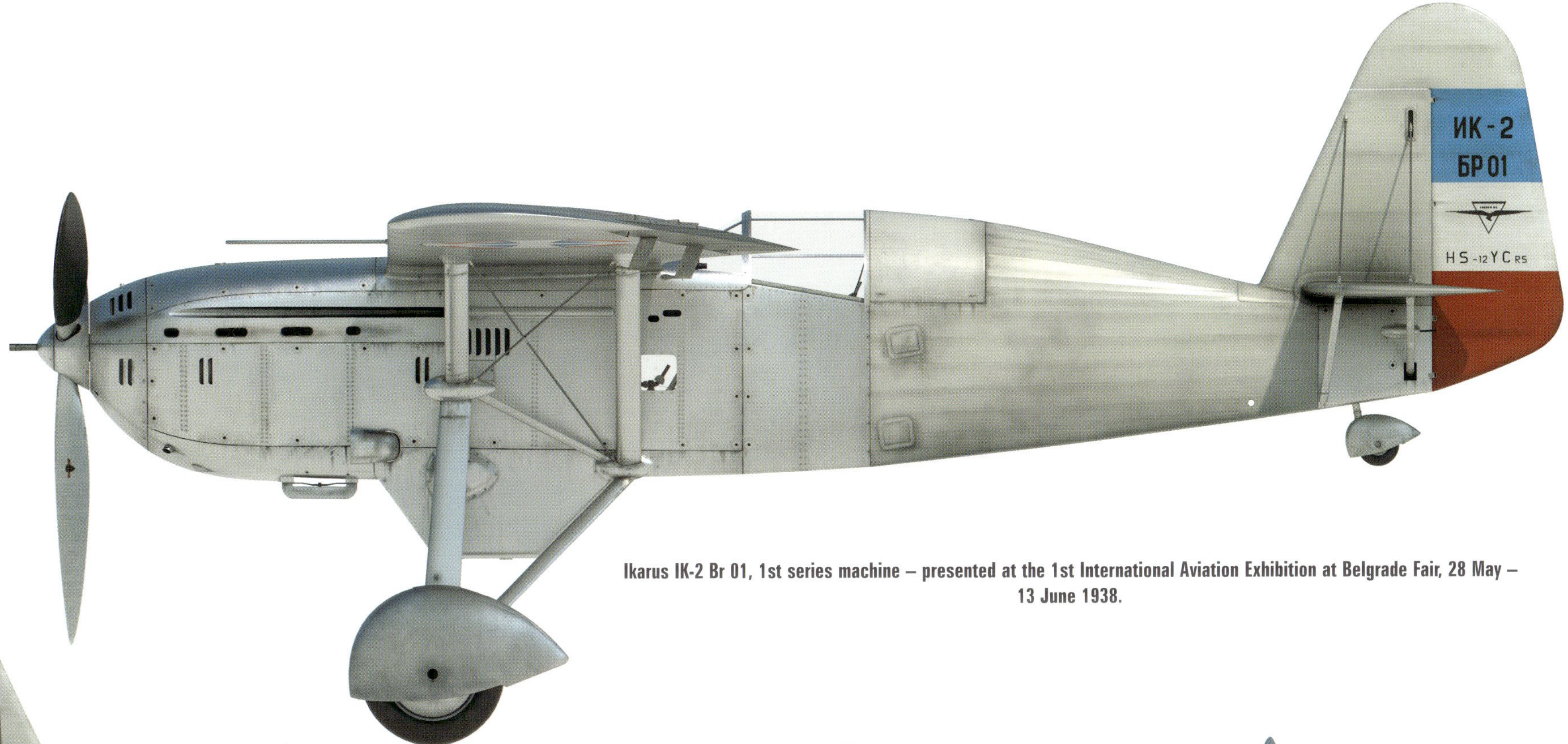


Ikarus IK-2 Br 01, 1st series machine – presented at the 1st International Aviation Exhibition at Belgrade Fair, 28 May – 13 June 1938.

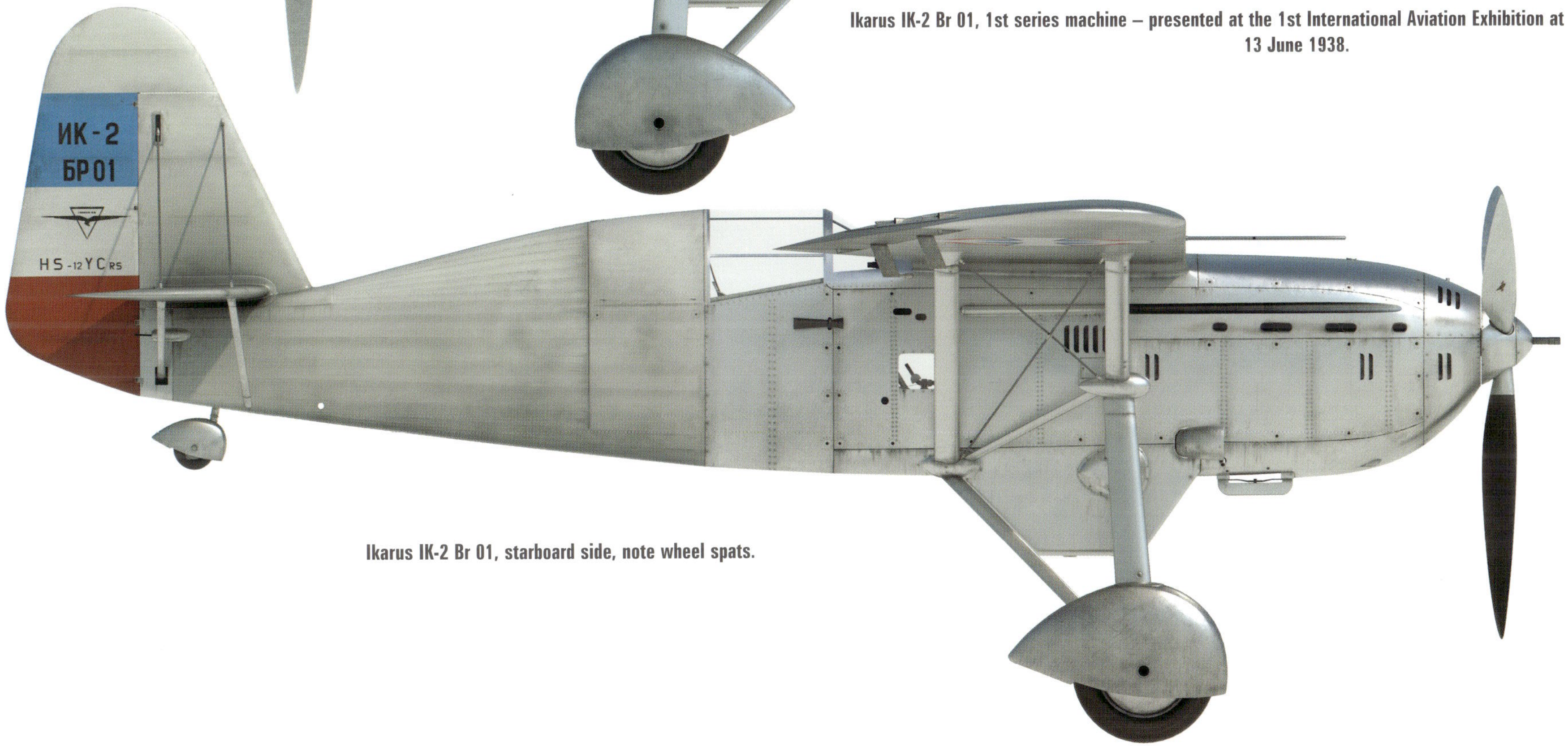


Ikarus IK-2 Br 01, starboard side, note wheel spats.

Ikarus IK-2 Br.2110, "black 2", 107. Escadrille/34. Aviation Group/4. Fighter Regiment VVKJ. Zagreb – Borongaj airport, 1940. Standard VVKJ peacetime scheme – overall natural aluminum and silver dope painting. Large Kosovo Cross insignias (120 cm) applied in four wing positions, large state flag over entire rudder.

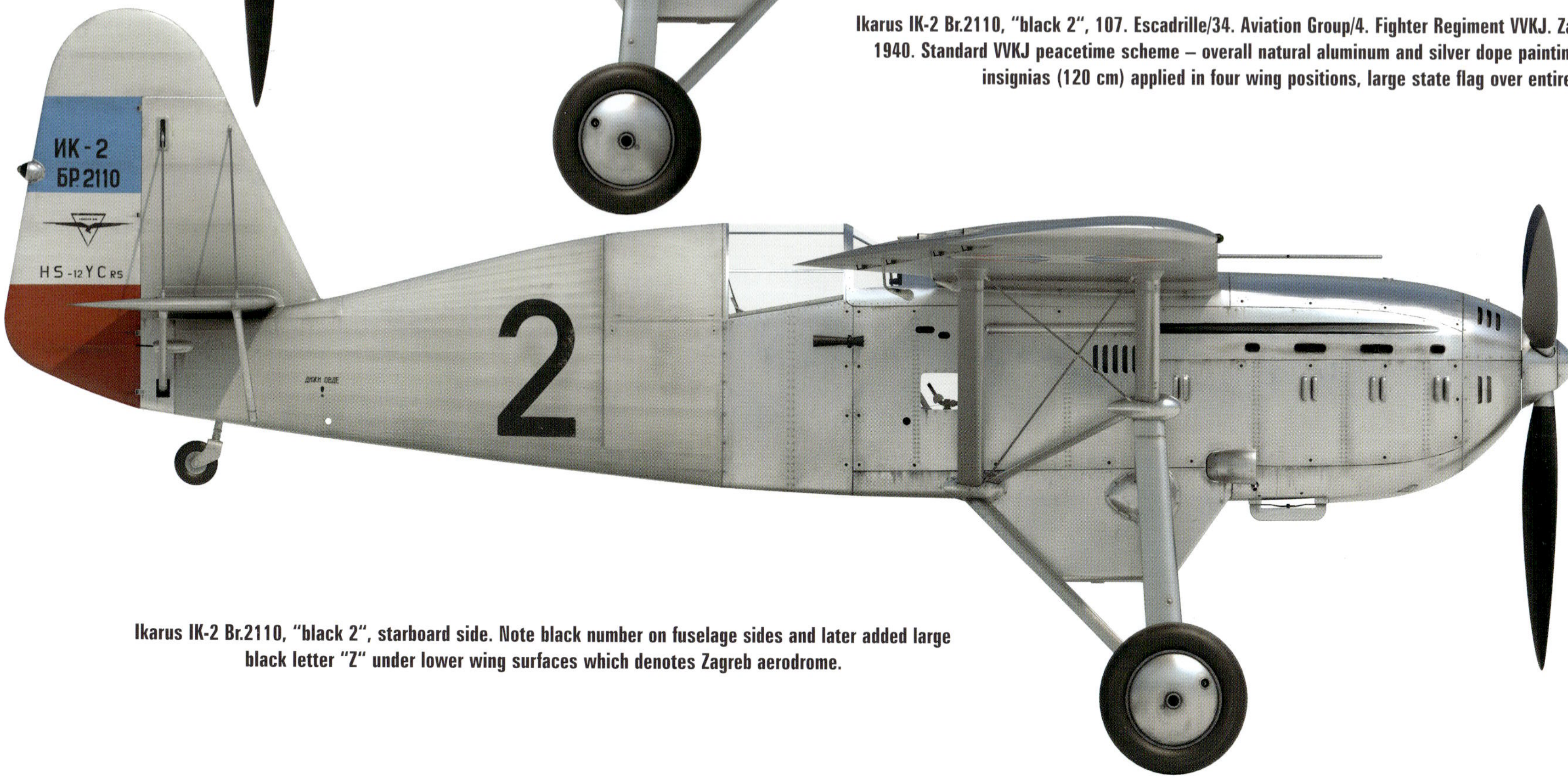


Ikarus IK-2 Br.2110, "black 2", starboard side. Note black number on fuselage sides and later added large black letter "Z" under lower wing surfaces which denotes Zagreb aerodrome.

Ikarus IK-2 Br.2112, "black 4", port side – 51. Aviation Group/6. Fighter Regiment VVKJ. Belgrade airport, October 1939.

Ikarus IK-2 Br.2112, "black 4". It was factory painted in overall silver dope with polished aluminum parts.

Ikarus IK-2 No2104, 107. Escadrille/34. Aviation Group/4. Fighter Regiment VVKJ. 4. Fighter Regiment homebase – Zagreb – Borongaj airport, 1940/1941.

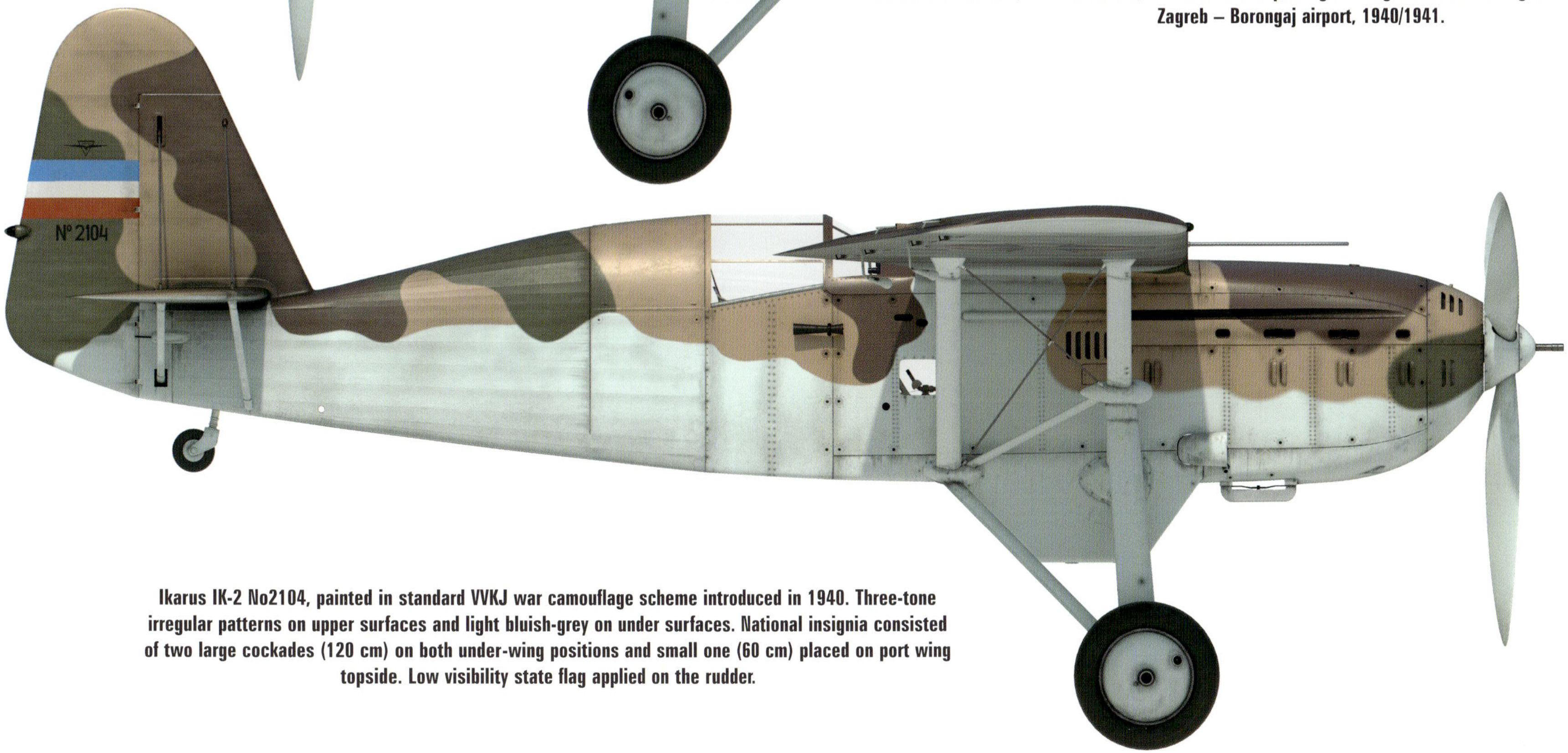


Ikarus IK-2 No2104, painted in standard VVKJ war camouflage scheme introduced in 1940. Three-tone irregular patterns on upper surfaces and light bluish-grey on under surfaces. National insignia consisted of two large cockades (120 cm) on both under-wing positions and small one (60 cm) placed on port wing topside. Low visibility state flag applied on the rudder.

Ikarus IK-2 No2105, "white 29", 107.E/34.AG/4.FR, port side. Zagreb – Borongaj airport, 1940.

Ikarus IK-2 No2105, "white 29", 107.E/34.AG/4.FR, starboard side with large white numbers on fuselage sides introduced in late 1940.

Ikarus IK-2 No2107, "white 31", 107.E/34.AG/4.FR, Zagreb – Borongaj airport, 1940.

Ikarus IK-2 No2107, "white 31", starboard side.

Ikarus IK-2 unknown s/n, field camouflage, 107.E/4.FR, port side Ikarus IK-2 unknown c/n, 107th E, 34th AG, 4th FR, Bosanski Aleksandrovac auxiliary airfield, April 1941.

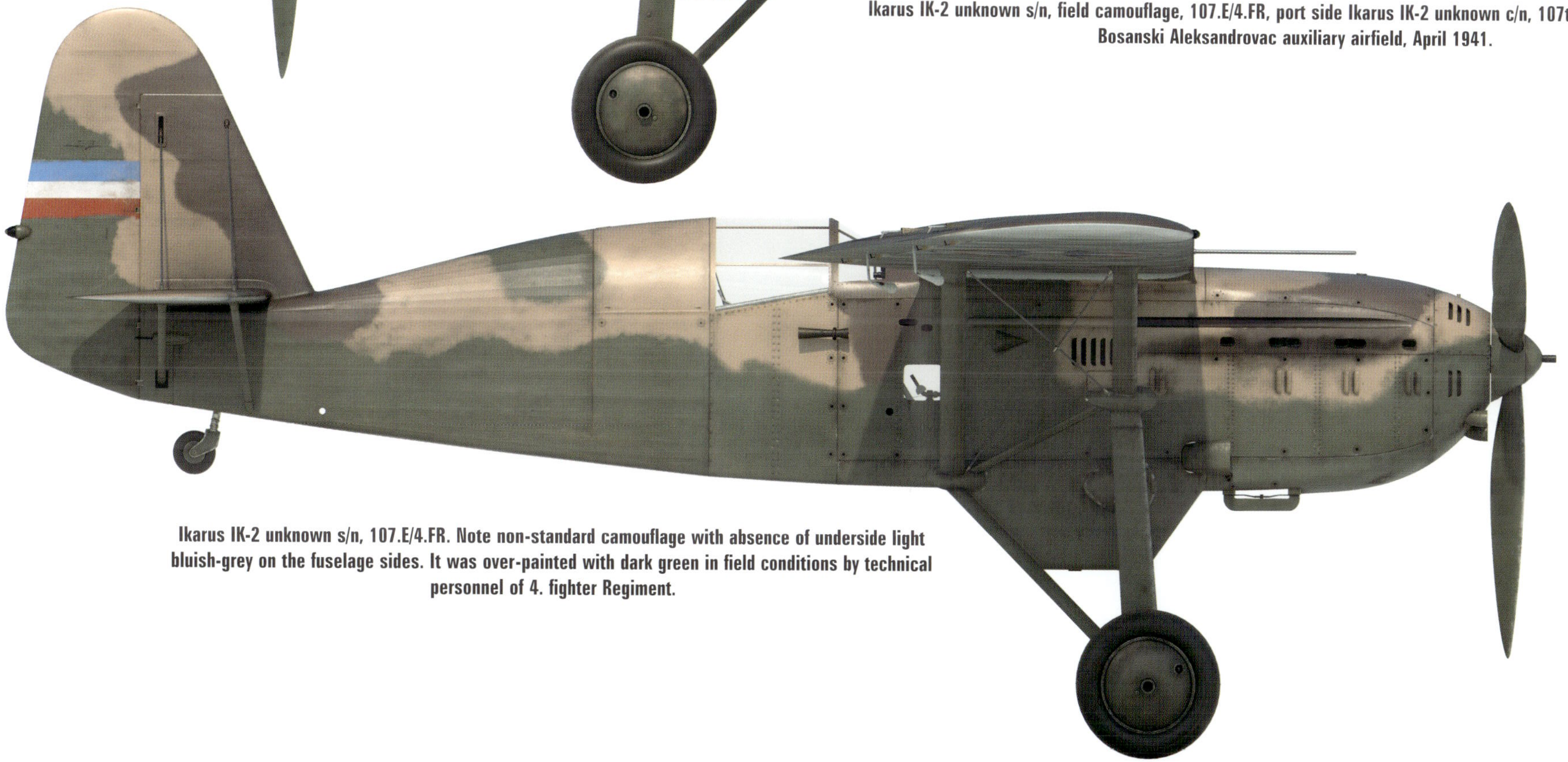

Ikarus IK-2 unknown s/n, 107.E/4.FR. Note non-standard camouflage with absence of underside light bluish-grey on the fuselage sides. It was over-painted with dark green in field conditions by technical personnel of 4. fighter Regiment.

Ikarus IK-2 2901, Independent State of Croatia Air Force (ZNDH), 5. Recce Escadrille (ZJ), 2. Air Base (ZB) ZNDH, Sarajevo – Rajlovac, 1941-1942.

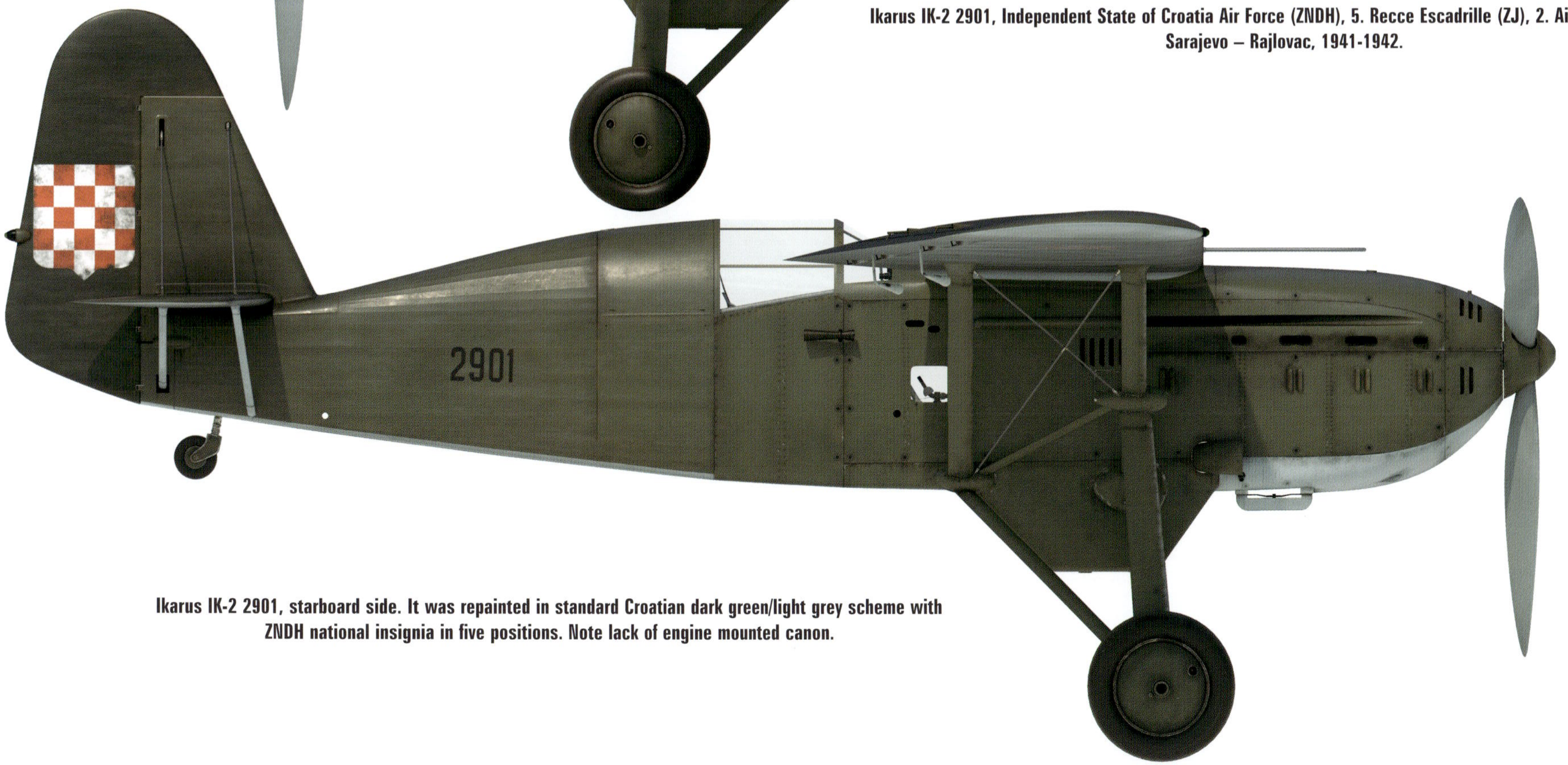


Ikarus IK-2 2901, starboard side. It was repainted in standard Croatian dark green/light grey scheme with ZNDH national insignia in five positions. Note lack of engine mounted canon.

Ikarus IK-2 2902, 5.ZJ/2.ZB ZNDH, Sarajevo – Rajlovac airfield, 1941-1942.

Ikarus IK-2 2902. Note standard VVKJ three-tone scheme (applied at Ikarus factory after overhauling) and newly applied standard Axis tactical markings – yellow fuselage band and wing tips.

Table with warious factory logos.